Oxford Junior Thesaurus

Compiled by Sheila Dignen
Literacy consultant: Kate Ruttle

OXFORD
UNIVERSITY PRESS

OXFORD

UNIVERSITY PRESS

Great Clarendon Street, Oxford OX2 6DP

Oxford University Press is a department of the University of Oxford.
It furthers the University's objective of excellence in research,
scholarship, and education by publishing worldwide in

Oxford New York

Auckland Cape Town Dar es Salaam Hong Kong Karachi
Kuala Lumpur Madrid Melbourne Mexico City Nairobi
New Delhi Shanghai Taipei Toronto

With offices in

Argentina Austria Brazil Chile Czech Republic France Greece
Guatemala Hungary Italy Japan Poland Portugal Singapore
South Korea Switzerland Thailand Turkey Ukraine Vietnam

Oxford is a registered trade mark of Oxford University Press
in the UK and in certain other countries

First published 2003
New edition 2007

British Library Cataloguing in Publication Data

Data available

ISBN-13: 978-0-19-911513 6

10 9 8 7 6

Printed in Malaysia.

www.schooldictionaries.co.uk

Contents

Preface

The *Oxford Junior Thesaurus* has been specially written for primary school children aged 7 and above. In the UK, it fulfils the Primary National Strategy requirements for KS2 YR2–YR4 and the Scottish Guidelines P3, 4, and 5.

This thesaurus uses a straightforward approach to help primary school children build and enrich their vocabulary and master the skills of using a thesaurus. The entries are arranged alphabetically: all the **headwords** have been carefully chosen and are words that children are most likely to look up. The **synonyms** and alternative words offered are a mixture of familiar words and unfamiliar words that will stretch children's vocabulary. Words across the **curriculum subjects** such as Science, Information Technology, Sports, and Music have been included. The tinted Word Web panels provide lists of words relating to a wide range of topics, including *birds*, *dogs*, *cars*, *boats*, *rain*, *wind*, and *water*. Special attention has been given to overused words such as *big*, *go*, *good*, *nice*, and *say*, to encourage children to be creative and imaginative in their writing. Also, context and example sentences support children to choose words effectively and correctly.

The extensive Word Explorer section is an indispensable guide for creative writing and effective use of English. It explores the basic tools needed for writing, focusing on punctuation, grammar, and words that are easily confused. It also offers useful tips to help with writing.

The *Oxford Junior Thesaurus* forms an excellent companion volume to the *Oxford Junior Dictionary*, which offers further support with reading, writing, and understanding meaning.

The publisher and editors are indebted to all the advisors, consultants, and teachers who were involved in planning and compiling this dictionary. Special thanks go to Susan Rennie for her helpful advice on the Word Explorer section.

Introduction
What is a thesaurus for?

Here are some good reasons why you should use a thesaurus:

✓ to find a more *interesting word*

Are there any alternative words to describe clothes that are very *dirty*?
Look up *dirty* to find some other adjectives to describe dirty clothes.

✓ to find the *right word*

What word might you use to describe how a *duck* walks?
Look up *duck* to find the right word.

✓ to make your *writing more interesting*

Imagine you are writing about what you did at the weekend.
You might start like this:

> *I had a good weekend. The weather was not very nice so we went to the shops. I got a new top that is really nice. I met up with my friend and we went to see a film. I thought it was good but my friend didn't like it.*

Can you see that the words *good* and *nice* are used over and over again?
It would be more interesting and tell the reader much more about the
weekend if you used different words instead. If you look up these words
in the thesaurus you will find a number of synonyms with a similar
meaning. Think carefully about what you are describing and choose
alternative words. You could write this instead:

> *I had a brilliant weekend. The weather was not very sunny so we went to the shops. I got a new top and it is really stylish. I met up with my friend and we went to see a film. I thought it was amusing but my friend didn't like it.*

What is the difference between a thesaurus and a dictionary?

A **dictionary** tells you what a word means, so it gives you a **definition** of the word. A **thesaurus** tells you what other words have the same meaning, so it gives you **synonyms** of a word. A thesaurus also gives you **related words** that you can use when you are describing something or writing about it.

For example, if you look up the word **boat** in a dictionary, it will tell you that a boat is something that floats on water and can carry people and goods. But a thesaurus will give you some other words for a boat (*a ship, a vessel, a craft*). A thesaurus will also give you some words for different kinds of boats (*a canoe, a ferry, a raft, a speed boat*) and words you can use to describe boats (*bob up and down, float, drift, capsize*).

You often use a dictionary when you have read or heard a new word and want to know what it means. You use a thesaurus when you want to write or say something yourself and you want to choose the best word.

Features in this thesaurus

The **headword** is the word you look up.
Headwords are in alphabetical order.

The **word class** (part of speech) tells you whether a word is a
noun, *verb*, *adjective*, or *adverb*.

The **numbered senses** show you that a word has more than
one meaning.

The **example sentence** shows how you might use a word.

The **synonyms** are words that words that mean the same, or
nearly the same, as the headword. You will find help on using
synonyms in the **Become a Word explorer** section at the
back of this thesaurus.

An **opposite** (antonym) is a word that has an opposite
meaning to the headword. Sometimes each meaning has its
own opposite.

The **extra help** explains the difference between some of the
synonyms, and helps you to choose the best one.

How to use this thesaurus

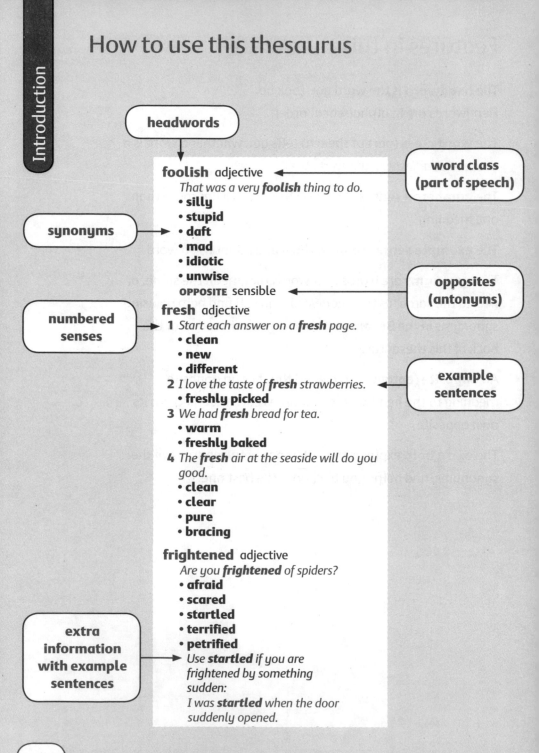

headwords

word class (part of speech)

synonyms

opposites (antonyms)

numbered senses

example sentences

extra information with example sentences

foolish adjective
*That was a very **foolish** thing to do.*
- **silly**
- **stupid**
- **daft**
- **mad**
- **idiotic**
- **unwise**
OPPOSITE **sensible**

fresh adjective
1 *Start each answer on a **fresh** page.*
- **clean**
- **new**
- **different**
2 *I love the taste of **fresh** strawberries.*
- **freshly picked**
3 *We had **fresh** bread for tea.*
- **warm**
- **freshly baked**
4 *The **fresh** air at the seaside will do you good.*
- **clean**
- **clear**
- **pure**
- **bracing**

frightened adjective
*Are you **frightened** of spiders?*
- **afraid**
- **scared**
- **startled**
- **terrified**
- **petrified**
*Use **startled** if you are frightened by something sudden:*
*I was **startled** when the door suddenly opened.*

fruit noun

WORD WEB
some types of fruit
- an apple
- an apricot
- a banana
- blackberries
- cherries
- figs
- gooseberries
- a grapefruit
- a guava
- a kiwi fruit
- a lemon
- a lychee
- a mango
- rhubarb
- strawberries
- a tangerine
- a tomato
- a watermelon

Word Web panel

good adjective

⚠ OVERUSED WORD
Try to vary the words you use to mean *good*. Here are some other words you can use instead.

1 *This is a really **good** book.*
- **wonderful**
- **brilliant**
- **excellent**
- **fantastic**
- **great**
- **entertaining**
  Use **wonderful**, **brilliant**, **excellent**, **fantastic**, or **great** if something is very good:
  *He told us some **wonderful** stories about his travels.*

2 *William is a very **good** footballer.*
- **skilful**
- **talented**
- **competent**

3 *I hope the weather is **good** for sports day.*
- **fine**
- **nice**
- **dry**
- **sunny**
- **warm**

Overused word panel

Special panels

The tinted boxes in this thesaurus give you extra help on choosing the best word to use. There are three kinds of panel: **Overused word**, **Word Web**, and **Writing tips**.

⚠ Overused word panels

The **Overused word** symbol shows you that a headword is very common and often overused. If you use these words too often, your writing will seem dull and boring. The thesaurus gives you lots of more interesting and creative words you can use instead.

bad	look
big	nice
bit	put
do	run
get	say
go	walk
good	

Word Web panels

The **Word Web** panels list words that are related to each other. For example, the **Word Web** panel at **house** includes words for different types of house such as a *bungalow*, a *cottage*, a *farmhouse*, and a *mansion*. Choosing one of these words can help make your writing more detailed and accurate.

aeroplane	farm
bag	film
bat	flower
bed	fruit
bell	group
bicycle	gun
bird	hair
boat	hat
body	horse
book	house
bridge	insect
building	job
cage	jewel
camera	knife
car	light
cat	material
chair	meat
clock	meal
clothes	metal
colour	monster
computer	music
cook	musical instrument
cup	tool
dance	tree
dog	vegetable
duck	weapon
	writer

Writing tips panels

The **Writing tips** panels include words and example sentences to show you ways of writing about the headword. For example, the **Writing tips** panel at the word **bird** shows you how you can use words such as *soar*, *hover*, *glide*, *swoop*, and *flutter* when you are writing about birds.

aeroplane	duck
bird	horse
boat	insect
car	light
cat	monster
dog	water

Aa

ability noun

1 You have the **ability** to do very well at school.
   - **capability**
   - **intelligence**
2 He's a young footballer with a lot of **ability**.
   - **talent**
   - **skill**
   - **flair**

about adverb

There are **about** thirty children in our class.
   - **roughly**
   - **approximately**

accept verb

The children stepped forward to **accept** their prizes.
   - **to take**
   - **to receive**
   OPPOSITE reject

accident noun

1 There was an **accident** on the main road.
   - **a crash**
   - **a smash**
   - **a collision**
   - **a pile-up**
   - **a bump**
   A **pile-up** is a bad accident with a lot of cars:
   There was a huge **pile-up** on the motorway.

A **bump** is an accident that is not very bad:
We had a bit of a **bump** on the way to the supermarket.

2 I'm sorry, it was an **accident**.
   - **a mistake**

accidentally adverb

I **accidentally** knocked the lamp over.
   - **unintentionally**
   - **inadvertently**
   OPPOSITE deliberately

accurate adjective

She gave the police an **accurate** description of the thief.
   - **exact**
   - **precise**
   - **correct**
   OPPOSITE inaccurate

achieve verb

You have **achieved** a lot this term.
   - **to do**
   - **to accomplish**

achievement noun

Winning a gold medal is a great **achievement**.
   - **an accomplishment**
   - **a feat**
   - **a success**

act verb

1 We must **act** quickly to save these animals.
   - **to do something**
   - **to take action**
2 I would love to **act** on the stage.
   - **to perform**
   - **to appear**

a
b
c
d
e
f
g
h
i
j
k
l
m
n
o
p
q
r
s
t
u
v
w
x
y
z

a
b
c
d
e
f
g
h
i
j
k
l
m
n
o
p
q
r
s
t
u
v
w
x
y
z

action noun
1 *I like films that are full of **action**.*
- **excitement**
- **suspense**
2 *His brave **action** saved his sister's life.*
- **an act**
- **a deed**

active adjective
*Most children enjoy being **active**.*
- **busy**
- **lively**
- **energetic**
- **on the go** (*informal*)
OPPOSITE inactive

activity noun
*What **activities** do you do outside school?*
- **a hobby**
- **a pastime**
- **an interest**

actual adjective
*This is the **actual** ship that Nelson sailed on.*
- **real**
- **genuine**
- **very**

add verb
*Mix the butter and sugar together, then **add** the eggs.*
- **to mix in**

admire verb
1 *Which sports stars do you **admire**?*
- **to respect**
- **to look up to**
- **to idolize**
- **to hero-worship**

2 *We stood and **admired** the lovely view.*
- **to enjoy**
- **to appreciate**

admit verb
*He **admitted** that he had broken the window.*
- **to confess**
- **to own up**
OPPOSITE deny

adult noun
*You must be accompanied by an **adult**.*
- **a grown-up**

advantage noun
*Being tall is an **advantage** in some sports.*
- **a help**
- **an asset**
OPPOSITE disadvantage

adventure noun
*He told us about all his exciting **adventures**.*
- **an escapade**
- **an exploit**

advertise verb
*We made some posters to **advertise** the jumble sale.*
- **to publicize**
- **to promote**

advice noun
*He gave me some very useful **advice**.*
- **help**
- **guidance**
- **a suggestion** *He made a useful suggestion.*

aeroplane noun
*He had never been in an **aeroplane** before.*
- **a plane**
- **an aircraft**

> **WORD WEB**
> **Some types of aeroplane:**
> - an airliner
> - a fighter plane
> - a glider
> - a jet
> - a jumbo jet

> **WRITING TIPS**
> Here are some useful words for writing about aeroplanes.
> - The aeroplane **was flying** high above the clouds.
> - The jumbo jet **soared** up into the sky.
> - Our plane **took off** at six o'clock and landed at ten o'clock.

afraid adjective
1 *Are you **afraid** of spiders?*
- **frightened**
- **scared**
- **terrified**
- **petrified**
  *Use **terrified** or **petrified** if you are very afraid:*
  *I'm absolutely **terrified** of snakes.*
2 *I was **afraid** the boat might capsize.*
- **worried**
- **nervous**

aggressive adjective
1 *Tigers are very **aggressive** animals.*
- **fierce**
2 *You shouldn't be so **aggressive** with your brother.*
- **rough**
- **violent**

aim verb
*He **aimed** his water pistol at his aunt.*
- **to point**

alarm noun
*The fire **alarm** went off.*
- **a signal**
- **a siren**

alert adjective
*The sentries on duty must remain **alert**.*
- **ready**
- **awake**
- **on the lookout**

alive adjective
*The bird was injured but still **alive**.*
- **living**
- **breathing**
OPPOSITE dead

allow verb
*They **allowed** us to use their swimming pool.*
- **to let** *They let us use their swimming pool.*
- **to permit** *They permitted us to use their swimming pool.*
- **to give someone permission** *They gave us permission to use their swimming pool.*
OPPOSITE forbid

all right adjective
1 *Are you **all right**?*
- **well**
- **safe**
- **unhurt**
- **healthy** →

a b c d e f g h i j k l m n o p q r s t u v w x y z

a
b
c
d
e
f
g
h
i
j
k
l
m
n
o
p
q
r
s
t
u
v
w
x
y
z

2 *The food was **all right**, but not brilliant.*
- **OK**
- **acceptable**
- **satisfactory**

almost adverb
*I've **almost** finished.*
- **nearly**
- **virtually**
- **practically**

amaze verb
*He **amazed** us with his magic tricks.*
- **to astonish**
- **to astound**

amazed adjective
*I was **amazed** when I saw his new bike.*
- **astonished**
- **staggered**
- **flabbergasted** (*informal*)
- **stunned**

amazing adjective
*What an **amazing** car!*
- **wonderful**
- **fantastic**
- **incredible**
- **phenomenal**

ambition noun
*Her **ambition** is to be a doctor.*
- **a dream**
- **a goal**
- **an aim**
- **a wish**

amount noun
*They ate a huge **amount** of food!*
- **a quantity**

amuse verb
*His jokes **amused** us all.*
- **to entertain**
- **to make someone laugh**

amusing adjective
*He told us a very **amusing** story.*
- **funny**
- **humorous**
- **entertaining**

anger noun
*She couldn't hide her **anger**.*
- **annoyance**
- **irritation**
- **fury**
- **rage**
  *Use **irritation** for slight anger:*
  *He waved the flies away in **irritation**.*
  *Use **fury** or **rage** for very great anger:*
  *Mr Evans turned crimson with **rage**.*

angry adjective
*Mum looked very **angry**.*
- **cross**
- **annoyed**
- **irritated**
- **furious**
- **livid**
- **mad**
  *Use **irritated** if someone is slightly angry:*
  *My mum gets a bit **irritated** if I keep asking her questions.*
  *Use **furious** or **livid** if someone is very angry:*
  *My dad was absolutely **livid** when he saw what we'd done.*

animal noun
*What sort of **animal** was it?*
- **a creature**

WORD WEB

some types of animal
- a mammal
- a bird
- a fish
- a reptile
- an amphibian
- an insect

some farm animals
- chicken
- cow
- duck
- goose
- horse
- pig
- sheep

some animals that are popular as pets
- cat
- dog
- gerbil
- guinea pig
- hamster
- pony
- rabbit
- tropical fish

some wild animals you might see in Britain
- badger
- deer
- fox
- hare
- hedgehog
- mole
- mouse
- rabbit
- rat
- squirrel

some wild animals from hot countries
- baboon
- camel
- cheetah
- chimpanzee
- crocodile
- elephant
- gazelle
- giraffe
- gorilla
- hippopotamus
- leopard
- lion
- monkey
- panther
- penguin
- rhinoceros
- tiger
- zebra

some wild animals from cold countries
- penguin
- polar bear
- reindeer
- wolf

some wild animals from Australia
- kangaroo
- koala
- kookaburra
- wallaby
- wombat

some wild animals that live in the sea
- dolphin
- fish
- octopus
- seal
- sea-lion
- shark
- turtle
- walrus
- whale

annoy verb
1 *The loud music was **annoying** me.*
   - **to irritate**
   - **to get on someone's nerves**
2 *My little brother keeps **annoying** me!*
   - **to pester**
   - **to bother**
   - **to tease**
   - **to bug**
   OPPOSITE please

a
b
c
d
e
f
g
h
i
j
k
l
m
n
o
p
q
r
s
t
u
v
w
x
y
z

5

a
b
c
d
e
f
g
h
i
j
k
l
m
n
o
p
q
r
s
t
u
v
w
x
y
z

annoyed adjective
*My mum was quite **annoyed** with me.*
- **cross**
- **angry**
- **irritated**
- **exasperated**
OPPOSITE pleased

annoying adjective
*Sometimes my sister can be very **annoying**.*
- **irritating**
- **tiresome**

answer noun
*I called his name, but there was no **answer**.*
- **a reply**
- **a response**

answer verb
*I shouted to her, but she didn't **answer**.*
- **to reply**
- **to respond**

apologize verb
*I **apologized** for being rude.*
- **to say sorry**

appear verb
*The ship **appeared** on the horizon.*
- **to arrive**
- **to come into view**
- **to become visible**
OPPOSITE disappear

appointment noun
*Your **appointment** is at two o'clock.*
- **a meeting**
- **an interview**

approach verb
*I started to feel nervous as we **approached** the theatre.*
- **to come near to**
- **to come towards**

appropriate adjective
*Those clothes are not **appropriate** for church.*
- **suitable**
- **acceptable**
- **right**

area noun
1 *There is a special **area** where you can play.*
- **a place**
- **a space**
- **a patch**
2 *This is a very nice **area** of the city.*
- **a part**
- **a district**

argue verb
*Why are you two always **arguing**?*
- **to quarrel**
- **to squabble**
- **to fight**
- **to fall out**
- **to bicker**
  To **bicker** means to argue about small things that are not important:
  *The two girls were **bickering** about whose pencil it was.*
OPPOSITE agree

argument noun
*They had a big **argument**.*
- **a quarrel**
- **a disagreement**
- **a row**
- **a fight**

arrange verb
1 She **arranged** the books carefully on the shelf.
   • **to place**
   • **to set out**
2 We have **arranged** to meet at ten o'clock.
   • **to plan**
   • **to agree**
3 My mother has **arranged** everything for my party.
   • **to organize**
   • **to plan**

arrest verb
   The police have **arrested** the robbers.
   • **to catch**
   • **to capture**
   • **to take prisoner** The police have taken the robbers prisoner.
   • **to take into custody** The police have taken the robbers into custody.

arrive verb
1 We finally **arrived** in London.
   • **to reach**
   • **to get to**
2 Jessica **arrived** at the party two hours late.
   • **to come**
   • **to turn up**
3 When does the plane **arrive** in New York?
   • **to land**
   • **to touch down**
   • **to get in**
4 The boat should **arrive** at ten o'clock.
   • **to dock**
   • **to get in**
   OPPOSITE depart

art noun
   I really enjoy doing **art** at school.
   • **drawing**
   • **painting**
   • **sketching**
   • **modelling**
   • **pottery**
   • **sculpture**
   • **graphics**

ashamed adjective
   He was **ashamed** of what he had done.
   • **sorry** He was sorry for what he had done.
   • **upset** He was upset about what he had done.
   • **remorseful** He was remorseful for what he had done.

ask verb
   He **asked** me what my name was.
   • **to enquire**

ask for verb
   I've **asked for** a new bike for my birthday.
   • **to request**
   • **to demand**
   • **to beg for**
   To **demand** something means to say that you must have it:
   He held out his hand and **demanded** the money.
   To **beg** for something means to ask someone very strongly for it:
   'Please, please can I go?' she begged.

asleep adjective
   Grandfather was **asleep** in front of the fire.
   • **sleeping**
   • **dozing**
   • **resting**
   • **slumbering**
   • **snoozing**
   • **having a nap**
   OPPOSITE awake

a
b
c
d
e
f
g
h
i
j
k
l
m
n
o
p
q
r
s
t
u
v
w
x
y
z

a
b
c
d
e
f
g
h
i
j
k
l
m
n
o
p
q
r
s
t
u
v
w
x
y
z
.

astonish verb

*She **astonished** us with her skilful tricks.*
- to amaze
- to astound

astonished adjective

*I was **astonished** when he told me how much his bike cost.*
- amazed
- staggered
- flabbergasted
- stunned

athlete noun

*They are very talented **athletes**.*
- a sportsman
- a sportswoman
- a runner
- a sprinter
- a high jumper
- a long jumper

athletics noun

*Do you enjoy doing **athletics**?*
- running
- sprinting
- hurdles
- the high jump
- the long jump
- the triple jump

attach verb

*You must **attach** the string firmly to the kite.*
- to fix
- to fasten
- to join
- to connect
- to tie
- to stick
- to glue

attack verb

*The two robbers **attacked** them and stole their money.*
- to assault
- to set upon
- to ambush
- to mug

To **ambush** someone means to jump out from a hiding place and attack them:
*Robbers hide in the hills and **ambush** travellers.*
To **mug** someone means to attack and rob them in the street:
*Two men **mugged** an old lady in the High Street.*

attractive adjective

1 *She's a very **attractive** girl.*
That's an attractive colour.
- beautiful
- pretty
- lovely
- gorgeous

2 *He's an attractive boy.*
- handsome
- good-looking

OPPOSITE unattractive

average adjective

*What is the **average** number of children in a class?*
- normal
- usual
- ordinary
- typical

avoid verb

1 *I'm allergic to cats, so I try to **avoid** them.*
- to keep away from
- to steer clear of

2 *He always tries to **avoid** doing the washing up.*
- to get out of

award noun
> He got a special **award** for his bravery.
> • **a prize**
> • **a reward**
> • **a trophy**
> • **a cup**
> • **a medal**

awful adjective
> What an **awful** smell!
> • **terrible**
> • **dreadful**
> • **horrible**

awkward adjective
> 1 The box was an **awkward** shape.
> • **difficult**
> • **bulky**
> 2 They arrived at a very **awkward** time.
> • **inconvenient**

a
b
c
d
e
f
g
h
i
j
k
l
m
n
o
p
q
r
s
t
u
v
w
x
y
z

Bb

a
b
c
d
e
f
g
h
i
j
k
l
m
n
o
p
q
r
s
t
u
v
w
x
y
z

baby noun
- **a child**
- **an infant**
- **a toddler**
  A **toddler** is a baby that is just learning to walk.

back noun
1 We sat at the **back** of the hall.
- **the rear**
2 I was at the **back** of the queue.
- **the end**
- **the rear**
OPPOSITE front

bad adjective

> ⚠️ **OVERUSED WORD**
> Try to vary the words you use to mean bad. Here are some other words you can use instead.
> 1 He's a **bad** man.
> - **wicked**
> - **evil**
> - **cruel**
> - **nasty**
> Use **wicked** for a very bad person: The country was ruled by a **wicked** king.
> Use **evil** for something that is very bad and frightening: I sensed that there was something **evil** in that cave.
> Use **cruel** for someone who is very unkind and enjoys hurting people: The two horses were bought by a **cruel** master.
> Use **nasty** for someone who is mean or unkind: He's a mean and **nasty** boy!

2 You **bad** dog!
- **naughty**
- **disobedient**
3 There has been a **bad** accident on the motorway.
- **terrible**
- **awful**
- **dreadful**
- **horrible**
- **shocking**
4 I'm very **bad** at maths.
- **hopeless**
- **useless**
- **poor**
- **terrible**
- **weak**
- **incompetent**
5 Sara's got a **bad** knee.
- **sore**
- **injured**
- **painful**
6 Food goes **bad** if you don't keep it in the fridge.
- **off**
- **rotten**
- **mouldy**
- **sour**
  Use **off** for meat and fish: The meat has gone **off**.
  Use **rotten** for fruit: The apples were brown and **rotten**.
  Use **mouldy** for cheese: The cheese was **mouldy** and smelly.
  Use **sour** for milk or cream: This milk has gone **sour**.
OPPOSITE good

badly adverb
1 Our team played **badly**.
- **terribly**
- **appallingly**
- **poorly**

2 *Is she badly injured?*
- **seriously**

bad-tempered adjective
*Why are you so **bad-tempered** today?*
- **grumpy**
- **moody**
- **irritable**
OPPOSITE good-tempered

bag noun
*She packed her books into her **bag**.*

> 🕸 **WORD WEB**
> **some types of bag**
> - a backpack
> - a briefcase
> - a carrier bag
> - a handbag
> - a holdall
> - a rucksack
> - a school bag
> - a suitcase
> - a trunk

baggy adjective
*He was wearing a pair of **baggy** trousers.*
- **loose**
- **loose-fitting**
- **large**

ball noun
*She made the dough into the shape of a **ball**.*
- **a sphere**
- **a globe**

ban verb
*Our school has **banned** mobile phones.*
- **to forbid**
- **to prohibit**

Use **forbid** when a person tells someone not to do something:
*The teacher has **forbidden** us to talk.*
Use **prohibit** when something is not allowed because of a rule or law:
*Smoking in public places is now **prohibited**.*

band noun
*I play the drums in the school **band**.*
- **a group**
- **a brass band**
- **an orchestra**
A **group** is any band, especially one that plays pop music.
A **brass band** is a group playing trumpets and other brass instruments.
An **orchestra** is a large group of musicians playing classical music.

bang noun
*We heard a loud **bang**.*
- **a crash**
- **a thud**
- **a thump**
- **a boom**
- **an explosion**

bang verb
1 *He **banged** on the door.*
- **to knock**
- **to rap**
- **to tap**
- **to hammer**
To **rap** or **tap** means to bang lightly:
*She **tapped** gently on the window.*
To **hammer** means to bang loudly:
*He **hammered** loudly on the door.* →

a
b
c
d
e
f
g
h
i
j
k
l
m
n
o
p
q
r
s
t
u
v
w
x
y
z

2 *I fell and **banged** my head.*
- **to bump**
- **to knock**
- **to hit**
- **to bash**

bar noun
*There were iron **bars** on the windows to stop people from escaping.*
- **a pole**
- **a rail**
- **a stick**
- **a rod**

bare adjective
*The baby was **bare**.*
- **naked**
- **undressed**
- **nude**

barrier noun
*The police put up a **barrier** to keep people out.*
- **a fence**
- **a railing**
- **a wall**
- **a barricade**
- **a roadblock**
  A **roadblock** is a barrier the police put up to stop cars going along a road.

base noun
1 *There were plants growing along the **base** of the wall.*
- **the bottom**
- **the foot**
2 *The soldiers returned to their **base**.*
- **a headquarters**
- **a camp**

basic adjective
*You must learn the **basic** skills first.*
- **main**
- **key**
- **essential**
- **elementary**

bat noun

> **WORD WEB**
> **some types of bat**
> - a baseball bat
> - a cricket bat
> - a golf club
> - a hockey stick
> - a tennis racket

battle noun
*There was an important **battle** here in 1066.*
- **a fight**
- **an attack**
- **a skirmish**
- **a siege**
  A **skirmish** is a small battle between a few people or soldiers:
  There were a few **skirmishes** in the playground.
  A **siege** is a long battle in which one army is trapped inside a place and cannot get out:
  There was a **siege** of the castle in 1232.

bay noun
*The ship took shelter in the **bay**.*
- **a cove**
- **an inlet**

beach noun
*The children played on the **beach**.*
- **the sand**
- **the seaside**
- **the seashore**

a
b
c
d
e
f
g
h
i
j
k
l
m
n
o
p
q
r
s
t
u
v
w
x
y
z

- **the shore**
- **the shingle**
  Shingle is a pebbly beach:
  We walked over the **shingle**, looking
  for colourful pebbles.

beam noun
1 Old oak **beams** supported the
  ceiling.
  - **a rafter**
  - **a joist**
  - **a girder**
2 A **beam** of light shone onto the
  table.
  - **a ray**
  - **a shaft**

bear verb
1 The ice may not **bear** your weight.
  - **to support**
  - **to hold**
2 I can't **bear** loud music!
  - **to stand**
  - **to put up with**

beast noun
  A huge **beast** roamed the forest.
  - **a creature**
  - **a monster**
  - **a brute**
  - **a wild animal**

beat verb
1 We **beat** the other team 1–0.
  - **to defeat**
  - **to thrash**
    To **thrash** someone means to beat
    them very easily:
    They **thrashed** us 6–0.
2 It's cruel to **beat** animals.
  - **to hit**
  - **to thrash**
  - **to whip**

3 **Beat** the eggs and sugar
  together.
  - **to mix**
  - **to blend**
  - **to stir**
  - **to whip**

beautiful adjective
1 He married the **beautiful**
  princess.
  - **lovely**
  - **pretty**
  - **fair**
  - **attractive**
  - **gorgeous**
  - **stunning**
  - **glamorous**
    Use **gorgeous** or **stunning** if someone
    is very beautiful:
    You look absolutely **stunning** in that
    dress!
    Use **glamorous** if someone looks
    beautiful and rich:
    She looked like a **glamorous** film
    star.
    OPPOSITE ugly
2 The weather was **beautiful** for sports
  day.
  - **lovely**
  - **gorgeous**
  - **wonderful**
  - **fantastic**
  - **fine**
  OPPOSITE awful

become verb
1 A tadpole will **become**
  a frog.
  - **to change into**
  - **to grow into**
  - **to turn into**
2 He **became** angry.
  - **to get**
  - **to grow**

a
b
c
d
e
f
g
h
i
j
k
l
m
n
o
p
q
r
s
t
u
v
w
x
y
z

bed noun

some types of bed
- a berth (*a bed on a ship*)
- a bunk (*one of two beds on top of each other*)
- a cot (*a bed with sides for a baby*)
- a four-poster bed (*a bed with curtains around it*)
- a hammock (*a piece of cloth that you hang up and use as a bed*)

beg verb

*We **begged** him to let us go.*
- **to plead with** *We pleaded with him to let us go.*
- **to ask**
- **to implore** *We implored him to let us go.*

begin verb

1 *The little girl **began** to laugh.*
- **to start**
2 *What time does the film **begin**?*
- **to start**
- **to commence**
OPPOSITE end

beginning noun

*I was scared at the **beginning** of the film.*
- **the start**
- **the opening**
OPPOSITE ending

behave verb

1 *She was **behaving** rather strangely.*
- **to act**
2 *Make sure you **behave** at the party.*
- **to be good**
- **to behave yourself**
- **to be on your best behaviour**

behaviour noun

*The children's **behaviour** was excellent.*
- **conduct**
- **manners**
- **attitude**

belief noun

*People have different religious **beliefs**.*
- **a faith**
- **an opinion**
- **a view**

believe verb

1 *I don't **believe** you.*
- **to trust**
2 *I **believe** that she is innocent.*
- **to think**
- **to be sure**
- **to be convinced**
3 *The ancient Greeks **believed** in many gods.*
- **to have faith in**
- **to put your faith in**

bell noun

WRITING TIPS
Here are some useful words for writing about bells.
- The school bell **rings** at ten to nine.
- The grandfather clock in the hall **chimes** every hour.
- The sleigh bells **jingled** as we rode along.
- The tiny bells on the Christmas tree **tinkled** as I walked past.
- The huge church bell began to **toll**.

belong verb

1 *This book **belongs** to me.*
- **to be owned by**
2 *Ali **belongs** to the football club.*
- **to be a member of**
- **to be in** *Ali is in the football club.*

3 *These pencils **belong** in the cupboard.*
- **to go**

belongings noun
*Be sure to take your **belongings** when you get off the train.*
- **possessions**
- **property**
- **things**

bend noun
*There are a lot of sharp **bends** in this road.*
- **a corner**
- **a turn**
- **a twist**
- **a curve**

bend verb
1 *He **bent** the wire into the correct shape.*
- **to twist**
- **to curve**
- **to curl**
- **to coil**
- **to wind**
OPPOSITE straighten
2 *She **bent** down to tie her shoelaces.*
- **to stoop**
- **to crouch**
- **to duck**

bent adjective
*The back wheel of the bicycle was **bent**.*
- **twisted**
- **crooked**
- **distorted**
- **warped**
OPPOSITE straight

best adjective
*She is the **best** swimmer in the world.*
- **finest**
- **greatest**

- **number-one**
- **top**
OPPOSITE worst

better adjective
*Tom has been ill, but he's **better** now.*
- **all right**
- **recovered**
- **cured**

beware verb
***Beware** of the dog.*
- **to be careful of**
- **to watch out for**

bicycle noun
- **a bike**
- **a cycle**

> **WORD WEB**
> **some types of bicycle**
> - a mountain bike
> - a racing bike
> - a tandem (*for two people*)
> - a tricycle (*with three wheels*)
> - a unicycle (*with one wheel*)

big adjective

> ⚠ **OVERUSED WORD**
> Try to vary the words you use to mean *big*. Here are some other words you can use instead.
> **1** *He put the books into a big box.*
> - **large**
> - **huge**
> - **enormous**
> - **massive**
> - **gigantic**
> - **colossal**
>   Use **large** with the same meaning as **big**:
>   *There was a **large** wooden* →

crate in the middle of the room.
Use **huge** or **enormous** for
something that is very big:
*We had to climb over some **huge**
rocks.*
Use **massive**, **gigantic**, or **colossal**
for something that is very big
indeed:
*The dragon swept the ship aside
with one of its **colossal** claws.*

2 *There are lots of big buildings in the
city centre.*
- **large**
- **tall**
- **high**
- **spacious**
- **vast**
- **grand**
- **magnificent**
Use **spacious** for houses and flats
that have plenty of space inside:
*Inside, the flat was quite **spacious**.*
Use **vast** for very big buildings or
rooms:
*Underneath the house was a **vast**
cellar.*
Use **grand** or **magnificent** for
buildings that are big and beautiful:
*We were amazed by the
magnificent mountains.*

3 *Tom is quite big for his age.*
- **tall**
- **broad**
- **well-built**
Use **broad** or **well-built** for someone
who looks strong and not very thin:
*He was a strong, **well-built** boy.*

4 *This T-shirt is too big for me.*
- **long**
- **loose**
- **baggy**

5 *Mice are a big problem for farmers.*
- **important**

- **serious**
- **significant**
OPPOSITE small

bird noun

WORD WEB

some familiar British birds
- blackbird
- blue tit
- chaffinch
- crow
- cuckoo
- dove
- house martin
- lark
- magpie
- pigeon
- robin
- sparrow
- swallow
- thrush
- woodpecker
- wren

some birds of prey
- buzzard
- eagle
- hawk
- kestrel
- kite
- owl
- vulture

some farm birds
- chicken
- duck
- goose

some waterbirds
- flamingo
- heron
- kingfisher
- moorhen
- pelican
- swan

some seabirds
- albatross
- puffin
- seagull

some tropical birds
- budgerigar
- canary
- cockatoo
- macaw
- magpie
- mynah bird
- parakeet
- parrot
- toucan

WRITING TIPS

Here are some useful words for writing about birds.
- A strange-looking bird **flew** past me.
- The eagle **soared** high in the sky.
- I watched the large bird **hover** and **glide**, then **swoop** down on its prey.
- Some sparrows **fluttered** about in the trees.
- A robin **hopped** onto the branch next to me.
- I could hear birds **singing**.
- The little birds **twittered** and **chirped** in trees.
- Owls **screeched** and **hooted** in the wood.

biscuit noun
- **a cookie**
- **a cracker**
- **a wafer**

A **cracker** is a dry biscuit for eating with cheese. A **wafer** is a very thin biscuit.

bit noun

WORD WEB

Use **piece** with the same meaning as **bit**:
I've lost a **piece** of my jigsaw.
Use **chunk**, **lump**, **block**, or **slab** for a big bit of something:
He picked up a big **lump** of rock.

Use **fragment** for a small bit of something:
We found some tiny **fragments** of Roman pottery.
Use **slice** or **sliver** for a thin bit of something:
Would you like a **slice** of cake?
Use **scrap** for a small bit of paper or cloth:
I wrote the address down on a **scrap** of paper.
Use **chip** for a small bit that has broken off something:
He found a **chip** of glass on the floor.
Use **bite, mouthful, nibble,** or **taste** for a small bit of something you eat:
Can I have a **bite** of your biscuit?

bite verb
1 Be careful that dog doesn't **bite** you.
- **to nip**
- **to snap at**
2 Mice have **bitten** a hole in the carpet.
- **to chew**
- **to gnaw**
- **to nibble**

bitter adjective
The medicine had a **bitter** taste.
- **sour**
- **sharp**
- **acid**
OPPOSITE sweet

black adjective
1 It was a cold, **black** night.
- **dark**
- **pitch black**
- **moonless**
- **starless** →

a
b
c
d
e
f
g
h
i
j
k
l
m
n
o
p
q
r
s
t
u
v
w
x
y
z

a
b
c
d
e
f
g
h
i
j
k
l
m
n
o
p
q
r
s
t
u
v
w
x
y
z

2 She had **black** hair.
- **dark**
- **jet black**
- **ebony**

blame verb
The teacher **blamed** me for breaking the window.
- **to accuse** The teacher accused me of breaking the window.
- **to tell off** The teacher told me off for breaking the window.
- **to scold** The teacher scolded me for breaking the window.

blank adjective
We started with **a blank** piece of paper.
- **clean**
- **fresh**
- **unused**

blaze verb
The fire was **blazing** merrily.
- **to burn**
- **to flicker**
- **to glow**

blob noun
There was a **blob** of jam on the table.
- **a lump**
- **a dollop**
- **a drop**

block noun
They covered the hole with a **block** of concrete.
- **a piece**
- **a lump**
- **a slab**

block verb
A huge lorry had **blocked** the road.
- **to obstruct**
- **to clog up**

blow verb
He **blew** on his food to cool it down.
- **to breathe**
- **to puff**

blow up verb
1 Shall I help you **blow up** the balloons?
- **to inflate**
2 The car **blew up**.
- **to explode**

blue adjective
- **navy blue**
- **sky-blue**
- **royal blue**
- **turquoise**
- **azure** (bright blue)

blush verb
She **blushed** whenever a boy spoke to her.
- **to go red**
- **to redden**
- **to flush**

boast verb
He's always **boasting** about how good he is at football.
- **to brag**
- **to show off**
- **to gloat**

boat noun
We need a **boat** to get across the lake.
- **a ship**
- **a vessel**
- **a craft**

> **WORD WEB**
> **some types of boat**
> - an aircraft carrier
> - a barge
> - a battleship

- a canoe
- a dinghy
- a ferry
- a fishing boat
- a lifeboat
- a motor boat
- a raft
- a rowing boat
- a sailing boat
- a speedboat
- a tanker
- a trawler
- a warship
- a yacht

WRITING TIPS

Here are some useful words for writing about boats.
- The little fishing boat **bobbed up and down** in the water.
- The dinghy **drifted** slowly out to sea.
- We **floated** down the river on our raft.
- The barge **chugged along** slowly.
- The speedboat **sped** through the water.
- We **sailed** the yacht into the harbour and **moored** it to the jetty.
- We were worried our little rowing boat would **capsize** in the storm.

body noun

WORD WEB

some parts of your body
- ankle
- arm
- armpit
- calf
- cheek
- chest
- chin
- ear
- elbow
- eye
- finger
- foot
- forehead
- hand
- head
- heel
- hip
- knee
- leg
- lip
- mouth
- navel
- neck
- nose
- shin
- shoulder
- skin
- stomach
- thigh
- throat
- thumb
- toe
- waist
- wrist

bog noun
*They didn't want to get lost in the **bog**.*
- **a marsh**
- **a swamp**

boggy adjective
*The ground was very **boggy**.*
- **wet**
- **soft**
- **sticky**
- **marshy**

boil verb
*Is the water **boiling** yet?*
- **to bubble**
- **to simmer**

boiling adjective
1 *It was a **boiling** hot day.*
- **hot**
- **baking** →

- **scorching**
- **sweltering**

2 *The radiator's **boiling**!*
- **hot**
- **red hot**

bolt verb

1 *He **bolted** the door.*
- **to lock**
- **to fasten**

2 *The horse **bolted**.*
- **to run away**
- **to flee**

3 *She **bolted** her food.*
- **to gobble down**
- **to guzzle**
- **to wolf**

book noun

> **WORD WEB**
> **some types of book**
> - an annual
> - an atlas
> - a brochure
> - a catalogue
> - a dictionary
> - a directory
> - an encyclopedia
> - a novel
> - a picture book
> - a reference book
> - a story book
> - a textbook
> - a thesaurus

bored adjective
*I'm **bored** with this!*
- **fed up**
- **tired**

boring adjective
*This film is really **boring**!*
- **dull**
- **tedious**

- **dreary**
- **unexciting**
- **uneventful**
- **monotonous**
  Use **uneventful** or **unexciting** when nothing interesting happens:
  *It was a very **uneventful** day.*
  Use **monotonous** to describe a boring voice:
  *The doctor spoke in a low, **monotonous** voice.*
  OPPOSITE interesting

borrow verb
*Can I **borrow** your pen for a minute, please?*
- **to use**
- **to take**

boss noun
1 *Who's the **boss** here?*
- **the person in charge**
- **the leader**
- **the chief**
- **the head**

2 *Her **boss** said she could have the day off.*
- **an employer**
- **a manager**
- **a supervisor**
- **a director**

bossy adjective
*She can be **bossy** sometimes.*
- **domineering**
- **bullying**

bother verb
1 *Is the loud music **bothering** you?*
- **to annoy**
- **to disturb**

- **to upset**
- **to irritate**

2 They didn't **bother** to clear up their mess.
- **to make the effort**
- **to take the trouble**

bottom noun

1 We'll wait at the **bottom** of the hill.
- **the foot**
- **the base**
OPPOSITE top

2 She fell and landed on her **bottom**.
- **backside**
- **rear**

bounce verb

The ball **bounced** off the wall.
- **to rebound**
- **to ricochet**

bowl noun

She put the fruit into a **bowl**.
- **a dish**
- **a basin**

box noun

1 I bought a **box** of cereal.
- **a packet**
- **a carton**

2 We packed the books into a **box**.
- **a case**
- **a crate**
- **a chest**
- **a trunk**

boy noun
- **a lad**
- **a kid**
- **a child**
- **a youngster**
- **a teenager**

brain noun

He's got a very good **brain**.
- **a mind**

branch noun

A large **branch** had fallen off the tree.
- **a bough**

brand noun

He likes expensive **brands** of trainers.
- **a make**
- **a sort**
- **a label**

brave adjective

Are you **brave** enough to fight the dragon?
- **courageous**
- **bold**
- **daring**
- **fearless**
- **heroic**
- **adventurous**

Use **fearless** if someone seems to feel no fear:
The captain was **fearless** in battle.
Use **heroic** if someone helps another person in a very brave way:
The firemen were rewarded for their **heroic** rescue of the children.
Use **adventurous** if someone is brave enough to start a new adventure:
Are you **adventurous** enough to take on this challenge?
OPPOSITE cowardly

bravery noun

He got a medal for his **bravery**.
- **courage**
- **heroism**
- **valour**
OPPOSITE cowardice

a
b
c
d
e
f
g
h
i
j
k
l
m
n
o
p
q
r
s
t
u
v
w
x
y
z

break verb

1 *I dropped a cup and it **broke**.*
- **to crack**
- **to chip**
- **to smash**
- **to shatter**
- **to splinter**

Use **chip** when a small piece breaks off something:
*I **chipped** my favourite mug.*
Use **smash**, **shatter**, and **splinter** when something breaks into a lot of pieces:
*The glass **shattered** into hundreds of tiny pieces.*

2 *The stick **broke** in two.*
- **to snap**
- **to split**

3 *The bridge will **break** if there is too much weight on it.*
- **to collapse**
- **to fall down**
- **to fall apart**

4 *My brother **broke** my CD player.*
- **to damage**
- **to ruin**

5 *She fell and **broke** her wrist.*
- **to fracture**

6 *You will be punished if you **break** the rules.*
- **to disobey**

break noun

1 *We climbed through a **break** in the hedge.*
- **a gap**
- **a hole**
- **an opening**

2 *There was a **break** in the pipe.*
- **a crack**
- **a split**
- **a hole**

3 *Let's stop for a short **break**.*
- **a rest**
- **a pause**

4 *There will be a fifteen-minute **break** halfway through the show.*
- **an interval**
- **an intermission**

break off verb

1 *The strap on my bag has **broken** off.*
- **to fall off**
- **to come off**
- **to drop off**
- **to snap off**

2 *She picked up the bar of chocolate and **broke** a piece off.*
- **to pull off**
- **to cut off**
- **to snap off**
- **to rip off**
- **to tear off**

bridge noun

> **WORD WEB**
> **some types of bridge**
> - a flyover (*over a motorway*)
> - a footbridge (*for people*)
> - a viaduct (*over a river or valley*)

brief adjective

1 *We only had time for a **brief** visit.*
- **short**
- **quick**
- **fleeting**

2 *He wrote a **brief** letter to his aunt.*
- **short**
- **concise**
- OPPOSITE **long**

bright adjective

1 *We saw a **bright** light in the sky.*
- **shining**
- **dazzling**

- **brilliant**
- **glaring**
- **blinding**
- **glowing**
- **gleaming**
  Use **dazzling** and **brilliant** for a light that is very bright:
  We watched the **dazzling** firework display.
  Use **glaring** and **blinding** for a light that is so bright you cannot look at it:
  We turned away from the **blinding** headlights.
  Use **glowing** and **gleaming** for a soft, gentle light:
  We could see the **glowing** light of the fire in the distance.
  OPPOSITE dull
2 I like wearing **bright** colours.
  - **vivid**
  - **strong**
  - **rich**
  OPPOSITE dull
3 He's a very **bright** boy.
  - **clever**
  - **intelligent**
  - **brainy**
  - **quick**
  - **sharp**
  - **smart**
  OPPOSITE stupid
4 It was a lovely **bright** day.
  - **clear**
  - **fine**
  - **sunny**
  - **brilliant**
    Use **brilliant** for a very bright day:
    The next morning was a **brilliant** day of blue skies and hot sun.
  OPPOSITE gloomy

brilliant adjective
1 He is a **brilliant** scientist.
  - **intelligent**
  - **clever**

  - **talented**
  OPPOSITE stupid
2 It's a **brilliant** film.
  - **great**
  - **excellent**
  - **wonderful**
  - **fantastic**
  - **marvellous**
  OPPOSITE terrible

bring verb
1 I'll **bring** the shopping in.
  - **to carry**
  - **to take**
2 Please **bring** me a drink.
  - **to get**
  - **to fetch**

broad adjective
  The river is quite **broad** here.
  - **wide**
  - **big**
  - **large**
  OPPOSITE narrow

brown adjective
  He was wearing **brown** trousers.
  - **beige**
  - **fawn**
  - **khaki**
  - **chocolate brown**

brush verb
  We had to **brush** the floor.
  - **to sweep**
  - **to clean**

bubbles noun
  She picked up a handful of **bubbles** from the bath.
  - **foam**
  - **lather**
  - **suds**

a
b
c
d
e
f
g
h
i
j
k
l
m
n
o
p
q
r
s
t
u
v
w
x
y
z

a
b
c
d
e
f
g
h
i
j
k
l
m
n
o
p
q
r
s
t
u
v
w
x
y
z

bucket noun
  • **a pail**

bug noun
  1 *You can find lots of interesting bugs in your garden.*
  • **an insect**
  • **a creepy-crawly** (*informal*)
  2 *She has been off school with a bug.*
  • **a virus**
  • **a germ**
  • **an illness**
  3 *The computer program had a bug in it.*
  • **a fault**
  • **an error**
  • **a virus**

build verb
  It takes about six months to build a new house.
  • **to construct**
  • **to put up**

building noun

🕸 **WORD WEB**
some buildings where people live
• bungalow
• castle
• cottage
• farmhouse
• flat
• house
• mansion
• palace
• skyscraper
• tower
• villa

some buildings where people worship
• cathedral
• chapel
• church
• gurdwara
• monastery
• mosque
• synagogue
• temple

other types of building
• cafe
• cinema
• factory
• fire station
• garage
• hospital
• hotel
• library
• mill
• museum
• office
• police station
• post office
• prison
• school
• shop
• theatre

bully verb
  Some of the older boys were bullying him.
  • **to tease**
  • **to torment**
  • **to terrorize**
  • **to persecute**
    *Use **terrorize** and **persecute** when someone bullies a person badly:*
    *He used to **terrorize** the younger kids and take all their money off them.*

bump noun
  1 *The book fell to the ground with a bump.*
  • **a bang**
  • **a crash**
  • **a thud**
  • **a thump**

2 She's got a nasty **bump** on her head.
- **a lump**
- **a swelling**

bump verb
  I fell and **bumped** my head.
- **to bang**
- **to knock**
- **to hit**
- **to bash**

bumpy adjective
  We drove along the **bumpy** road.
- **rough**
- **uneven**

bunch noun
  1 He bought me a **bunch** of flowers.
- **a bouquet**
- **a posy**
  2 She handed me a large **bunch** of keys.
- **a collection**
- **a set**
- **a quantity**
  3 I went to the cinema with a **bunch** of friends.
- **a group**
- **a crowd**
- **a gang**

bundle noun
  He brought a **bundle** of old newspapers.
- **a pile**
- **a heap**

burglar noun
  The police arrested the **burglars**.
- **a robber**
- **a thief**
- **an intruder**
- **a housebreaker**

burn verb
  1 Paper **burns** easily.
- **to catch fire**
- **to catch light**
- **to burst into flames**
  2 A fire was **burning** in the grate.
- **to blaze**
- **to glow**
- **to smoulder**
- **to flicker**
    Use **blaze** when a fire burns quickly, with a lot of heat:
    A warm fire **blazed** in the corner of the room.
    Use **glow** or **smoulder** when a fire burns slowly, without big flames:
    Last night's bonfire was still **smouldering** in the garden.
    Use **flicker** when a fire burns with small flames:
    The camp fire **flickered** merrily.
  3 We can **burn** all this rubbish.
- **to set fire to**
- **to set alight**
- **to incinerate**
  4 He **burnt** his shirt on the iron.
- **to scorch**
- **to singe**

burst verb
  My balloon's **burst**!
- **to pop**
- **to go bang**
- **to split**

bus noun
- **a coach**
- **a minibus**

bush noun
  We hid in the **bushes**.
- **a shrub**

a
b
c
d
e
f
g
h
i
j
k
l
m
n
o
p
q
r
s
t
u
v
w
x
y
z

business noun

1 *His parents run their own business.*
  - **a company**
  - **a firm**
  - **an organization**

2 *Her dad works in business.*
  - **commerce**
  - **industry**
  - **trade**

busy adjective

1 *Dad was busy in the garden.*
  - **occupied**
  - **working**
  OPPOSITE idle

2 *I've had a very busy morning.*
  - **active**
  - **energetic**
  OPPOSITE idle

3 *London is a very busy place.*
  - **crowded**
  - **bustling**
  - **lively**
  OPPOSITE peaceful

buy verb

1 *Where's the best place to buy a bike?*
  - **to get**
  - **to purchase**
  - **to obtain**

2 *My friend bought me some sweets.*
  - **to get** *My friend got me some sweets.*
  - **to treat someone to** *My friend treated me to some sweets.*
  - **to pay for** *My friend paid for some sweets for me.*
  OPPOSITE sell

Cc

cabin noun
> They lived in a log **cabin**.
> - a hut
> - a chalet
> - a shed

cafe noun
> We went to a **cafe** for lunch.
> - a restaurant
> - a snack bar
> - a coffee bar
> - a tearoom
> - a cafeteria

cage noun

> **WORD WEB**
> **some types of cage**
> - a hutch (*for rabbits*)
> - an enclosure (*in a zoo*)
> - an aviary (*for birds*)
> - a pen (*for farm animals*)

calculate verb
> Can you **calculate** the amount we have to pay?
> - to work out
> - to add up

call verb
> 1 'Hello,' she **called**.
>   - to shout
>   - to yell
>   - to cry
> 2 We've decided to **call** the puppy Lucky.
>   - to name

3 I'll **call** you when I get home.
> - to phone
> - to ring
> - to telephone

calm adjective
> 1 The little village was very **calm**.
>   - peaceful
>   - quiet
>   OPPOSITE noisy
> 2 The sea was **calm** now after the storm.
>   - flat
>   - smooth
>   - still
>   OPPOSITE stormy
> 3 It was a lovely **calm** day.
>   - still
>   - windless
>   OPPOSITE windy
> 4 She told the children to keep **calm**.
>   - quiet
>   - relaxed
>   - cool
>   - patient
>   OPPOSITE excited

camera noun

> **WORD WEB**
> **some types of camera**
> - a camcorder
> - a digital camera
> - a video camera

cancel verb
> We had to **cancel** the football match.
> - to call off
> - to abandon
> - to postpone
>   To **postpone** something means to cancel it until a later time:
>   The match has been **postponed** until next Sunday.

a
b
c
d
e
f
g
h
i
j
k
l
m
n
o
p
q
r
s
t
u
v
w
x
y
z

capture verb

*The police have **captured** the robbers.*

- **to catch**
- **to arrest**
- **to take prisoner** *The police have taken the robbers prisoner.*

car noun

*There are too many **cars** on the roads.*

- **a motor car**

WORD WEB

some types of car
- a convertible
- an eco-friendly car
- an estate car
- a four-wheel drive (4x4)
- a hatchback
- a limousine
- a people carrier
- a racing car
- a saloon
- a sports car
- a taxi
- a van

WRITING TIPS

Here are some useful words for writing about cars.

- The little car **accelerated** down the hill then **slowed down** and stopped at the traffic lights.
- The sports car was **speeding** along.
- Cars **zoomed** past us on the motorway.
- The taxi **raced** away towards the airport.
- The old estate car **crawled along** at 40 kilometres per hour.

care verb

*I don't **care** who wins the game.*

- **to mind** *I don't mind who wins.*
- **to be bothered** *I'm not bothered who wins.*

careful adjective

1 *Be **careful** when you cross the busy road.*
- **cautious**
- **alert**
- **attentive**
- **watchful**

2 *This is good, **careful** work.*
- **neat**
- **thorough**
- **conscientious**
- **accurate**

OPPOSITE careless

careless adjective

1 *This work is untidy and **careless**!*
- **messy**
- **untidy**
- **sloppy**
- **shoddy**

2 *She was **careless** and left the door open.*
- **silly**
- **foolish**
- **thoughtless**
- **irresponsible**

OPPOSITE careful

carnival noun
- **a festival**
- **a celebration**
- **a parade**
- **a procession**

carry verb

*We **carried** the boxes into the house.*

- **to lift**
- **to move**

- **to bring**
- **to take**

carry on verb
*The children **carried on** talking.*
- **to continue**
- **to keep on**
- **to go on**

case noun
1 *We packed the books into wooden cases.*
- **a box**
- **a crate**
- **a container**

2 *He left his **case** on the train.*
- **a suitcase**
- **a bag**
- **a holdall**
- **a trunk**
- **a rucksack**

castle noun
- **a fort**
- **a fortress**
- **a stronghold**

cat noun
*A large black **cat** was sitting on the wall.*
- **a pussy**
- **a pussy cat**
- **a moggy** (*informal*)
- **a kitten**
- **a tomcat**
  A **kitten** is a young cat. A **tomcat** is a male cat.

WORD WEB
some types of domestic cat
- a Manx cat
- a Persian cat
- a Siamese cat
- a tabby cat
- a tortoiseshell cat

---

some types of wild cat
- a cheetah
- a leopard
- a lion
- a lynx
- an ocelot
- a panther
- a puma
- a tiger

WRITING TIPS
Here are some useful words for writing about cats.
- Cats can **creep** or **slink** along very quietly.
- They **prowl** around when they are looking for food, then they **crouch down** and **spring** on their prey.
- Cats **miaow** or **mew** when they are hungry. They **purr** when they are happy, and they **hiss** and **spit** when they are angry.

---

catch verb
1 *The police have **caught** the thieves.*
- **to capture**
- **to arrest**
- **to take prisoner** *The police have taken the thieves prisoner.*

2 *We **caught** wild rabbits to eat.*
- **to trap**
- **to snare**

3 *I've **caught** a fish!*
- **to hook**
- **to net**

4 *Try to **catch** the ball.*
- **to get hold of**
- **to take hold of**
- **to hold**
- **to grip**
- **to grab**

5 *She **caught** chickenpox.*
- **to get**
- **to come down with**
- **to be infected with**

a
b
c
d
e
f
g
h
i
j
k
l
m
n
o
p
q
r
s
t
u
v
w
x
y
z

a
b
c
d
e
f
g
h
i
j
k
l
m
n
o
p
q
r
s
t
u
v
w
x
y
z

catching adjective
*I hope your cold isn't **catching**.*
- **infectious**
- **contagious**

cause verb
*The heavy rain **caused** a lot of flooding.*
- **to bring about**
- **to lead to**
- **to result in**
- **to produce**

cave noun
- **a cavern**
- **a grotto**

celebration noun
*There was a huge **celebration** when the new king was crowned.*
- **a party**
- **a feast**
- **a carnival**

centre noun
1 *There was a fire in the **centre** of the room.*
- **the middle**
2 *They live right in the **centre** of the city.*
- **the middle**
- **the heart**
3 *The **centre** of the planet is very hot.*
- **the core**
- **the middle**

certain adjective
1 *I'm **certain** I saw her in town.*
- **sure**
- **positive**
- **convinced**
OPPOSITE uncertain

chair noun
*He sat in his usual **chair** by the fire.*
- **a seat**

WORD WEB
some types of chair
- an armchair
- a bench
- a couch
- a deckchair
- a rocking chair
- a settee
- a sofa
- a stool

champion noun
*I want to win the competition and become the world **champion**.*
- **the winner**
- **the best**
- **the victor**

chance noun
1 *This is our last **chance** to escape.*
- **an opportunity**
2 *There is a **chance** that we will fail.*
- **a possibility**
- **a risk**
3 *We met by **chance**.*
- **luck**
- **coincidence**
- **fate**

change noun
1 *Have you got some **change** for the sweet machine?*
- **coins**
- **loose change**
2 *At the weekend there will be a **change** in the weather.*
- **an alteration**

change verb
1 *Our school has **changed** a lot in the last five years.*
- **to alter**

2 *My design didn't work, so I had to* ***change*** *it.*
- **to alter**
- **to modify**
- **to adjust**

3 *Tadpoles* ***change*** *into frogs.*
- **to turn into**
- **to grow into**
- **to develop into**
- **to become**

4 *I took the dress back to the shop and* ***changed*** *it.*
- **to exchange**
- **to swap**

chaos noun
There was ***chaos*** *when the lights went out.*
- **confusion**
- **pandemonium**
- **mayhem**

character noun
1 *Which* ***character*** *in the pantomime do you want to play?*
- **a part**
- **a role**

2 *Tom has got a lovely* ***character***.
- **a personality**
- **a nature**
- **a temperament**

charge noun
There is no ***charge*** *to go into the museum.*
- **a fee**
- **a payment**

charge verb
1 *How much do they* ***charge*** *for orange juice?*
- **to ask**

2 *The bull was about to* ***charge***.
- **to attack**
- **to rush**
- **to stampede**

charming adjective
What a ***charming*** *little dog!*
- **lovely**
- **pretty**
- **beautiful**
- **delightful**
- **cute**

chart noun
We made a ***chart*** *to show the results of the school's sponsored swim.*
- **a graph**
- **a diagram**
- **a table**

chase verb
1 *The policeman* ***chased*** *the thief down the road.*
- **to run after**
- **to follow**
- **to pursue**

2 *It is natural for cats to* ***chase*** *birds.*
- **to hunt**
- **to track**
- **to catch**

chat verb
Stop ***chatting***!
- **to talk**
- **to chatter**
- **to natter**
- **to gossip**
  To ***gossip*** means to talk about other people:
  I thought all the other girls were ***gossiping*** about me.

cheap adjective
*These trainers are quite **cheap**.*
- **inexpensive**
- **reasonable**
- **cut-price**
OPPOSITE expensive

cheat verb
1 *The other team won, but they **cheated**!*
- **to break the rules**
- **to not play fair**
2 *They **cheated** me out of my money.*
- **to trick**
- **to swindle**
- **to fool**

check verb
1 *Always **check** your spellings.*
- **to look at**
- **to examine**
- **to double-check**
2 *All the cars are carefully **checked** before they are sold.*
- **to inspect**
- **to test**

cheeky adjective
*Don't be so **cheeky**!*
- **rude**
- **impertinent**
- **impudent**
- **insolent**
- **disrespectful**
OPPOSITE respectful

cheer verb
*Everyone **cheered** when our team scored.*
- **to shout**
- **to shout hurray**
- **to applaud**

cheerful adjective
*He seems very **cheerful** today.*
- **happy**
- **smiling**
- **joyful**
- **light-hearted**
- **in a good mood**
OPPOSITE sad

chew verb
1 *She was **chewing** on a sweet.*
- **to bite**
- **to crunch**
- **to suck**
- **to munch**
- **to nibble**
2 *Mice had **chewed** through the wires.*
- **to bite**
- **to gnaw**
- **to nibble**

child noun
- **a boy**
- **a girl**
- **a kid**
- **a youngster**
- **a toddler**
- **a brat**
  *A **toddler** is a young child who is just starting to walk. A **brat** is a badly-behaved child.*

childish adjective
*This behaviour is very **childish**!*
- **silly**
- **immature**
- **juvenile**
- **babyish**
OPPOSITE mature

chilly adjective
*It's a **chilly** evening.*
- **cold**
- **cool**

- **nippy**
- **fresh**
- **frosty**

OPPOSITE warm

choice noun

1 You can have first **choice**.
- **pick**

2 There's a choice of vanilla, strawberry, and chocolate ice cream.
- **a selection**

choke verb

1 The thick smoke was **choking** us.
- **to suffocate**
- **to asphyxiate**

2 The tight collar was **choking** him.
- **to strangle**
- **to throttle**

choose verb

1 Which cake shall I **choose**?
- **to pick**
- **to select**
- **to decide on**

2 We need to **choose** a new class representative.
- **to elect**
- **to vote for**

chop verb

My dad was **chopping** wood.
- **to cut**
- **to saw**
- **to split**

chunk noun

He gave me a slice of bread and a **chunk** of cheese.
- **a piece**
- **a lump**
- **a block**

- **a slab**
- **a wedge**

citizen noun

All the **citizens** of the town came to the meeting.
- **a resident**
- **an inhabitant**

claim verb

She walked up to **claim** her prize.
- **to ask for**
- **to collect**
- **to request**
- **to demand**

clap verb

The audience **clapped**.
- **to applaud**
- **to cheer**

class noun

Which **class** are you in?
- **a form**
- **a group**
- **a set**

clean adjective

1 After two hours, the whole house was **clean**.
- **spotless**
- **tidy**
- **spick and span**

OPPOSITE dirty

2 The water in this river is very **clean**.
- **fresh**
- **pure**
- **clear**
- **unpolluted**

OPPOSITE polluted

3 Start again on a **clean** sheet of paper.
- **blank**
- **unused**
- **new**

a
b
c
d
e
f
g
h
i
j
k
l
m
n
o
p
q
r
s
t
u
v
w
x
y
z

a
b
c
d
e
f
g
h
i
j
k
l
m
n
o
p
q
r
s
t
u
v
w
x
y
z

clean verb

1 *They had to stay at home and **clean** the floors.*
- **to brush**
- **to sweep**
- **to hoover**
- **to vacuum**
- **to wash**
- **to mop**
- **to scrub**

2 *Whose job is it to **clean** the furniture?*
- **to dust**
- **to wipe**
- **to polish**

3 *Go and **clean** your hands.*
- **to wash**
- **to scrub**
- **to rinse**

4 *Don't forget to **clean** your teeth.*
- **to brush**

clear adjective

1 *Make sure you write nice **clear** instructions.*
- **simple**
- **plain**
- **understandable**

2 *Her voice was loud and **clear**.*
- **audible**
- **distinct**
- **understandable**

3 *It was **clear** that he was very angry.*
- **obvious**
- **evident**

4 *Windows are usually made of **clear** glass.*
- **see-through**
- **transparent**
OPPOSITE opaque

5 *The water in the lake was lovely and **clear**.*
- **clean**
- **pure**
OPPOSITE dirty

6 *The next morning the sky was **clear**.*
- **blue**
- **sunny**
- **cloudless**
OPPOSITE cloudy

clear verb

*We need to **clear** these chairs out of the way.*
- **to move**
- **to remove**
- **to take away**

clever adjective

1 *You're so **clever**!*
- **intelligent**
- **bright**
- **brainy**
- **quick**
- **sharp**
- **smart**

2 *That's a very **clever** idea.*
- **good**
- **brilliant**
- **sensible**
- **ingenious**

3 *The old fox was very **clever**.*
- **cunning**
- **crafty**
OPPOSITE stupid

climb verb

1 *He **climbed** the stairs.*
- **to go up**
- **to run up**

2 *The plane **climbed** into the air.*
- **to rise**
- **to ascend**
- **to go up**

3 *They **climbed** over the rocks.*
- **to clamber**
- **to scramble**

cling verb
> He was **clinging** to the
> handrail.
> - **to hold onto**
> - **to grip**
> - **to grasp**

clock noun

> ⊕ **WORD WEB**
> some types of clock
> - an alarm clock
> - a cuckoo clock
> - a digital clock
> - a grandfather clock

close adjective
1 He sat **close** to the fire.
> - **near to**
> - **next to**
> - **beside**
> OPPOSITE far away
2 I took a **close** look at
> the map.
> - **careful**
> - **detailed**

close verb
> Please **close** the door.
> - **to shut**
> - **to lock**
> - **to slam**
> Use **slam** when someone closes a
> door very noisily:
> She ran out and **slammed** the door
> angrily.
> OPPOSITE open

clothes noun
> He was dressed in old-fashioned
> **clothes**.
> - **clothing**
> - **attire**

> ⊕ **WORD WEB**
> **some clothes for warm weather**
> - a blouse
> - a dress
> - a shirt
> - shorts
> - a skirt
> - a sunhat
> - trousers
> - a t-shirt
>
> **some clothes for cold weather**
> - an anorak
> - a cardigan
> - a cloak
> - a coat
> - a duffel coat
> - a fleece
> - gloves
> - a jumper
> - mittens
> - a muffler
> - a pullover
> - a raincoat
> - a scarf
> - a sweater
> - a sweatshirt
> - a woolly hat
>
> **some smart clothes**
> - a blazer
> - a jacket
> - a suit
> - a tie
> - a uniform
> - a waistcoat
>
> **some informal clothes**
> - jeans
> - a polo shirt
> - a sweatshirt
> - a t-shirt
> - a training suit
>
> **some clothes from around the world**
> - a djellaba
> - a kimono →

a
b
c
d
e
f
g
h
i
j
k
l
m
n
o
p
q
r
s
t
u
v
w
x
y
z

a
b
c
d
e
f
g
h
i
j
k
l
m
n
o
p
q
r
s
t
u
v
w
x
y
z

- a salwar kameez
- a sari
- a sarong
- a yashmak

cloudy adjective
*It was a **cloudy** day.*
- **grey**
- **dull**
- **overcast**
- **gloomy**
OPPOSITE clear

club noun
*She joined her local drama **club**.*
- **a society**
- **a group**
- **an association**

clumsy adjective
*I can be quite **clumsy** sometimes.*
- **careless**
- **accident-prone**

coach noun
1 *We went to London on the **coach**.*
- **a bus**
2 *A football **coach** trains the team.*
- **a trainer**
- **an instructor**

coil verb
*She **coiled** the rope around a tree.*
- **to wind**
- **to loop**
- **to twist**
- **to curl**

cold adjective
1 *It's quite **cold** outside today.*
- **chilly**
- **cool**

- **nippy**
- **freezing**
- **bitter**
- **frosty**
- **icy**
- **snowy**
- **wintry**
Use **chilly**, **cool**, and **nippy** for
weather that is slightly cold:
*I put my sweatshirt on because it was
getting a bit **chilly**.*
Use **freezing** or **bitter** for weather
that is very cold:
*It was a **bitter** winter's day.*
Use **frosty**, **icy**, **snowy**, or **wintry**
when there is frost, ice, or snow:
*It was a lovely **frosty** morning.*
2 *I'm **cold**!*
- **chilly**
- **freezing**
- **frozen**
Use **chilly** when you feel slightly
cold:
*I was feeling a bit **chilly** after my swim
in the sea.*
Use **freezing** or **frozen** when you feel
very cold:
*After two hours in the snow, I was
absolutely **frozen**.*
OPPOSITE hot

collapse verb
1 *Some of the old buildings **collapsed** in
the storm.*
- **to fall down**
- **to cave in**
2 *The old man **collapsed** in the street.*
- **to faint**
- **to pass out**
- **to fall down**

collect verb
1 *I **collect** old coins.*
- **to keep**
- **to save**

2 *We have **collected** a lot of things for our nature table.*
- **to accumulate**
- **to bring together**
- **to gather together**

3 *My mum **collected** me from school.*
- **to fetch**
- **to pick up**

collection noun
*He's got a huge **collection** of CDs.*
- **a set**
- **a hoard**
- **an assortment**

collide verb
*Their car **collided** with a van.*
- **to hit**
- **to bump into**
- **to crash into**
- **to smash into**

colour noun
*I think we should paint the room a different **colour**.*
- **a shade**

colour noun

> **WORD WEB**
> **some shades of red**
> - crimson
> - maroon
> - ruby
> - scarlet
>
> **some shades of blue**
> - aquamarine
> - azure
> - navy blue
> - royal blue
> - sapphire
>
> - sky blue
> - turquoise
>
> **some shades of green**
> - bottle green
> - emerald
> - lime green
>
> **some shades of yellow**
> - gold
> - lemon
> - primrose
>
> **some shades of black**
> - ebony
> - jet black
>
> **some shades of white**
> - cream
> - ivory
> - snow white
>
> **some shades of grey**
> - charcoal grey
> - dove grey
> - silver
>
> **some shades of brown**
> - beige
> - bronze
> - chocolate
> - fawn
> - khaki
> - tan

colourful adjective
*Everyone was wearing **colourful** clothes.*
- **bright**
- **multicoloured**

OPPOSITE dull

combine verb
1 ***Combine** all the ingredients in a bowl.*
- **to put together**
- **to mix together**
- **to add together**
- **to blend** →

a
b
c
d
e
f
g
h
i
j
k
l
m
n
o
p
q
r
s
t
u
v
w
x
y
z

a
b
c
d
e
f
g
h
i
j
k
l
m
n
o
p
q
r
s
t
u
v
w
x
y
z

2 *The two groups **combined** to make one big group.*
- **to come together**
- **to join together**
- **to unite**
- **to merge**

come verb
1 *We saw a car **coming** towards us.*
- **to move**
- **to approach** *We saw a car approaching us.*
- **to draw near** *We saw a car drawing near to us.*
2 *Would you like to **come** to my house?*
- **to visit**
3 *A letter **came** this morning.*
- **to arrive**
- **to turn up**

comfort verb
*I **comforted** the little boy because he was upset.*
- **to reassure**
- **to calm down**
- **to cheer up**

comfortable adjective
1 *This chair is very **comfortable**.*
- **soft**
- **cosy**
- **relaxing**
2 *Are you **comfortable** there?*
- **relaxed**
- **cosy**
- **warm**
- **happy**
- **snug**
OPPOSITE uncomfortable

command verb
*She **commanded** us to leave.*
- **to tell**
- **to order**
- **to instruct**

comment noun
*One of the boys kept making silly **comments**.*
- **a remark**
- **an observation**

commit verb
*He has **committed** a terrible crime.*
- **to carry out**
- **to be guilty of** *He is guilty of a terrible crime.*

common adjective
1 *These birds are quite **common** in Europe.*
- **widespread**
2 *Earthquakes are **common** in this part of the world.*
- **frequent**
3 *Having your tonsils out is a **common** operation.*
- **routine**
- **standard**
4 *It is very **common** for children to feel nervous before injections.*
- **ordinary**
- **usual**
- **normal**
OPPOSITE rare

commotion noun
*There was a terrible **commotion**.*
- **an uproar**
- **a row**
- **confusion**
- **chaos**

company noun
1 *I took my sister with me for **company**.*
- **friendship**
- **companionship**

2 *They run a **company** that makes sweets and biscuits.*
- **a business**
- **a factory**
- **a firm**

compare verb
*Please **compare** the two stories.*
- **to contrast**

competition noun
1 *Let's have a **competition** to see who's the best.*
- **a contest**
- **a game**
- **a race**
2 *Our team won the football **competition**.*
- **a tournament**
- **a championship**

complain verb
*Everyone **complained** about the food.*
- **to moan**
- **to grumble**
- **to whinge**

complete adjective
1 *I haven't got a **complete** set.*
- **full**
- **whole**
- **entire**
OPPOSITE incomplete
2 *At last the work was **complete**.*
- **finished**
OPPOSITE unfinished
3 *The show was a **complete** disaster.*
- **total**
- **absolute**
- **utter**

completely adverb
*I'm **completely** exhausted!*
- **totally**
- **utterly**
- **absolutely**

complicated adjective
1 *This is a very **complicated** machine.*
- **complex**
- **sophisticated**
- **intricate**
2 *We had to do some **complicated** sums.*
- **difficult**
- **hard**
OPPOSITE simple

computer noun

> **WORD WEB**
> **some types of computer**
> - a desktop
> - a laptop
> - a notebook
> - a PC
> - a palmtop
> - a personal computer
> - a portable computer

concentrate verb
*There was so much noise that I couldn't **concentrate**.*
- **to think**
- **to work**
- **to pay attention**
- **to focus**

concern verb
*This doesn't **concern** you.*
- **to affect**
- **to be important to**
- **to involve**

a
b
c
d
e
f
g
h
i
j
k
l
m
n
o
p
q
r
s
t
u
v
w
x
y
z

a
b
c
d
e
f
g
h
i
j
k
l
m
n
o
p
q
r
s
t
u
v
w
x
y
z

concerned adjective
*We were all very **concerned** about you.*
- **worried**
- **anxious**

condemn verb
*The judge **condemned** him to death.*
- **to sentence**

condition noun
*The amount your bike is worth will depend on the **condition** it is in.*
- **the state**

confess verb
*She **confessed** that she had stolen the money.*
- **to admit**
- **to own up**
- **to tell the truth**

confident adjective
1 *She looked very calm and **confident**.*
- **self-assured**
- **unafraid**
- **assertive**
2 *We are **confident** that we can win.*
- **sure**
- **certain**
- **convinced**
- **positive**

confuse verb
*The instructions for the game **confused** me.*
- **to puzzle**
- **to baffle**
- **to bewilder**
- **to perplex**

confused adjective
*I was feeling very **confused**.*
- **puzzled**
- **bewildered**
- **baffled**

congratulate verb
*I **congratulated** Salim on winning the race.*
- **to compliment**

connect verb
*You need to **connect** this wire to the battery.*
- **to join**
- **to attach**
- **to fix**

considerate adjective
*Please try to be more **considerate**.*
- **thoughtful**
- **kind**
- **helpful**
- **unselfish**
OPPOSITE selfish

constant adjective
*I'm fed up with this **constant** noise.*
- **incessant**
- **continuous**
- **relentless**
- **never-ending**

construct verb
*We **constructed** a model aeroplane.*
- **to build**
- **to make**
- **to assemble**

contain verb
*The bag **contained** some gold coins.*
- **to hold**
- **to have inside**

contest noun
*We're having a jumping **contest**.*
- **a competition**
- **a match**
- **a championship**

continual adjective
*Stop this **continual** arguing!*
- **constant**
- **repeated**
- **incessant**

continue verb
1 *Continue reading until the end of the chapter.*
- **to go on**
- **to keep on**
- **to carry on**
2 *The rain **continued** all afternoon.*
- **to last**
- **to go on**
- **to carry on**

continuous adjective
*In the factory there was the **continuous** noise of machines.*
- **constant**
- **incessant**

contribute verb
1 *They **contributed** money to the school repair fund.*
- **to give**
- **to donate**
- **to make a donation** *They made a donation to the school repair fund.*
2 *He **contributed** ideas to the class discussion.*
- **to add**
- **to put forward**

control verb
*The pilot uses these levers to **control** the aeroplane.*
- **to guide**
- **to move**
- **to direct**

convenient adjective
*The shop is just around the corner, so it's quite **convenient**.*
- **handy**
- **useful**
OPPOSITE inconvenient

conversation noun
*We had a long **conversation** about sport.*
- **a talk**
- **a discussion**
- **a chat**

convince verb
*My dad finally **convinced** me that ghosts are not real.*
- **to persuade**

convinced adjective
*I'm **convinced** that she is lying.*
- **sure**
- **certain**
- **confident**
- **positive**

cook verb

> **WORD WEB**
> **some ways to cook meat**
> - to barbecue
> - to casserole
> - to fry
> - to grill
> - to roast
> - to stew
>
> **some ways to cook bread or cakes**
> - to bake
> - to toast →

a
b
c
d
e
f
g
h
i
j
k
l
m
n
o
p
q
r
s
t
u
v
w
x
y
z

a
b
c
d
e
f
g
h
i
j
k
l
m
n
o
p
q
r
s
t
u
v
w
x
y
z

some ways to cook vegetables
• to bake
• to boil
• to roast
• to simmer
• to steam
• to stir-fry

some ways to cook eggs
• to boil
• to fry
• to poach
• to scramble

cool adjective
1 *It's quite **cool** outside today.*
• **cold**
• **chilly**
• **nippy**
2 *I could do with a nice **cool** drink.*
• **cold**
• **ice-cold**
OPPOSITE hot

cope verb
*Can you **cope** with all this work?*
• **to manage** *Can you manage all this work?*

copy verb
1 *See if you can **copy** this picture.*
• **to reproduce**
• **to make a copy of**
2 *Sam can **copy** his teacher's voice.*
• **to imitate**
• **to mimic**
• **to impersonate**

corner noun
*I'll meet you on the **corner**, by the school.*
• **a crossroads**
• **a turning**

• **a junction**
• **a bend**

correct adjective
1 *That is the **correct** answer.*
• **right**
2 *Make sure all your measurements are* **correct**.
• **accurate**
• **exact**
• **right**
OPPOSITE wrong

correct verb
*Shall I **correct** my mistakes?*
• **to put right**
• **to rectify**

costume noun
*We had to wear special **costumes** for the play.*
• **clothes**
• **a disguise**
• **fancy dress**
• **an outfit**

cosy adjective
*The room was small and **cosy**.*
• **comfortable**
• **snug**
• **warm**

count verb
*Can you **count** how many people there are altogether?*
• **to add up**
• **to calculate**
• **to work out**

country noun
1 *Australia is a big **country**.*
• **a land**
• **a nation**

2 *Do you live in the **country** or in a town?*
- **the countryside**

courage noun
We were all impressed with his courage.
- **bravery**
- **heroism**
- **valour**

cover noun
1 *She put a **cover** over the dish.*
- **a lid**
- **a top**
- **a covering**
2 *He laid a **cover** over the sleeping baby.*
- **a blanket**
- **a duvet**

cover verb
1 *He pulled his sleeve down to **cover** the scar on his arm.*
- **to hide**
- **to conceal**
2 *She **covered** him with a blanket.*
- **to wrap someone in** *She wrapped him in a blanket.*

coward noun
*He's a real **coward**!*
- **a wimp**
- **a chicken**

crack noun
1 *He handed me an old cup with a **crack** in it.*
- **a break**
- **a chip**
2 *There was a **crack** in the wall.*
- **a hole**
- **a gap**
- **a split**

crack verb
*Mind you don't **crack** the glass.*
- **to break**
- **to chip**
- **to smash**
- **to shatter**
  Use **smash** or **shatter** when something cracks and breaks into lots of pieces:
  *The mirror **smashed** into tiny pieces.*

crafty adjective
*Foxes are **crafty** animals.*
- **clever**
- **cunning**
- **sly**
- **sneaky**
- **wily**

crash noun
1 *There was a **crash** on the motorway.*
- **an accident**
- **a smash**
- **a collision**
- **a pile-up**
  A **pile-up** is a crash with a lot of cars:
  *There was a huge **pile-up** on the motorway.*
2 *The tree fell down with a loud **crash**.*
- **a bang**
- **a thud**
- **a clatter**
- **a bump**
- **a thump**

crash verb
1 *The car **crashed** into a wall.*
- **to smash into**
- **to bang into**
- **to hit** *The car hit a wall.*
2 *Two lorries **crashed** on the motorway.*
- **to collide**
- **to have an accident** →

a
b
c
d
e
f
g
h
i
j
k
l
m
n
o
p
q
r
s
t
u
v
w
x
y
z

3 *My computer has just **crashed**.*
- **to go down**

crawl verb
*We **crawled** through the tunnel.*
- **to creep**
- **to climb**
- **to slither**
- **to wriggle**
To **slither** means to crawl along on your stomach, like a snake:
*He **slithered** under the gate.*
To **wriggle** means to squeeze through a very small space:
*I managed to **wriggle** through a gap in the hedge.*

crazy adjective
1 *Everyone thought he was just a **crazy** old man.*
- **mad**
- **silly**
- **stupid**
OPPOSITE sensible
2 *The children went **crazy** when they saw the clown.*
- **mad**
- **berserk**

creak verb
*The old door **creaked** as it opened.*
- **to squeak**
- **to scrape**

crease verb
*Mind you don't **crease** your skirt.*
- **to crumple**
- **to crush**

creep verb
1 *We **crept** out through the window.*
- **to crawl**
- **to climb**
- **to slither**
- **to wriggle**
Use **slither** when you creep along on your stomach, like a snake:
*He **slithered** under the side of the tent.*
Use **wriggle** when you squeeze through a very small space:
*She managed to **wriggle** through the gap.*
2 *He **crept** away when no one was looking.*
- **to sneak**
- **to slip**
- **to steal**
- **to tiptoe**
To **tiptoe** means to creep quietly on your toes:
*I **tiptoed** past the sleeping guards.*

crime noun
*You have committed a terrible **crime**.*
- **an offence**
- **a sin**

criminal noun
*These **criminals** must be caught.*
- **a crook**
- **a villain**
- **a wrongdoer**
- **a thief**
- **a robber**
- **a murderer**
- **an offender**

crisp adjective
*She bit into the **crisp** toast.*
- **crunchy**
- **hard**
OPPOSITE soft

criticize verb

1 Stop **criticizing** me!
- **to blame**
- **to get at** (informal) Stop getting at me!
- **to put down** (informal) Stop putting me down!

2 You shouldn't **criticize** other people's work.
- **to find fault with**
- **to pick holes in**

OPPOSITE praise

crooked adjective

1 We sat down by an old, **crooked** tree.
- **bent**
- **twisted**
- **misshapen**

2 They climbed up the **crooked** path.
- **winding**
- **twisting**
- **bendy**

OPPOSITE straight

cross adjective

My mum was really **cross** with me.
- **angry**
- **annoyed**
- **irritated**
- **furious**
- **livid**

Use **irritated** when someone is slightly cross:
My sister wouldn't shut up, and I was beginning to get a bit **irritated** with her.
Use **furious** or **livid** when someone is very cross:
My brother was absolutely **furious** when I broke his MP3 player.

OPPOSITE pleased

cross verb

Take care when you **cross** the road.
- **to go across**
- **to go over**

cross out verb

I **crossed out** my name.
- **to erase**
- **to delete**
- **to rub out**

crouch verb

She **crouched** down to pick up a shell.
- **to bend**
- **to stoop**
- **to squat**

crowd noun

A **crowd** of people was waiting outside the cinema.
- **a group**
- **a mass**
- **a horde**
- **a mob**
- **a rabble**
  Use **mob** and **rabble** to talk about a noisy crowd:
  There was a **rabble** of boys outside the museum.

crowded adjective

The airport was very **crowded**.
- **busy**
- **full**
- **packed**
- **swarming with people**
- **teeming with people**

OPPOSITE empty

cruel adjective

1 The king was a **cruel** man.
- **wicked**
- **heartless**
- **cold-hearted**
- **brutal** →

a
b
c
d
e
f
g
h
i
j
k
l
m
n
o
p
q
r
s
t
u
v
w
x
y
z

a
b
c
d
e
f
g
h
i
j
k
l
m
n
o
p
q
r
s
t
u
v
w
x
y
z

2 *Some people think bullfighting is a* **cruel** *sport.*
• **barbaric**
• **inhumane**
OPPOSITE kind

crunch verb
He **crunched** *his apple noisily.*
• **to chew**
• **to munch**
• **to chomp**

crush verb
Mind you don't **crush** *the flowers.*
• **to squash**
• **to flatten**
• **to damage**
• **to break**

cry verb
1 *Some of the children were* **crying**.
• **to weep**
• **to wail**
• **to howl**
• **to sob**
• **to snivel**
• **to blubber**
Use **weep** *if someone is crying quietly:*
A young girl was **weeping** *in the garden.*
Use **wail**, **howl**, *or* **sob** *if someone is crying noisily, or speaking as they are crying:*
'What shall I do now?' she **wailed**.
Use **snivel** *or* **blubber** *if someone is making a lot of noise in a way that you find annoying:*
'Crying won't do any good, so stop **snivelling***!' he said.*
2 *'Look out!' she cried.*
• **to shout**
• **to yell**
• **to call**

• **to scream**
• **to shriek**
• **to exclaim**
Use **scream** *or* **shriek** *when someone shouts something in a loud high voice because they are frightened or annoyed:*
'Get out of here!' she **screamed** *angrily.*
Use **exclaim** *when someone is surprised or excited:*
'How wonderful!' she **exclaimed.**

cuddle verb
She **cuddled** *her little brother.*
• **to hug**
• **to embrace**
• **to hold**

cunning adjective
He thought of a **cunning** *plan to escape.*
• **clever**
• **crafty**
• **ingenious**
• **sneaky**

cup noun

> **WORD WEB**
> **some types of cup**
> • a beaker
> • a glass
> • a goblet
> • a mug
> • a teacup
> • a tumbler

cure verb
Doctors can **cure** *this disease.*
• **to treat**
• **to heal**

46

curious adjective

1 We were all very **curious** about the new teacher.
- **inquisitive**
- **nosy**

2 There was a **curious** smell in the kitchen.
- **strange**
- **funny**
- **odd**
- **peculiar**

curtain noun
- **a drape**
- **a blind**

curve noun

1 There was a **curve** in the road ahead of us.
- **a bend**
- **a turn**

2 We can make a pattern using straight lines and **curves**.
- **a loop**
- **a curl**
- **a swirl**
- **an arc**

custom noun

It's the **custom** to give someone presents on their birthday.
- **a tradition**

cut noun

She had a **cut** on her arm.
- **a wound**
- **a graze**
- **a nick**
- **a gash**
  A **nick** is a small cut:
  He had a little **nick** on his finger.

A **gash** is a big cut:
Blood was pouring from the **gash** on his leg.

cut verb

1 I fell over and **cut** my knee.
- **to graze**
- **to scratch**
- **to wound**
- **to gash**
  Use **graze** or **scratch** when you cut yourself not very badly:
  I'm OK. I've just **grazed** my knee a bit.
  Use **wound** or **gash** when you cut yourself badly:
  He **gashed** his leg and had to have stitches.

2 **Cut** the meat into small pieces.
- **to chop**
- **to chop up**
- **to slice**
- **to dice**
- **to mince**
  Use **slice** when you cut something into thin pieces:
  She **sliced** the bread and put it on a plate.
  Use **dice** when you cut something into small square pieces:
  Dice the onion and carrot.
  Use **mince** when you cut something into tiny pieces:
  For this recipe you need **minced** beef.

3 The hairdresser **cut** my hair.
- **to trim**
- **to snip**

4 The older boys **cut** some wood.
- **to chop**
- **to saw**
- **to carve**
  Use **carve** when you cut wood into a special shape:
  He **carved** a statue from the block of wood. →

a b c d e f g h i j k l m n o p q r s t u v w x y z

a
b
c
d
e
f
g
h
i
j
k
l
m
n
o
p
q
r
s
t
u
v
w
x
y
z

5 *We need to **cut** the grass.*
- **to mow**

6 *Dad **cut** the hedge.*
- **to prune**
- **to trim**
- **to clip**

cut off verb
*He had an accident and **cut off** one of his fingers.*

- **to chop off**
- **to sever**
- **to amputate**
*To **amputate** someone's arm or leg means to cut it off in a special operation:*
*Doctors had to **amputate** his leg because it was so badly injured.*

Dd

damage verb

1 Mind you don't **damage** any of the books.
   - **to spoil**
   - **to ruin**
     Use **ruin** when you damage something badly:
     I dropped my mobile in the bath and **ruined** it.

2 She dropped the box and **damaged** some of the plates.
   - **to break**
   - **to chip**
   - **to scratch**
   - **to smash**
     Use **chip** when you break a little bit off something:
     I **chipped** the paint on my new bike.
     Use **scratch** when you leave a mark on something:
     You'll **scratch** the dining room table if you dump your school bag on it.
     Use **smash** when you break something into pieces:
     I dropped the vase and **smashed** it.

3 The explosion **damaged** several buildings.
   - **to destroy**

4 The crash **damaged** our car quite badly.
   - **to dent**
   - **to wreck**

5 Someone has deliberately **damaged** the new fence.
   - **to vandalize**

damp adjective

The grass was rather **damp**.
   - **wet**
   - **moist**
   OPPOSITE dry

dance verb

1 Everyone was **dancing** to the music.
   - **to jig about**
   - **to leap about**

2 The younger children were all **dancing** about with excitement.
   - **to skip about**
   - **to jump about**
   - **to leap about**
   - **to prance about**

dance noun

He did a little **dance**.
   - **a jig**

WORD WEB
some types of dance
- ballet
- ballroom dancing
- breakdancing
- the cancan
- country dancing
- disco dancing
- folk dancing
- Irish dancing
- the jive
- line dancing
- rock and roll
- salsa
- Scottish dancing
- the tango
- tap dancing
- the waltz

---

danger noun

1 The animals could sense **danger**.
   - **trouble**

2 There is a **danger** that you might fall.
   - **a risk**
   - **a chance**
   - **a possibility**

dangerous adjective
1 It's **dangerous** to play with matches.
 • **risky**
 • **unsafe**
 OPPOSITE safe
2 A knife is a **dangerous** weapon.
 • **lethal**
 • **deadly**
3 The factory produces some very **dangerous** chemicals.
 • **harmful**
 • **poisonous**
 • **toxic**
 • **hazardous**
4 This man is a **dangerous** criminal.
 • **violent**

dare verb
1 Come and catch me, if you **dare!**
 • **to be brave enough**
 • **to have the courage**
 • **to have the nerve**
2 I **dare** you to climb that tree.
 • **to challenge**

daring adjective
Which of you boys is the most **daring**?
 • **brave**
 • **bold**
 • **courageous**
 • **fearless**
 • **adventurous**
 OPPOSITE timid

dark adjective
1 It was **dark** outside.
 • **black**
 • **pitch-black**
 Use **pitch-black** if it is completely dark:
 It was **pitch-black** in the tunnel.
 OPPOSITE light

2 He was left alone in a **dark** room.
 • **gloomy**
 • **dingy**
 • **unlit**
 Use **gloomy** or **dingy** if a room is dark and unpleasant:
 The cellar was damp and **gloomy** and slightly spooky.
 Use **unlit** if there are no lights in the room:
 We walked along a long **unlit** corridor.
 OPPOSITE bright
3 They walked through the **dark** woods.
 • **shady**
 • **shadowy**
 Use **shady** if a place is nice and cool:
 We found a lovely **shady** spot under some trees for our picnic.
 Use **shadowy** if there are lots of big shadows:
 Helen hated walking through the cold, **shadowy** forest.
 OPPOSITE bright
4 She has **dark** hair.
 • **black**
 • **brown**
 • **ebony**
 • **jet-black**
 Use **ebony** or **jet-black** if someone's hair is very dark:
 She had beautiful long **jet-black** hair.
 OPPOSITE light

darling noun
Take care, **darling**.
 • **dear**
 • **love**
 • **sweetheart**

dash verb
She **dashed** out of the room.
 • **to run**
 • **to rush**

a
b
c
d
e
f
g
h
i
j
k
l
m
n
o
p
q
r
s
t
u
v
w
x
y
z

50

- to sprint
- to fly
- to dart
- to hurry

dawdle verb
*They **dawdled** along.*
- to stroll
- to amble
- to wander

dead adjective
1 *My grandmother is **dead** now.*
- deceased
- passed away *My grandmother has passed away.*
2 *We found the **dead** body of a fox.*
- lifeless

deadly adjective
*This poison is **deadly**.*
- dangerous
- lethal
- fatal
OPPOSITE harmless

deal with verb
*I will **deal with** this problem.*
- to handle
- to sort out
- to cope with

dear adjective
*He was delighted to see his **dear** daughter again.*
- beloved
- darling

deceive verb
*He tried to **deceive** us.*
- to trick
- to mislead
- to fool

decide verb
1 *He **decided** to tell his parents everything.*
- to make up your mind *He made up his mind to tell his parents everything.*
- to resolve *He resolved to tell his parents everything.*
2 *I can't **decide** which cake to have.*
- to choose

decorate verb
1 *They **decorated** the Christmas tree with tinsel.*
- to adorn
- to beautify
2 *This summer we need to **decorate** your bedroom.*
- to paint
- to wallpaper

deep adjective
*The treasure was hidden at the bottom of a **deep** hole.*
- bottomless
OPPOSITE shallow

defeat verb
1 *They finally **defeated** their enemies.*
- to beat
- to overcome
- to conquer
2 *We **defeated** the other team quite easily.*
- to beat
- to thrash
*Use **thrash** if you defeat someone easily:*
*We **thrashed** the other team 9–0.*

defend verb
*We must stay and **defend** the city.*
- to protect
- to guard

a
b
c
d
e
f
g
h
i
j
k
l
m
n
o
p
q
r
s
t
u
v
w
x
y
z

definite adjective
1 *The party will probably be next Saturday, but it's not **definite** yet.*
- **certain**
- **fixed**
- **settled**
2 *I can see a **definite** improvement in your work.*
- **clear**
- **obvious**
- **positive**

delay verb
1 *The bad weather **delayed** us.*
- **to hold someone up** *The bad weather held us up.*
- **to make someone late** *The bad weather made us late.*
2 *We had to **delay** the start of the race.*
- **to postpone**
- **to put off**

deliberate adjective
*He said it was a **deliberate** mistake.*
- **intentional**
- **planned**
OPPOSITE accidental

deliberately adverb
*She **deliberately** left the gate open.*
- **on purpose**
- **intentionally**
- **knowingly**
OPPOSITE accidentally

delicate adjective
*A lot of the objects in the museum are very old and **delicate**.*
- **fragile**
- **flimsy**

delicious adjective
*This food is **delicious**!*
- **lovely**
- **tasty**

- **scrumptious**
- **gorgeous**
- **succulent**
- **mouthwatering**
Use **tasty**, **scrumptious**, **gorgeous**, and **succulent** if food tastes delicious: *Mmm, this cake is **gorgeous**!*
Use **mouthwatering** if food looks delicious:
*The table was covered with **mouthwatering** food.*
OPPOSITE horrible

delighted adjective
*I was **delighted** with your present.*
- **pleased**
- **thrilled**
- **overjoyed**
- **ecstatic**

deliver verb
*We will **deliver** the new computer to your house.*
- **to bring**
- **to take**

demand verb
*She **demanded** an explanation.*
- **to insist on**
- **to ask for**
- **to request**

demolish verb
*They are going to **demolish** the old school building.*
- **to knock down**
- **to pull down**
- **to bulldoze**
- **to flatten**

deny verb
*She **denied** that she had stolen the money.*
- **to refuse to admit** *She refused*

to admit that she had stolen
the money.
OPPOSITE admit

depend on verb
The young chicks **depend on** their
mother for food.
• **to need**
• **to rely on**

depressed adjective
He was feeling **depressed**.
• **sad**
• **unhappy**
• **upset**
• **low**
• **dejected**

describe verb
1 She **described** the animal she had
seen.
• **to give a description of** She gave a
description of the animal.
2 The boy **described** how he had
escaped.
• **to explain**
• **to relate**
• **to recount**

deserted adjective
They walked through the **deserted**
village.
• **empty**
• **abandoned**

design verb
They have **designed** a new type of
engine.
• **to create**
• **to make**
• **to invent**
• **to devise**
• **to plan**

destroy verb
1 The explosion **destroyed** several
buildings.
• **to demolish**
• **to flatten**
• **to crush**
2 The storm **destroyed** their small boat.
• **to smash**
• **to wreck**
3 The fire **destroyed** many valuable old
books.
• **to ruin**

determined adjective
1 We are **determined** to win.
• **resolved**
2 You have to be very **determined** if you
want to succeed.
• **single-minded**
• **strong-willed**

develop verb
Tadpoles gradually **develop** into frogs.
• **to change into**
• **to grow into**
• **to evolve into**

device noun
They use a special **device** for opening
the bottles.
• **a gadget**
• **a tool**
• **an implement**

diagram noun
We drew a **diagram** of the machine.
• **a plan**
• **a drawing**
• **a sketch**

diary noun
I am keeping a **diary** of our holiday.
• **a journal**
• **a daily record**

a
b
c
d
e
f
g
h
i
j
k
l
m
n
o
p
q
r
s
t
u
v
w
x
y
z

a
b
c
d
e
f
g
h
i
j
k
l
m
n
o
p
q
r
s
t
u
v
w
x
y
z

die verb
1 *My grandfather **died** last year.*
- **to pass away**
2 *Hundreds of people **died** in the fire.*
- **to perish**
- **to be killed** *Hundreds of people were killed in the fire.*
3 *The plants **died** because I forgot to water them.*
- **to shrivel**
- **to wither**

difference noun
*Can you see any **differences** between the two pictures?*
- **a discrepancy**
- **an inconsistency**
- **a variation**
OPPOSITE similarity

different adjective
1 *Your book is **different** from mine.*
- **dissimilar**
- **unlike**
OPPOSITE similar
2 *Our ice cream is available in five **different** flavours.*
- **assorted**
- **various**
3 *Each one of the puppies is slightly **different**.*
- **special**
- **distinctive**
- **individual**
- **unique**
4 *Let's do something **different** for a change!*
- **new**
- **exciting**
- **unusual**
- **extraordinary**
5 *Our new neighbours are certainly **different**!*
- **strange**
- **peculiar**
- **odd**
- **unusual**
- **bizarre**

difficult adjective
*The teacher gave us some very **difficult** work to do.*
- **hard**
- **tough**
- **tricky**
- **complicated**
OPPOSITE easy

difficulty noun
*We have had a few **difficulties**.*
- **a problem**
- **a snag**
  *A **snag** is a small difficulty: There's just one little **snag**.*

dig verb
1 *We **dug** a hole in the garden.*
- **to make**
- **to excavate**
2 *We'll have to **dig** our way out of here!*
- **to tunnel**
- **to burrow**
3 *They **dig** stone out of the ground here.*
- **to quarry**
- **to mine**
  *You **quarry** stone and **mine** coal: Coal has been **mined** here for 200 years.*

dim adjective
*A **dim** light was shining in the window.*
- **faint**
- **dull**
- **pale**
OPPOSITE bright

dip verb
> She **dipped** her hand into the water.
> • to lower
> • to drop
> • to plunge
> • to immerse

dirt noun
> Their clothes were covered in **dirt**.
> • mud
> • muck
> • dust
> • grime
> • filth

dirty adjective
> 1 Why are your clothes so **dirty**?
> • mucky
> • grubby
> • muddy
> • greasy
> • filthy
> • grimy
> • stained
> Use **mucky** or **grubby** if something is slightly dirty:
> His sweatshirt was old and slightly **grubby**.
> Use **muddy** if something is covered in mud:
> Take your **muddy** boots off!
> Use **greasy** if something is covered in oil or grease:
> He handed me a horrible **greasy** spoon.
> Use **filthy** or **grimy** if something is very dirty:
> Go and wash your hands. They're **filthy**!
> Use **stained** if something has dirty marks on it:
> His shirt was **stained** with ink.
> 2 The room was very **dirty**.
> • dusty
> • messy
> • filthy

> 3 The water in some rivers is too **dirty** to drink.
> • polluted
> • foul
> OPPOSITE clean

disagree verb
> The two boys always seem to **disagree** about everything.
> • to argue
> • to quarrel
> • to have different opinions
> OPPOSITE agree

disappear verb
> The dog **disappeared** into some bushes.
> • to vanish
> OPPOSITE appear

disappointed adjective
> I was very **disappointed** when the trip was cancelled.
> • upset
> • sad
> • dejected
> • downcast

disaster noun
> The plane crash was a terrible **disaster**.
> • a tragedy
> • a catastrophe
> • a calamity

discover verb
> We **discovered** an old map in the attic.
> • to find
> • to come across
> • to uncover
> • to unearth

discuss verb
> We will **discuss** this later.
> • to talk about
> • to debate

a
b
c
d
e
f
g
h
i
j
k
l
m
n
o
p
q
r
s
t
u
v
w
x
y
z

discussion noun
*We had a **discussion** about different religions.*
- **a talk**
- **a conversation**
- **a chat**

disease noun
*Quite a lot of children suffer from this **disease**.*
- **an illness**
- **a complaint**
- **a sickness**
- **an infection**

disgusting adjective
*This food is **disgusting**!*
- **horrible**
- **revolting**
- **foul**
OPPOSITE lovely

dish noun
*She put the vegetables in a **dish**.*
- **a bowl**
- **a plate**
- **a platter**

display noun
*We made a **display** of our paintings.*
- **an exhibition**
- **a presentation**

display verb
*We will **display** the best pictures in the hall.*
- **to show**
- **to hang up**
- **to exhibit**

distance noun
*We measured the **distance** between the two posts.*
- **the space**
- **the gap**
- **the length**
- **the width**

distant adjective
*They travelled to many **distant** lands.*
- **faraway**
- **far off**
- **remote**

disturb verb
1 *I'm working, so please don't **disturb** me.*
- **to interrupt**
- **to bother**
- **to pester**
- **to hassle**
  To **pester** or **hassle** someone means to keep disturbing them:
  *My little brother's been **pestering** me all morning!*
2 *The sight of so many soldiers **disturbed** me.*
- **to worry**
- **to trouble**
- **to alarm**
- **to distress**

dive verb
*She **dived** into the water.*
- **to plunge**
- **to leap**
- **to jump**

divide verb
1 *We can **divide** the sweets between us.*
- **to share**
- **to split**
2 *She **divided** the cake into ten pieces.*
- **to cut**
- **to split**
- **to separate**

a b c d e f g h i j k l m n o p q r s t u v w x y z

dizzy adjective

I felt weak and **dizzy**.
- **giddy**
- **faint**
- **light-headed**
- **unsteady**

do verb

⚠ **OVERUSED WORD**

Try to vary the words you use to mean **do**. Here are some other words you can use instead.

1 I usually try to **do** my work quickly.
- **to get on with**
- **to finish**
- **to complete**

2 We're going to **do** an experiment.
- **to carry out**
- **to conduct**

3 I can't **do** this sum.
- **to work out**
- **to calculate**
- **to solve**
- **to answer**

4 What are you **doing**?
- **to be up to** What are you up to?

5 They are in danger—we must **do** something!
- **to take action**
- **to act**

6 You have **done** very well.
- **to get on**
- **to perform**

doctor noun

🕸 **WORD WEB**
some types of doctor
- a consultant (*a doctor in a hospital*)
- a general practitioner
- a G.P.

- a paediatrician (*a doctor who looks after children*)
- a specialist (*a doctor who knows a lot about one type of illness*)
- a surgeon (*a doctor who performs operations*)

dog noun
- **a hound**
- **a bitch** (*a female dog*)
- **a puppy** (*a young dog*)

🕸 **WORD WEB**
some types of dog
- a beagle
- a boxer
- a bulldog
- a chihuahua
- a collie
- a dachshund
- a Dalmatian
- a German Shepherd
- a Great Dane
- a greyhound
- a Labrador
- a mongrel (*a mixture of different breeds*)
- a poodle
- a retriever
- a sheepdog
- a spaniel
- a terrier

✏ **WRITING TIPS**
Here are some useful words for writing about dogs.
- The dogs **barked** and **yapped** excitedly when they heard us coming.
- The guard dog **growled** and **snarled** at us.
- Our dog always **whines** by the kitchen door when it wants to go out.
- The little dog **yelped** when I accidentally trod on its tail.
- The dog was **panting** after it had run up the hill.

a
b
c
d
e
f
g
h
i
j
k
l
m
n
o
p
q
r
s
t
u
v
w
x
y
z

dot noun

*There were red **dots** all over the wall.*
- **a spot**
- **a mark**
- **a speck**

doubt noun

*There's some **doubt** about whether she will be well enough to play.*
- **concern**
- **worry**
- **anxiety**
- **uncertainty**

doubt verb

*I **doubt** whether she'll be well enough to sing in the concert.*
- **to question**
- **to wonder**
- **to be uncertain about**

drag verb

*We **dragged** the box out into the hall.*
- **to pull**
- **to haul**
- **to tug**

draw verb

1 *Are you good at **drawing** pictures?*
- **to sketch**
- **to paint**
- **to trace**
- **to doodle**

2 *She **drew** the curtains.*
- **to close**
- **to open**
- **to pull back**

3 *The two teams **drew** in the last game.*
- **to finish equal**
- **to tie**

dreadful adjective

*The whole house was in a **dreadful** mess.*
- **terrible**
- **awful**
- **horrible**
- **appalling**

dream noun

1 *Do you ever remember your **dreams**?*
- **a bad dream** (*a horrible dream*)
- **a nightmare** (*a frightening dream*)

2 *Her **dream** is to be a famous ballet dancer.*
- **an ambition**
- **a wish**
- **a goal**
- **a fantasy**
  *A **fantasy** is a dream you have which you know will never come true:*
  *Indira has this **fantasy** about being a pop star.*

dress noun

*She was wearing a red **dress**.*
- **a frock**
- **a gown**

dress verb

1 *Hurry up and get **dressed**.*
- **to put clothes on**

2 *He was **dressed** in a black suit.*
- **to be attired in** *He was attired in a black suit.*
- **to be wearing** *He was wearing a black suit.*
- **to have on** *He had a black suit on.*

drift verb

*The little boat **drifted** out to sea.*
- **to float**
- **to be carried**

drink verb

1 He picked up the glass of milk and **drank** it.
- **to swallow**
- **to sip**
- **to gulp down**
- **to swig**
- **to knock back**
- **to guzzle**
- **to slurp**

Use **swallow** when someone drinks something quickly without tasting it: She took a deep breath and **swallowed** the disgusting medicine.
Use **sip** when someone drinks slowly: She **sipped** the lovely cool apple juice.
Use **gulp** or **swig** when someone drinks very quickly: He **gulped** down a whole bottle of water.
Use **guzzle** or **slurp** when someone drinks quickly and noisily: She **slurped** the hot tea.

2 The dog drank its water.
- **to lap up**

drip verb

Water was **dripping** from the trees above us.
- **to drop**
- **to splash**
- **to trickle**
- **to dribble**

drive verb

1 She got into her car and **drove** off.
- **to speed**
- **to zoom**
- **to crawl**

Use **speed** or **zoom** when someone drives quickly: They **zoomed** along the motorway.
Use **crawl** when someone drives slowly: We **crawled** along behind the tractor.

2 She **drove** the car carefully into the parking space.
- **to steer**
- **to guide**
- **to manoeuvre**

droop verb

The flowers were beginning to **droop**.
- **to wilt**
- **to flop**

drop noun

I felt a few **drops** of rain on my face.
- **a drip**
- **a spot**
- **a droplet**

drop verb

He accidentally **dropped** his glass.
- **to let go of**

dry adjective

1 The ground was very **dry**.
- **hard**
- **parched**
- **arid**
OPPOSITE wet

2 They lived on **dry** bread and water.
- **hard**
- **stale**

duck noun
- **a drake** (a male duck)
- **a duckling** (a young duck)

WRITING TIPS

Here are some useful words for writing about ducks.
- The ducks **waddled** down towards the pond and **swam** out into the water.
- There were some ducks **dabbling** and **diving** for food in the middle of the lake.
- The mother duck **quacked** loudly to call her ducklings to her.

a
b
c
d
e
f
g
h
i
j
k
l
m
n
o
p
q
r
s
t
u
v
w
x
y
z

dull adjective

1 *I think this television show is very **dull**.*
- **boring**
- **tedious**
- **uninteresting**
OPPOSITE interesting

2 *She was wearing a **dull** green dress.*
- **drab**
- **dark**
- **dreary**
- **dowdy**
OPPOSITE bright

3 *It was a rather **dull** day.*
- **grey**
- **cloudy**
- **overcast**
- **dismal**
- **miserable**
OPPOSITE bright

dump noun

*All the rubbish is taken to the rubbish **dump**.*
- **a tip**
- **a rubbish heap**

dump verb

1 *Some people **dump** rubbish by the side of the road.*
- **to leave**
- **to throw away**
- **to discard**

2 *She **dumped** her bags on the kitchen floor.*
- **to drop**
- **to throw**
- **to fling**

dusty adjective

*The room was very **dusty**.*
- **dirty**
- **mucky**
- **filthy**
OPPOSITE clean

duty noun

*It is your **duty** to look after the younger children.*
- **a responsibility**
- **a job**

Ee

eager adjective
*We were **eager** to go out and play.*
- keen
- impatient
- anxious

OPPOSITE reluctant

earn verb
*You can **earn** money by delivering newspapers.*
- to make
- to get

earth noun
1 *This is the largest lake on **earth**.*
- the world
- the globe
- the planet

2 *Bulbs will start to grow when you plant them in the **earth**.*
- the soil
- the ground

easy adjective
*These sums are **easy**.*
- simple
- straightforward
- obvious

OPPOSITE difficult

eat verb
*Someone has **eaten** all the cake.*
- to guzzle
- to polish off
- to scoff
- to wolf down
- to bolt
- to gobble
- to devour
- to munch
- to crunch
- to chomp
- to chew
- to suck
- to nibble

Use **guzzle**, **polish off**, and **scoff** when someone eats something quickly:
*We soon **polished off** the rest of the sandwiches.*
Use **wolf down**, **bolt**, **gobble**, and **devour** when someone eats something very quickly and greedily:
*The hungry children **wolfed down** the pizza.*
Use **munch**, **crunch**, and **chomp** when someone eats noisily:
*Anita **munched** noisily on an apple.*
Use **chew** and **suck** when someone eats something without biting it:
*She was **sucking** a large sweet.*
Use **nibble** when someone eats something slowly, taking small bites:
*She was **nibbling** on a biscuit.*

edge noun
1 *I bumped my leg on the **edge** of the table.*
- the side

2 *There was a pattern around the **edge** of the plate.*
- the outside

3 *The **edge** of the cup was cracked.*
- the rim

4 *We walked right to the **edge** of the field.*
- the boundary

5 *Keep close to the **edge** of the road when you are walking.*
- the side
- the verge
- the kerb →

a
b
c
d
e
f
g
h
i
j
k
l
m
n
o
p
q
r
s
t
u
v
w
x
y
z

61

6 *We live on the **edge** of the town.*
- **the outskirts**
- **the suburbs**

effect noun
*What will be the **effect** of the hot sun on these plants?*
- **the result**
- **the impact**
- **the consequence**

effort noun
1 *You should put more **effort** into your spellings.*
- **work**
2 *I made an **effort** to be cheerful.*
- **an attempt**

elect verb
*We **elect** a new school captain each year.*
- **to choose**
- **to pick**
- **to vote for**
- **to appoint**

embarrassed adjective
*I felt really **embarrassed**.*
- **uncomfortable**
- **awkward**
- **ashamed**
- **shy**
- **self-conscious**

emergency noun
*Be quick, it's an **emergency**!*
- **a crisis**

empty adjective
1 *There was an **empty** lemonade bottle on the table.*
- **unfilled**
OPPOSITE full

2 *They've moved away, so their house is **empty**.*
- **unoccupied**
- **vacant**
- **bare**
- **unfurnished**
Use **unoccupied** or **vacant** if nobody is living in a house:
*The house will be **vacant** next month, so we'll be able to move in.*
Use **bare** or **unfurnished** if there is nothing inside a room or house:
*The room was completely **bare**.*
OPPOSITE occupied

3 *It was raining, so the town centre was **empty**.*
- **deserted**
OPPOSITE crowded

encourage verb
1 *My parents **encouraged** me to learn the violin.*
- **to persuade**
- **to urge**
2 *We all cheered to **encourage** our team.*
- **to support**
- **to cheer on**
- **to inspire**
OPPOSITE discourage

end noun
1 *We walked right to the **end** of the lane.*
- **the limit**
- **the boundary**
2 *Please go to the **end** of the queue.*
- **the back**
- **the rear**
3 *He tied a balloon to the **end** of the stick.*
- **the tip**
- **the top**
- **the bottom**

4 *This book has a happy **end**.*
- **an ending**
- **a finish**
- **a conclusion**

end verb
*When will the concert **end**?*
- **to stop**
- **to finish**
- **to cease**
- **to conclude**
   *Use **cease** when something finally ends, after a long time:*
   *The rain finally **ceased**.*

enemy noun
*He fought bravely against his **enemy**.*
- **an opponent**
- **a foe**
- **a rival**
OPPOSITE friend

energetic adjective
*I'm feeling quite **energetic** this morning.*
- **active**
- **lively**
- **full of beans**

energy noun
*The children seem to have a lot of **energy** today.*
- **strength**
- **stamina**

enjoy verb
*I really **enjoyed** that book.*
- **to like**
- **to love**
- **to take pleasure from**

enjoyable adjective
*It was a very **enjoyable** trip.*
- **pleasant**
- **pleasurable**

- **delightful**
OPPOSITE unpleasant

enough adjective
*Have you got **enough** money to buy an ice cream?*
- **sufficient**

enter verb
1 *She **entered** the room.*
- **to go into**
- **to come into**
- **to walk into**
- **to run into**
OPPOSITE leave
2 *Are you going to **enter** the competition?*
- **to go in for**
- **to take part in**
- **to join in**

entertain verb
*The clown **entertained** the children.*
- **to amuse**
- **to delight**
- **to make someone laugh**

enthusiastic adjective
*He is very **enthusiastic** about joining the football team.*
- **keen** *He is keen to join the football team.*
- **eager** *He is eager to join the football team.*

entrance noun
1 *We couldn't find the **entrance** to the building.*
- **the way in**
- **the door**
- **the gate**
OPPOSITE exit →

a
b
c
d
e
f
g
h
i
j
k
l
m
n
o
p
q
r
s
t
u
v
w
x
y
z

63

a
b
c
d
e
f
g
h
i
j
k
l
m
n
o
p
q
r
s
t
u
v
w
x
y
z

2 *They stood by the **entrance** to the cave.*
- **the mouth**
- **the opening**

equipment noun
*We keep the games **equipment** in the shed.*
- **things**
- **gear**
- **tackle**
- **apparatus**

escape verb
1 *The police arrived too late, and the robbers **escaped**.*
- **to get away**
- **to run away**
- **to break free**
- **to make your escape**
- **to give someone the slip**
  To **break free** means to escape when you have been tied up or held:
  Two policemen were holding him, but he managed to **break free**.
  To **give someone the slip** means to get away from someone who is following you:
  I knew someone was following me, but I managed to **give them the slip**.
2 *We went indoors to **escape** from the rain.*
- **to avoid**

estimate noun
*What is your **estimate** of how tall you are?*
- **a calculation**
- **a guess**

estimate verb
*I **estimate** that it will take us two hours to get there.*
- **to guess**
- **to calculate**
- **to reckon**

even adjective
1 *You need an **even** surface for cycling.*
- **flat**
- **smooth**
- **level**
OPPOSITE uneven
2 *Their scores were **even** at half time.*
- **equal**
- **level**
- **the same**
OPPOSITE different

evening noun
*We should be there by **evening**.*
- **dusk**
- **nightfall**
- **sunset**

event noun
1 *The party will be a big **event**.*
- **an occasion**
2 *Some strange **events** have been happening.*
- **an incident**

eventually adverb
*We got home **eventually**.*
- **finally**
- **at last**
- **in the end**

evidence noun
*Where is your **evidence** for this idea?*
- **proof**
- **facts**
- **information**

evil adjective
1 *This was an **evil** deed.*
- **wicked**
- **cruel**
- **vile**

2 *An **evil** king ruled over the land.*
- **wicked**
- **bad**
- **cruel**
- **black-hearted**

OPPOSITE good

exact adjective

*Make sure you add the **exact** amount of water.*
- **right**
- **correct**
- **precise**

exam noun

*We've got a maths **exam** tomorrow.*
- **a test**
- **an examination**

example noun

*Can you show us an **example** of your work?*
- **a sample**
- **a specimen**

excellent adjective

*This is an **excellent** piece of work.*
- **very good**
- **wonderful**
- **brilliant**
- **first-class**
- **superb**
- **outstanding**

OPPOSITE bad

exchange verb

*I **exchanged** my old bike for a new one.*
- **to change**
- **to swap**

excited adjective

*She was very **excited** because it was her birthday.*
- **happy**
- **thrilled**
- **enthusiastic**

OPPOSITE calm

excitement noun

*I like films with a lot of **excitement**.*
- **action**
- **activity**
- **drama**
- **suspense**

exciting adjective

1 *We had a very **exciting** day.*
- **thrilling**
- **exhilarating**
- **action-packed**
- **eventful**
  Use **action-packed** or **eventful** when a lot of different things happen:
  *We had an **action-packed** holiday.*

2 *This is a very **exciting** book.*
- **gripping**

3 *It was a very **exciting** game to watch.*
- **fast-moving**
- **tense**
- **nail-biting**

OPPOSITE boring

excuse verb

*Please **excuse** me for being late.*
- **to forgive**
- **to pardon**

exercise noun

*You should do more **exercise**.*
- **sport**
- **PE**
- **games**
- **running around**

a
b
c
d
e
f
g
h
i
j
k
l
m
n
o
p
q
r
s
t
u
v
w
x
y
z

a
b
c
d
e
f
g
h
i
j
k
l
m
n
o
p
q
r
s
t
u
v
w
x
y
z

exhausted adjective
*I was **exhausted** after my long walk.*
• **tired**
• **worn out**
• **shattered**

exhibition noun
*We made an **exhibition** of our paintings.*
• **a display**

expect verb
*I **expect** it will rain later.*
• **to think**
• **to believe**
• **to suppose**

expensive adjective
*Those trousers are very **expensive**.*
• **dear**
• **costly**
OPPOSITE cheap

explain verb
*He **explained** how the machine worked.*
• **to describe**
• **to show** *He showed us how the machine worked.*

explode verb
1 *The firework **exploded** with a shower of stars.*
• **to go off**
• **to burst**
• **to go bang**
2 *The car caught fire and **exploded**.*
• **to blow up**

explore verb
*Let's **explore** the cave.*
• **to look round**
• **to search**
• **to investigate**

expression noun
*He had a sad **expression** on his face.*
• **a look**

extra adjective
*I've brought some **extra** food in case we get hungry.*
• **more**
• **additional**

extraordinary adjective
*Standing before us was an **extraordinary** creature.*
• **strange**
• **bizarre**
• **incredible**
• **remarkable**
• **unusual**
• **amazing**
OPPOSITE ordinary

extreme adjective
*No plants can grow in the **extreme** heat of the desert.*
• **great**
• **intense**
• **severe**

extremely adverb
*You are **extremely** lucky.*
• **very**
• **incredibly**
• **exceptionally**
• **unbelievably**

Ff

face noun
> The little boy had a sad **face**.
> • an expression

fact noun
> We found out some interesting **facts** about the ancient Romans.
> • information
> • data

fade verb
> 1 The colour in my dress has **faded**.
> • to become lighter
> 2 It was evening, and the light was beginning to **fade**.
> • to go
> • to dwindle
> • to grow dim
> 3 The sound of the engine gradually **faded**.
> • to become faint
> • to disappear
> • to die away

fail verb
> Our attempt to launch the boat **failed**.
> • to be unsuccessful
> • to meet with disaster

failure noun
> The magician's trick was a complete **failure**!
> • a disaster
> • a flop
> OPPOSITE success

faint adjective
> 1 I heard a **faint** cry.
> • quiet
> • weak
> • muffled
> • dim
> OPPOSITE loud
> 2 The writing was quite **faint** and difficult to read.
> • unclear
> • indistinct
> • faded
> OPPOSITE clear

faint verb
> I **fainted** because it was so hot.
> • to pass out
> • to lose consciousness

fair adjective
> 1 Tom has **fair** hair.
> • blond (for a boy)
> • blonde (for a girl)
> • light
> • golden
> OPPOSITE dark
> 2 It's not **fair** if she gets more sweets than me.
> • right
> • reasonable
> OPPOSITE unfair
> 3 I don't think the referee was very **fair**.
> • impartial
> • unbiased
> • honest
> OPPOSITE biased
> 4 We've got a **fair** chance of winning.
> • reasonable
> • good
> • moderate

faithful adjective
> Joshua was his **faithful** friend.
> • loyal
> • devoted
> • true
> OPPOSITE unfaithful

a
b
c
d
e
f
g
h
i
j
k
l
m
n
o
p
q
r
s
t
u
v
w
x
y
z

67

fake noun
> He knew that the painting was
> a **fake**.
> - **a forgery**
> - **a copy**

fall verb
> 1 *Mind you don't **fall**.*
> - **to trip**
> - **to stumble**
> - **to slip**
> - **to tumble**
> - **to plunge**
> - **to lose your balance**
> Use **trip** or **stumble** when someone
> falls because their foot catches on
> something:
> I **tripped** over one of the
> wires.
> Use **slip** when someone falls on a
> slippery surface:
> I **slipped** on the ice.
> Use **tumble** when someone falls from
> a height:
> He **tumbled** off the wall.
> Use **plunge** when someone falls into
> water:
> She couldn't stop running and
> **plunged** head first into the
> pond.
> Use **lose your balance** when
> someone falls after they have been
> balancing on something:
> I **lost my balance** halfway across the
> tightrope.
> 2 *The book fell off the table.*
> - **to drop**
> - **to tumble**
> - **to crash**
> Use **crash** when something makes a
> loud noise as it falls:
> The pile of plates **crashed** to the
> floor.
> 3 *Snow began to fall.*
> - **to come down**

fall down verb
> The old school **fell down** a few years
> ago.
> - **to collapse**

false adjective
> 1 *He was wearing a **false** beard.*
> - **fake**
> - **artificial**
> - **pretend**
> OPPOSITE real
> 2 *He gave the police **false** information.*
> - **incorrect**
> - **misleading**
> OPPOSITE correct

family noun
> I really enjoy being with my **family** in
> the holidays.
> - **relatives**
> - **relations**

famous adjective
> One day she might be a **famous** pop
> star.
> - **well-known**
> - **world-famous**
> - **celebrated**
> OPPOSITE unknown

fan noun
> Are you a football **fan**?
> - **a supporter**
> - **a follower**
> - **an admirer**

fantastic adjective
> We had a **fantastic** time.
> - **wonderful**
> - **brilliant**

- **great**
- **fabulous**
- **marvellous**
- **sensational**
OPPOSITE terrible

farm noun

> 🕸 **WORD WEB**
> **some types of farm**
> - an arable farm (*one that grows crops*)
> - a dairy farm (*one that keeps cows for milk*)
> - a fruit farm
> - a poultry farm (*one with chickens, ducks, or turkeys*)
> - a ranch (*a cattle farm in North America*)
> - a smallholding (*a small farm*)

fashion noun

*These shoes are the latest **fashion**.*
- **a style**
- **a trend**
- **a craze**
- **a look**

fashionable adjective

1 *He wears very **fashionable** clothes.*
- **trendy**
- **stylish**
2 *These coats are **fashionable** at the moment.*
- **popular**
- **in fashion**
- **all the rage** (*informal*)
OPPOSITE unfashionable

fast adjective

1 *He's a very **fast** runner.*
- **quick**
- **speedy**
- **swift**
2 *He loves driving **fast** cars.*
- **powerful**

3 *We'll go on the **fast** train.*
- **high-speed**
- **express**
4 *Scientists are working on a new **fast** aeroplane.*
- **supersonic** (*faster than the speed of sound*)
5 *We were walking at quite a **fast** pace.*
- **brisk**
- **quick**
- **swift**
OPPOSITE slow

fast adverb

*She was walking quite **fast**.*
- **quickly**
- **rapidly**
- **swiftly**

fasten verb

1 ***Fasten** your seat belt.*
- **to do up**
- **to buckle**
2 *I stopped to **fasten** my shoelaces.*
- **to tie up**
- **to do up**
3 ***Fasten** the two bits of string together.*
- **to tie**
- **to fix**
- **to join**
- **to secure**

fat adjective

*The ticket collector was a little **fat** man.*
- **plump**
- **tubby**
- **chubby**
- **podgy**
- **stout**
- **portly**
- **overweight**
- **obese**
Use **plump**, **tubby**, **chubby**, or **podgy** for someone who is →

slightly fat in a nice way:
In the pushchair was a **chubby**
smiling baby.
Use **stout** or **portly** for an older
person who is quite fat:
My uncle Bill likes his food, and as a
result he's rather **stout**.
Use **overweight** or **obese** for
someone who is so fat that they are
unhealthy:
If you don't do enough exercise, you
can become **obese**.
OPPOSITE thin

fault noun
The heating system has a **fault**, but we
are trying to fix it.
- **a problem**
- **a defect**
- **a malfunction**

favour noun
Please will you do me a **favour**?
- **a good turn**

favourite adjective
What is your **favourite** book?
- **best-loved**
- **number-one**

fear noun
I could see **fear** in his eyes.
- **terror**
- **panic**
- **dread**
- **horror**
  Use **terror** for a very strong feeling of
  fear:
  Emily screamed in **terror** as the ogre
  came towards her.
  Use **panic** for a sudden feeling of fear
  when you are so frightened that you
  don't know what to do:
  A feeling of **panic** came over me as

our little boat began to sink.
Use **dread** or **horror** for a feeling of
fear and disgust:
He watched in **horror** as the huge
snake slid towards him.

feel verb
1 She put out her hand and **felt** the
  puppy's fur.
  - **to touch**
  - **to stroke**
2 I **felt** that I was in the right.
  - **to believe**
  - **to think**

feeling noun
1 Try to think about other people's
  feelings.
  - **an emotion**
2 I had a **feeling** that somebody was
  following me
  - **a sensation**

fence noun
There was a high **fence** around the
garden.
- **a railing**
- **a wall**

festival noun
Diwali is a Hindu religious
festival.
- **a celebration**

fetch verb
1 Shall I **fetch** your bag for you?
  - **to get**
  - **to bring**
2 I'll come and **fetch** you at
  five o'clock.
  - **to collect**
  - **to pick up**

fiction noun
*I like to read **fiction**.*
- **stories**
- **tales**
- **myths**
- **legends**
- **fantasies**

field noun
*The ponies have their own **field** behind the house.*
- **a paddock**
- **an enclosure**
- **a meadow**

fierce adjective
*Tigers are very **fierce** animals.*
- **ferocious**
- **savage**
- **aggressive**
- **dangerous**

fight verb
1 *I don't like watching people **fight**.*
- **to brawl**
- **to wrestle**
- **to grapple**
2 *Why are you two children always **fighting**?*
- **to argue**
- **to quarrel**
- **to bicker**

fight noun
*The two boys had a **fight** after school.*
- **a brawl**
- **a punch-up**
- **a battle**
- **a clash**
  Use **brawl** or **punch-up** for a small fight:
  The argument between the two boys
ended up as a **punch-up**.
Use **battle** or **clash** for a big fight between a lot of people:
*There was a huge **battle** going on in the street.*

fill verb
1 *We **filled** the boxes with toys.*
- **to pack**
- **to load**
- **to stuff**
- **to cram**
2 *They **filled** the huge balloon with air.*
- **to inflate**
OPPOSITE empty

film noun
*We watched a **film** on TV last night.*
- **a movie**

> **WORD WEB**
> **some types of film**
> - an adventure film
> - a cartoon
> - a comedy
> - a documentary (*a film that gives you information about something*)
> - a western (*a film about cowboys*)

filthy adjective
1 *The footballers were **filthy** by the end of the game.*
- **dirty**
- **muddy**
- **mucky**
- **grubby**
- **grimy**
2 *The room was **filthy**.*
- **dirty**
- **dusty**
- **messy**
3 *The water in this river is **filthy**.*
- **polluted**
OPPOSITE clean

a
b
c
d
e
f
g
h
i
j
k
l
m
n
o
p
q
r
s
t
u
v
w
x
y
z

final adjective
This is the **final** day of the holidays.
- **last**

finally adverb
We **finally** arrived home at seven o'clock.
- **eventually**
- **at last**

find verb
1 I can't **find** my homework.
- **to locate**
OPPOSITE lose
2 The children **found** an old map in the attic.
- **to discover**
- **to come across**
- **to stumble upon**
- **to notice**
- **to spot**
3 It took the police six months to **find** the missing man.
- **to trace**
- **to track down**
4 When the archaeologists started digging, they **found** some very interesting things.
- **to dig up**
- **to uncover**
- **to unearth**

fine adjective
1 You will need to use a very **fine** thread.
- **thin**
- **delicate**
- **light**
OPPOSITE thick
2 I hope the weather is **fine** for sports day.
- **sunny**
- **dry**
- **bright**
- **clear**
- **cloudless**
OPPOSITE dull
3 I felt ill yesterday, but today I feel **fine**.
- **okay**
- **all right**
OPPOSITE ill
4 The town hall is a very **fine** building.
- **beautiful**
- **magnificent**
- **splendid**

finish verb
1 What time does the film **finish**?
- **to end**
- **to stop**
2 Have you **finished** your homework?
- **to complete**
- **to do**
3 Hurry up and **finish** your meal.
- **to eat**
- **to eat up**
4 I haven't **finished** my drink.
- **to drink**
- **to drink up**
OPPOSITE start

fire noun
1 We lit a **fire** to keep us warm.
- **a bonfire** (a fire outside)
2 The explosion caused a huge fire.
- **a blaze**
- **an inferno**

fire verb
They were **firing** at a row of bottles on the wall.
- **to shoot**

firm adjective
1 The ladder didn't feel very **firm**.
- **stable**
- **secure**

a
b
c
d
e
f
g
h
i
j
k
l
m
n
o
p
q
r
s
t
u
v
w
x
y
z

- **steady**
- **solid**

OPPOSITE unsteady

2 *We patted the sand down until it was* ***firm***.

- **hard**
- **rigid**

OPPOSITE soft

first adjective

1 *We were the **first** to arrive.*

- **earliest**
- **soonest**

2 *Who designed the **first** aeroplane?*

- **earliest**
- **original**

fit adjective

1 *You have to be **fit** to play football.*

- **strong**
- **healthy**
- **well**

OPPOSITE unfit

2 *I don't think this food is **fit** to eat.*

- **suitable**
- **good enough**

OPPOSITE unsuitable

fit verb

1 *These shoes **fit** me.*

- **to be the right size** *These shoes are the right size for me.*

2 *This box won't **fit** in the back of the car.*

- **to go**

fix verb

1 *Mum **fixed** the shelves onto the wall.*

- **to attach**
- **to tie**
- **to stick**
- **to nail**
- **to fasten**

2 *Our TV is broken and we can't **fix** it.*

- **to mend**
- **to repair**

fizzy adjective

*She offered us a glass of **fizzy** lemonade.*

- **sparkling**
- **bubbly**

flap verb

*The loose sails were **flapping** in the wind.*

- **to flutter**
- **to wave about**

flat adjective

*You need a nice **flat** surface to work on.*

- **level**
- **even**
- **smooth**
- **horizontal**

OPPOSITE uneven

flavour noun

*This drink has got a lovely **flavour**.*

- **a taste**

flow verb

*Water was **flowing** along the pipe.*

- **to run**
- **to pour**
- **to stream**
- **to gush**
- **to spurt**
- **to drip**
- **to trickle**
- **to leak**
- **to gurgle**
- **to burble**
- **to babble**

*Use **pour**, **stream**, **gush**, and **spurt** when water flows very quickly:*
*The side of the pool split and water came **gushing** out.*
*Use **drip** and trickle when water flows very slowly:*
*Water was **dripping** from the tap.* →

a
b
c
d
e
f
g
h
i
j
k
l
m
n
o
p
q
r
s
t
u
v
w
x
y
z

Use **leak** when water flows through a small hole in something:
*Water was **leaking** into the house through a hole in the roof.*
Use **gurgle, burble,** and **babble** when water flows noisily over stones:
*A little stream **babbled** under the bridge.*

flower noun
*We admired the **flowers** on the rose bush.*
• **a bloom**
• **blossom**

WORD WEB
some garden flowers
• anemones
• bougainvillea
• carnations
• crocuses
• daffodils
• geraniums
• hibiscus
• jasmine
• lavender
• lilac
• lilies
• marigolds
• pansies
• petunia
• roses
• snowdrops
• sunflowers
• sweet peas
• tulips
• wallflowers

some wild flowers
• bluebells
• buttercups
• daisies
• dandelions
• foxgloves
• poppies
• primroses

fluffy adjective
*She picked up the small, **fluffy** kitten.*
• **furry**
• **soft**
• **woolly**

fly verb
*We watched the birds **flying** high above our heads.*
• **to glide**
• **to soar**
• **to hover**
• **to flutter**
• **to flit**
• **to dart**
• **to swoop**
• **to dive**
Use **glide** when something moves quietly through the sky:
*A hot-air balloon **glided** silently past us.*
Use **soar** when a bird or plane flies high in the sky:
*The eagle **soared** high above us.*
Use **hover** when something stays in the same place in the air:
*A helicopter **hovered** over the field.*
Use **flutter, flit,** and **dart** when something flies about quickly:
*Bats were **flitting** about in the barn.*
Use **swoop** or **dive** when something flies down towards the ground:
*The owl **swooped** down onto its prey.*

fog noun
*I couldn't see because of the **fog**.*
• **mist**

fold verb
***Fold** the paper along the dotted line.*
• **to bend**
• **to crease**

follow verb
1 *I had the feeling that someone was following me.*
- **to chase**
- **to run after**
- **to pursue**
- **to shadow**
- **to tail**
- **to track**
  Use **chase**, **run after**, and **pursue** when someone is trying to catch a person:
  *The policeman **pursued** the two robbers.*
  Use **shadow** and **tail** when someone follows a person secretly:
  *We **tailed** the professor as far as the library.*
  Use **track** when someone follows the tracks that a person has left:
  *They brought in dogs to **track** the criminals.*
2 ***Follow** this road until you come to a crossroads.*
- **to take**
- **to go along**
- **to continue along**
3 ***Follow** my instructions carefully.*
- **to pay attention to**
- **to obey**

food noun
1 *We were all tired and in need of **food**.*
- **something to eat**
- **refreshments**
- **nourishment**
- **grub** (*informal*)
- **a meal**
2 *We've got plenty of **food** for the animals.*
- **feed**
- **fodder**

fool noun
*Don't be such a **fool**!*
- **an idiot**
- **a twit**
- **an imbecile**
- **a clown**

fool verb
*You can't **fool** me.*
- **to trick**
- **to deceive**

foolish adjective
*That was a very **foolish** thing to do.*
- **silly**
- **stupid**
- **daft**
- **mad**
- **idiotic**
- **unwise**
OPPOSITE sensible

foot noun
- **a paw** (*a dog's or cat's foot*)
- **a hoof** (*a horse's foot*)
- **a trotter** (*a pig's foot*)

force noun
1 *We had to use **force** to open the door.*
- **strength**
- **might**
- **power**
2 *The criminals used **force** to get into the building.*
- **violence**

force verb
1 *He **forced** me to give him money.*
- **to make** *He made me give him the money.*
- **to order** *He ordered me to give him the money.* →

a
b
c
d
e
f
g
h
i
j
k
l
m
n
o
p
q
r
s
t
u
v
w
x
y
z

2 *They **forced** the door open.*
- **to push**
- **to break**
- **to smash**

forest noun
*Don't get lost in the **forest**!*
- **a wood**
- **a jungle** (*a tropical forest*)

forget verb
*I've **forgotten** my PE kit.*
- **to leave behind** *I've left my PE kit behind.*
- **to not bring** *I haven't brought my PE kit.*
OPPOSITE remember

forgive verb
*I'm sorry. Please **forgive** my terrible behaviour.*
- **to excuse**
- **to pardon**

form noun
1 *The bicycle is a **form** of transport.*
- **a type**
- **a sort**
- **a kind**
2 *He is a magician who can change himself into any **form** he chooses.*
- **a shape**

form verb
*These rocks **formed** millions of years ago.*
- **to develop**
- **to be made** *These rocks were made millions of years ago.*

foul adjective
*There was a **foul** smell in the kitchen.*
- **horrible**
- **disgusting**
- **nasty**
- **revolting**
- **repulsive**

fragile adjective
*Be careful, these glasses are **fragile**.*
- **delicate**
- **flimsy**
- **breakable**
- **brittle**
OPPOSITE strong

free adjective
1 *At last he was **free**!*
- **at liberty**
- **out of prison**
- **no longer in captivity**
2 *All the drinks are **free**.*
- **for nothing**
- **complimentary**

free verb
*The judge **freed** him.*
- **to release**
- **to liberate**
- **to set free**
The judge set him free.

fresh adjective
1 *Start each answer on a **fresh** page.*
- **clean**
- **new**
- **different**
2 *I love the taste of **fresh** strawberries.*
- **freshly picked**
3 *We had **fresh** bread for tea.*
- **warm**
- **freshly baked**
4 *The **fresh** air at the seaside will do you good.*
- **clean**
- **clear**
- **pure**
- **bracing**

5 *I felt lovely and **fresh** after my swim.*
- **lively**
- **energetic**
- **refreshed**
- **invigorated**

friend noun
- **a mate**
- **a pal**
- **a companion**
- **a partner**
- **a colleague**
- **an ally**

A **mate** or **pal** is a friend:
*Who's your best **mate**?*

A **companion** is someone you travel with or do things with:
*I took my dog with me as a travelling **companion**.*

A **partner** or **colleague** is someone you work with:
*I always choose Sam as my **partner** in class.*

An **ally** is someone who helps you in a fight:
*I needed an **ally** in my fight with the Jones boys.*

friendly adjective
1 *She's a very **friendly** person.*
- **kind**
- **nice**
- **pleasant**
- **amiable**
- **affectionate**

2 *Don't worry, our dog is very **friendly**.*
- **good-natured**
- **gentle**

3 *Tina and I are quite **friendly** now.*
- **pally**
- **matey** (*informal*)
- **close**

OPPOSITE unfriendly

frighten verb
*The noise **frightened** us.*
- **to scare**
- **to startle**
- **to shock**
- **to make someone jump**
- **to terrify**

Use **startle**, **shock**, or **make someone jump** if something frightens you suddenly:
*Sam **startled** me when he jumped out from behind a bush.*

Use **terrify** if something frightens you a lot:
*That film used to **terrify** me when I was young.*

frightened adjective
*Are you **frightened** of spiders?*
- **afraid**
- **scared**
- **startled**
- **terrified**
- **petrified**

Use **startled** if you are frightened by something sudden:
*I was **startled** when the door suddenly opened.*

Use **terrified** or **petrified** if you are very frightened:
*James was **petrified** when he saw the lion.*

frightening adjective
*The film was quite **frightening**.*
- **scary**
- **terrifying**

Use **terrifying** for something that is very frightening:
*It was **terrifying** going on such a big roller coaster.*

a
b
c
d
e
f
g
h
i
j
k
l
m
n
o
p
q
r
s
t
u
v
w
x
y
z

a
b
c
d
e
f
g
h
i
j
k
l
m
n
o
p
q
r
s
t
u
v
w
x
y
z

front noun

> At last we got to the **front** of the queue.
> • **the beginning**
> • **the head**
> OPPOSITE back

fruit noun

> WORD WEB
> **some types of fruit**
> • an apple
> • an apricot
> • a banana
> • blackberries
> • cherries
> • figs
> • gooseberries
> • a grapefruit
> • a guava
> • a kiwi fruit
> • a lemon
> • a lychee
> • a mango
> • a melon
> • a nectarine
> • an orange
> • a papaya
> • a peach
> • a pear
> • a pineapple
> • a plum
> • raspberries
> • rhubarb
> • strawberries
> • a tangerine
> • a tomato
> • a watermelon

full adjective

> **1** We poured water into the bucket until it was **full**.
> • **full to the brim**
> • **overflowing**
> **2** The school hall was **full**.
> • **packed**
> • **full to capacity**

3 The room was **full** of people.
> • **crowded**
> • **packed**
4 The basket was **full** of good things to eat.
> • **packed with**
> • **crammed with**
> • **bursting with**
> • **bulging with**
> OPPOSITE empty

fun noun

> We had lots of **fun** on the beach.
> • **enjoyment**
> • **pleasure**

funny adjective

> **1** He told us a very **funny** joke.
> • **amusing**
> • **hilarious**
> • **witty**
> Use **hilarious** for something that is very funny:
> The film was absolutely **hilarious**.
> Use **witty** for something that is funny and clever:
> Joe's very good at making **witty** jokes.
> OPPOSITE serious
> **2** We had to write a **funny** poem.
> • **humorous**
> **3** You look really **funny** in that hat.`
> • **comical**
> • **ridiculous**
> **4** This sauce tastes very **funny**.
> • **strange**
> • **peculiar**
> • **odd**
> • **curious**

furious adjective

> My dad was **furious** when he saw the mess.
> • **livid**
> • **fuming**

furry adjective

*I stroked the cat's **furry** head.*
- **fluffy**
- **woolly**
- **soft**

fuss noun

*There was a terrible **fuss** when we found a mouse in our classroom.*
- **a commotion**
- **an uproar**

fussy adjective

1 *Some children are quite **fussy** about their food.*
- **choosy**
- **picky**
- **hard to please**

2 *My sister is very **fussy** about keeping her room neat and tidy.*
- **particular**
- **fastidious**

a
b
c
d
e
f
g
h
i
j
k
l
m
n
o
p
q
r
s
t
u
v
w
x
y
z

Gg

game noun
*The children were playing a **game** of football.*
- **a match**
- **a tournament**
- **a competition**
- **a contest**

gang noun
*Do you want to join our **gang**?*
- **a group**
- **a crowd**
- **a band**

gap noun
*We climbed through a **gap** in the hedge.*
- **a hole**
- **an opening**
- **a space**
- **a break**

gather verb
1 *People **gathered** round to watch the jugglers.*
- **to crowd round**
- **to come together**
- **to assemble**
2 *We **gathered** blackberries from the fields.*
- **to pick**
- **to collect**
3 *I need to **gather** some information for my project.*
- **to collect**
- **to find**

general adjective
*The **general** opinion in our class is that school is fun.*

- **common**
- **popular**
- **widespread**

generous adjective
*My grandma is a very **generous** person.*
- **kind**
- **unselfish**
- **big-hearted**
OPPOSITE selfish

gentle adjective
1 *She's a very **gentle** person.*
- **kind**
- **quiet**
- **good-tempered**
- **sweet-tempered**
- **loving**
- **tender**
2 *I gave her a **gentle** tap on the shoulder.*
- **light**
- **soft**
OPPOSITE rough

gently adverb
*He stroked the puppy **gently**.*
- **softly**
- **lightly**
- **carefully**
OPPOSITE roughly

get verb

⚠ **OVERUSED WORD**
Try to vary the words you use to mean *get*. Here are some other words you can use instead.
1 *I **got** a new bike for my birthday.*
- **to receive**
- **to be given**
2 *Where can I **get** some paper?*
- **to find**
- **to obtain**

a b c d e f g h i j k l m n o p q r s t u v w x y z

3 We're going to the shop to **get** some food.
  • **to buy**
  • **to purchase**
4 How much money do you **get** for doing the paper round?
  • **to earn**
  • **to receive**
5 I wonder who will **get** the first prize.
  • **to win**
6 Our team **got** fifteen points.
  • **to score**
7 I'll go and **get** the drinks.
  • **to fetch**
  • **to bring**
8 I **got** chickenpox last winter.
  • **to catch**
9 What time will we **get** home?
  • **to arrive**
  • **to reach**
  • **to come**
10 It's **getting** colder.
  • **to become**
  • **to grow**
  • **to turn**

ghost noun
Have you ever seen a **ghost**?
  • **a phantom**
  • **an apparition**
  • **a spirit**
  • **a spook**

giant noun
A wicked **giant** lived in the castle.
  • **an ogre**

giggle verb
The girls were all **giggling**.
  • **to snigger**
  • **to titter**
  • **to chuckle**

girl noun
  • **a lass**
  • **a kid**
  • **a child**
  • **a youngster**
  • **a teenager**

give verb

⚠ **OVERUSED WORD**
Try to vary the words you use to mean give. Here are some other words you can use instead.
1 Mia **gave** me a sweet.
  • **to hand**
  • **to pass**
  • **to hand over**
2 I'm going to **give** Rebecca a CD for her birthday.
  • **to buy**
3 The school **gives** us pens and paper.
  • **to provide**
  • **to supply**
4 The judges **gave** the first prize to our team.
  • **to award**
  • **to present**
5 We **gave** our old toys to the children's hospital.
  • **to donate**

glad adjective
I'm **glad** you got here safely.
  • **pleased**
  • **relieved**
  • **happy**
  • **delighted**
    Use **delighted** if you are very glad about something:
    We were **delighted** when we won the competition.

glass noun
She poured some milk into a **glass**.
  • **a tumbler**
  • **a wine glass**

a
b
c
d
e
f
g
h
i
j
k
l
m
n
o
p
q
r
s
t
u
v
w
x
y
z

a
b
c
d
e
f
g
h
i
j
k
l
m
n
o
p
q
r
s
t
u
v
w
x
y
z

glasses noun

I can't see very well without my
***glasses**.*
• **spectacles**

glue noun

Stick the pieces of paper together with
***glue**.*
• **adhesive**
• **gum**
• **paste**

go verb

⚠ **OVERUSED WORD**

Try to vary the words you use to mean
go. Here are some other words you can
use instead.

1 *Let's **go** along this path.*
• **to walk**
• **to run**
• **to rush**
• **to hurry**
• **to race**
• **to march**
• **to stride**
• **to saunter**
• **to stroll**
• **to creep**
• **to sneak**
• **to tiptoe**
  *Use **run**, **rush**, **hurry**, or **race**
  when you go somewhere very
  quickly:*
  *I **rushed** home as fast as I could.*
  *Use **march** or **stride** when you go
  along taking big steps:*
  *Mr Hoggett **strode** angrily towards
  the house.*
  *Use **saunter** or stroll when you go
  along slowly, in a relaxed way:*
  *In the afternoon, we **strolled** through
  the park.*
  *Use **creep**, **sneak**, or **tiptoe** when you
  go somewhere quietly or secretly:*
  *I **sneaked** out of the class when no
  one was looking.*

2 *We **went** along the motorway for a few
miles.*
• **to drive**
• **to travel**
• **to speed**
3 *We're **going** at six o'clock.*
• **to leave**
• **to set out**
4 *This road **goes** to London.*
• **to lead**
5 *When we got back, our suitcases had
gone.*
• **to disappear**
• **to vanish**
6 *My watch doesn't **go**.*
• **to work**
7 *When the teacher talks, all of the
children **go** quiet.*
• **to become**
• **to grow**

go away verb

*He told me to **go away**.*
• **to leave**
• **to get lost** (*informal*)

go back verb

*I think we should **go back**
now.*
• **to return**

go down verb

***Go down** the stairs.*
• **to descend**

go into verb

***Go into** the kitchen.*
• **to enter**

go out of verb

***Go out of** the house.*
• **to leave**
• **to exit**

go up verb
Go up the stairs.
- **to climb**
- **to ascend**

good adjective

> ⚠️ **OVERUSED WORD**
>
> Try to vary the words you use to mean *good*. Here are some other words you can use instead.
>
> **1** *This is a really good book.*
> - **wonderful**
> - **brilliant**
> - **excellent**
> - **fantastic**
> - **great**
> - **enjoyable**
> - **exciting**
> - **interesting**
> - **amusing**
> - **entertaining**
>
>   Use **wonderful**, **brilliant**, **excellent**, **fantastic**, or **great** if something is very good:
>   *He told us some **wonderful** stories about his travels.*
>   Use **enjoyable, exciting,** or **interesting** for something you enjoy a lot:
>   *We had a very **enjoyable** time at the seaside.*
>   Use **amusing** or **entertaining** for something that makes you laugh:
>   *It was a very **entertaining** film.*
>
> **2** *William is a very good footballer.*
> - **skilful**
> - **talented**
> - **competent**
>
> **3** *I hope the weather is good for sports day.*
> - **fine**
> - **nice**
> - **dry**
> - **sunny**
> - **warm**
>
> **4** *Jessica has got a very good imagination.*
> - **lively**
> - **vivid**
>
> **5** *He gave the police a good description of the thief.*
> - **clear**
> - **vivid**
> - **precise**
>
> **6** *You have been a very good friend to me.*
> - **kind**
> - **caring**
> - **loving**
> - **loyal**
>
> **7** *The children have been very good all day.*
> - **well-behaved**
> - **polite**
>
> OPPOSITE bad

grab verb
1 *I grabbed my coat and ran out.*
- **to seize**
- **to snatch**
- **to pick up**

2 *Tom grabbed my arm.*
- **to take hold of**
- **to grasp**
- **to clutch**
- **to grip**

graceful adjective
She is a very graceful dancer.
- **elegant**
- **beautiful**
- **smooth**

OPPOSITE clumsy

gradually adverb
It gradually got darker.
- **slowly**
- **steadily**
- **progressively**
- **little by little**

OPPOSITE suddenly

a
b
c
d
e
f
g
h
i
j
k
l
m
n
o
p
q
r
s
t
u
v
w
x
y
z

83

a
b
c
d
e
f
g
h
i
j
k
l
m
n
o
p
q
r
s
t
u
v
w
x
y
z

grateful adjective
*We are very **grateful** for all your help.*
- **thankful**
- **appreciative** *We are very appreciative of all your help.*
OPPOSITE ungrateful

greedy adjective
*Don't be **greedy** – you've had three cakes already!*
- **piggish**
- **gluttonous**

great adjective
1 *The soldiers led us into a **great** hall.*
- **big**
- **large**
- **enormous**
- **huge**
- **vast**
OPPOSITE small
2 *The royal wedding was a **great** occasion.*
- **grand**
- **magnificent**
- **splendid**
OPPOSITE unimportant
3 *He was a **great** musician.*
- **famous**
- **well-known**
- **celebrated**
OPPOSITE terrible
4 *It's a **great** film!*
- **wonderful**
- **brilliant**
- **excellent**
- **fantastic**
OPPOSITE terrible

green adjective
*She was wearing a **green** dress.*
- **emerald**

- **lime green** (*bright green*)
- **bottle green** (*dark green*)

greet verb
*She went to the door to **greet** her guests.*
- **to welcome**

grey adjective
1 *The sky was **grey**.*
- **cloudy**
- **dull**
- **overcast**
- **grim**
- **forbidding**
2 *They met an old man with **grey** hair.*
- **white**
- **silver**

grin verb
*The boy **grinned** at me.*
- **to smile**
- **to beam**

grip verb
*The old lady **gripped** my arm.*
- **to hold on to**
- **to grasp**
- **to clutch**

groan verb
*We all **groaned** when the teacher told us we had to stay inside.*
- **to moan**
- **to sigh**
- **to protest**

ground noun
1 *Don't leave your bags on the wet **ground**.*
- **soil**
- **earth**

2 Who owns this piece of **ground**?
- **land**
- **territory**

group noun

1 There was a large **group** of people waiting outside the cinema.
- **a crowd**
- **a throng**
- **a mob**
  Use **mob** for a large, noisy group: There was an angry **mob** outside the school.

2 He was showing a **group** of tourists round the museum.
- **a party**

3 We met up with a **group** of our friends.
- **a bunch**
- **a crowd**
- **a gang**

4 What's your favourite pop **group**?
- **a band**

WORD WEB

collective nouns for some groups of animals
- a flock of birds
- a flock of sheep
- a gaggle of geese
- a herd of cattle
- a litter of puppies
- a pack of wolves
- a pride of lions
- a school of whales
- a shoal of fish
- a swarm of bees

---

group verb
We had to **group** the poems together according to their author.
- **to arrange**
- **to classify**
- **to sort**
- **to order**

grow verb

1 Anita has really **grown** this year.
- **to get bigger**
- **to get taller**
- **to shoot up**

2 The seeds are starting to **grow**.
- **to germinate**
- **to sprout**
- **to shoot up**
- **to spring up**
  Use **germinate** or **sprout** when seeds first start to grow:
  After three or four days the seeds will start to **germinate**.
  Use **shoot up** or **spring up** when the plant starts to grow taller:
  Weeds were **springing up** all over the garden.

3 The number of children in our school is **growing**.
- **to increase**

4 We **grow** vegetables in our garden.
- **to plant**
- **to produce**

grown-up noun
Ask a **grown-up** if you need help.
- **an adult**

grown-up adjective
You need to behave in a **grown-up** manner.
- **mature**
- **responsible**
- **sensible**

grumble verb
Stop **grumbling**!
- **to complain**
- **to moan**
- **to whinge**
- **to whine**

a b c d e f g h i j k l m n o p q r s t u v w x y z

grumpy adjective
*Why are you so **grumpy** today?*
- **cross**
- **bad-tempered**
- **sulky**
- **moody**
OPPOSITE good-tempered

guard verb
1 *Soldiers **guard** the castle.*
- **to protect**
- **to defend**
- **to watch**
2 *A mother elephant will **guard** her young.*
- **to look after**
- **to watch over**
- **to protect**

guard noun
*There was a **guard** by the door.*
- **a sentry**
- **a lookout**
- **a security officer** (in a bank, office, or shop)

guess verb
1 *Can you **guess** how many sweets are in the jar?*
- **to estimate**
2 *Because they were late, I **guessed** that their car must have broken down.*
- **to think**
- **to suppose**

- **to predict**
- **to infer**

guide verb
*He **guided** us through the wood to the main road.*
- **to lead**
- **to steer**
- **to escort**
- **to accompany**

guilty adjective
*I felt **guilty** because I had been mean to my sister.*
- **bad**
- **ashamed**
- **sorry**
- **remorseful**
- **sheepish**
OPPOSITE innocent

gun noun
*The man was holding a **gun** in his hand.*
- **a weapon**
- **a firearm**

WORD WEB
some types of gun
- an air pistol
- a machine gun
- a pistol
- a revolver
- a rifle
- a shotgun

a
b
c
d
e
f
g
h
i
j
k
l
m
n
o
p
q
r
s
t
u
v
w
x
y
z

Hh

hair noun

*She had blonde **hair**.*
- **locks**
- **curls**
  *Use **locks** for long hair and **curls** for curly hair:*
  *She looked in the mirror and admired her golden **locks**.*

WORD WEB

some words you might use to describe the colour of someone's hair
- auburn
- black
- blond(e)
- brown
- chestnut
- dark
- ebony
- fair
- ginger
- golden
- grey
- jet black
- mousy
- red
- sandy
- white

some words you might use to describe someone's hair
- beautiful
- curly
- dishevelled
- fine
- frizzy
- glossy
- long
- scruffy
- shiny
- short
- sleek
- straight
- thick
- tousled
- untidy
- wavy
- windswept

---

hairy adjective

*They were greeted by a large, **hairy** dog.*
- **furry**
- **shaggy**
- **woolly**

handsome adjective

*He is a very **handsome** man.*
- **good-looking**
- **attractive**
- **gorgeous**
  *Use **gorgeous** for a man who is very handsome:*
  *He's my favourite actor – he's absolutely **gorgeous**!*

OPPOSITE ugly

hang verb

1 *A bunch of keys was **hanging** from his belt.*
  - **to dangle**
  - **to swing**
2 *We **hung** the picture on the wall.*
  - **to attach**
  - **to fasten**
  - **to fix**
3 *He **hung** on to the rope.*
  - **to hold on to**
  - **to cling on to**

happen verb

*When did the accident **happen**?*
- **to take place**
- **to occur**

happy adjective
*I'm feeling very **happy** today.*
- **cheerful**
- **contented**
- **good-humoured**
- **pleased**
- **glad**
- **delighted**
- **thrilled**
- **overjoyed**

Use **cheerful**, **contented**, or **good-humoured** if you are in a good mood and not grumpy or upset about anything:
*Sara is a very **cheerful** person who's always smiling.*
Use **pleased** or **glad** if you are happy about something that has happened:
*I'll be very **glad** when this adventure is over!*
Use **delighted**, **thrilled**, or **overjoyed** if you are very happy:
*Everyone was **overjoyed** when the children were found safe and well.*
OPPOSITE unhappy

hard adjective
1 *The ground was **hard** and frozen.*
- **firm**
- **solid**
- **rigid**
OPPOSITE soft
2 *The teacher gave us some very **hard** sums to do.*
- **difficult**
- **complicated**
- **tricky**
- **challenging**
OPPOSITE easy
3 *Carrying the bricks was very **hard** work.*
- **tiring**
- **exhausting**
- **strenuous**
- **back-breaking**
OPPOSITE easy

hardly adverb
*I was so tired I could **hardly** walk.*
- **scarcely**
- **barely**
- **only just**

harm verb
1 *I didn't mean to **harm** you.*
- **to hurt**
- **to injure**
- **to wound**
2 *Smoking can **harm** your health.*
- **to damage**
- **to ruin**

harmful adjective
1 *Smoking is **harmful** to your health.*
- **bad for** *Smoking is bad for your health.*
- **damaging** *Smoking is damaging to your health.*
2 *Be careful of these **harmful** chemicals.*
- **dangerous**
- **poisonous**
- **toxic**
OPPOSITE harmless

harmless adjective
*Our dog seems fierce, but really he is **harmless**.*
- **safe**
OPPOSITE dangerous

harsh adjective
1 *The machine made a **harsh** sound.*
- **rough**
- **grating**
- **shrill**
- **piercing**
Use **rough** or **grating** for a low sound:
*The wheel made a loud **grating** sound as it turned.*

Use **shrill** or **piercing** for a high sound:
*They heard a **piercing** scream.*
OPPOSITE gentle

2 *That punishment seemed a bit **harsh**.*
- **hard**
- **severe**
- **strict**
- **unkind**
OPPOSITE lenient

hat noun

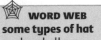

> **WORD WEB**
> **some types of hat**
> - a baseball cap
> - a beret
> - a boater
> - a bonnet
> - a bowler hat
> - a cap
> - a fedora
> - a fez
> - a helmet
> - a panama
> - a riding hat
> - a sombrero
> - a sun hat
> - a top hat
> - a turban
> - a woolly hat
> - a witches' hat

hate verb
*I **hate** cold weather!*
- **to dislike**
- **to detest**
- **to loathe**
- **to not be able to stand** *I can't stand cold weather!*
OPPOSITE love

have verb
1 *Our school **has** fifteen computers.*
- **to own**
- **to possess**

2 *I don't need this book now. You can **have** it.*
- **to keep**
3 *I **had** some lovely presents for my birthday.*
- **to get**
- **to receive**
4 *My brother is at home because he **has** chickenpox.*
- **to be suffering from**
- **to be infected with** *He is infected with chickenpox.*

heal verb
*That cut on your arm will soon **heal**.*
- **to get better**
- **to mend**

healthy adjective
1 *Most of the children here are very **healthy**.*
- **strong**
- **well**
- **fit**
2 *This food is very **healthy**.*
- **nutritious**
- **nourishing**
- **good for you**
OPPOSITE unhealthy

heap noun
*There was a **heap** of dirty clothes on the floor.*
- **a pile**
- **a mound**
- **a mass**
- **a stack**

hear verb
1 *I couldn't **hear** what he was saying.*
- **to make out**
- **to catch** →

a
b
c
d
e
f
g
h
i
j
k
l
m
n
o
p
q
r
s
t
u
v
w
x
y
z

a
b
c
d
e
f
g
h
i
j
k
l
m
n
o
p
q
r
s
t
u
v
w
x
y
z

2 *Have you **heard** the band's new single?*
• **to listen to**

heat noun
*I could feel the **heat** from the fire.*
• **warmth**

heat verb
*We can **heat** up a pizza for lunch.*
• **to warm up**

heavy adjective
*This bag is very **heavy**.*
• **weighty**
OPPOSITE light

help verb
1 *Shall I **help** you with your bags?*
• **to assist**
• **to lend a hand**
• **to give someone a hand**
2 *Members of a team must all **help** each other.*
• **to support**
• **to cooperate with**

help noun
*Do you need some **help**?*
• **assistance**
• **advice**
• **support**

helpful adjective
*She is always very **helpful** in class.*
• **kind**
• **considerate**
• **willing**
• **thoughtful**
OPPOSITE unhelpful

helping noun
*He gave me a huge **helping** of chips.*
• **a portion**
• **a serving**

here adjective
*Are all the children **here**?*
• **present**

hesitate verb
*She **hesitated** before diving into the water.*
• **to pause**
• **to wait**
• **to delay**
• **to dither**

hide verb
1 *We **hid** in the garden shed.*
• **to keep out of sight**
• **to go into hiding**
• **to lie low**
*Use **go into hiding** when someone hides for a long time:*
*The robbers **went into hiding** for several weeks after the robbery.*
*Use **lie low** when someone tries to avoid certain people:*
*I knew Mrs Flint would be furious with me, so I decided to **lie low** for a week or two.*
2 *They **hid** the money in a hollow tree.*
• **to conceal**
• **to stash**

high adjective
1 *There are a lot of **high** buildings in the city.*
• **tall**
• **big**
• **towering**
2 *Some shops charge very **high** prices.*
• **inflated**
• **exorbitant**

3 She spoke in a **high** voice.
- **high-pitched**
- **squeaky**
- **piercing**
- **shrill**
  Use **piercing** or **shrill** for a loud, unpleasant high voice:
  *'Get out!' she cried in a **shrill** voice.*
  OPPOSITE low

hill noun
  We walked up the **hill**.
- **a mountain**
- **a slope**

hit verb
1 You mustn't **hit** people.
- **to strike**
- **to punch**
- **to thump**
- **to slap**
- **to smack**
- **to beat**
- **to thrash**
  To **punch** or **thump** someone means to hit them with your fist:
  *'Get out of my way, or I'll **thump** you!' he shouted.*
  To **slap** someone means to hit them with your open hand:
  *She **slapped** the other girl's face.*
  To **smack** someone means to hit them as a punishment:
  *Some parents **smack** their children.*
  To **beat** or **thrash** someone means to hit them many times with a stick:
  *The cruel master used to **beat** the horses.*
2 I fell and **hit** my elbow.
- **to knock**
- **to bang**
- **to bash**
- **to bump**

3 The car went out of control and **hit** a lamp post.
- **to bump into**
- **to crash into**
- **to smash into**
- **to collide with**
4 He **hit** the ball as hard as he could.
- **to strike**
- **to whack**

hoarse adjective
  Dad's voice was **hoarse** because he had a cold.
- **croaking**
- **husky**
- **rough**

hobby noun
  Skateboarding is my favourite **hobby**.
- **a pastime**
- **an interest**
- **an activity**
- **a leisure activity**

hold verb
1 Can I **hold** the baby?
- **to carry**
- **to cuddle**
- **to hug**
- **to cradle**
2 She **held** the handrail tightly.
- **to grip**
- **to grasp**
- **to clutch**
3 One of the men was **holding** a knife.
- **to brandish**
- **to wield**
4 This box **holds** twenty pencils.
- **to take**
- **to contain**
- **to have space for** *This box has space for twenty pencils.*

a
b
c
d
e
f
g
h
i
j
k
l
m
n
o
p
q
r
s
t
u
v
w
x
y
z

a
b
c
d
e
f
g
h
i
j
k
l
m
n
o
p
q
r
s
t
u
v
w
x
y
z

hole noun
1 *We climbed through a **hole** in the hedge.*
  • **an opening**
  • **a gap**
  • **a space**
2 *There was a big **hole** in the ground.*
  • **a pit**
  • **a crater**
  • **a chasm**
3 *I could see them through a **hole** in the wall.*
  • **a crack**
  • **a slit**
  • **a chink**
4 *There's a **hole** in my shirt.*
  • **a split**
  • **a rip**
  • **a tear**
5 *There was a **hole** in one of the water pipes.*
  • **a crack**
  • **a leak**
6 *One of my bicycle tyres has a **hole** in it.*
  • **a puncture**
7 *The tiny animal escaped back into its **hole**.*
  • **a burrow**
  • **a den**
  • **a nest**

holy adjective
*He read to us from the **holy** book.*
  • **sacred**
  • **religious**

home noun
*This is my **home**.*
  • **a residence**
  • **a house**
  • **a flat**
  • **an apartment**

honest adjective
1 *I'm sure he is an **honest** man.*
  • **good**
  • **trustworthy**
  • **law-abiding**
  OPPOSITE dishonest
2 *Did you enjoy the film? Be **honest**.*
  • **truthful**
  • **sincere**
  • **frank**
  OPPOSITE insincere

hopeless adjective
*I'm **hopeless** at swimming.*
  • **bad**
  • **no good**
  • **terrible**
  • **useless**
  • **incompetent**
  OPPOSITE good

horrible adjective
1 *Don't be **horrible**!*
  • **nasty**
  • **unpleasant**
  • **mean**
  • **unkind**
  • **obnoxious**
  • **horrid**
2 *The food was **horrible**.*
  • **revolting**
  • **disgusting**
  • **tasteless**
  • **inedible**
3 *What a **horrible** dress!*
  • **vile**
  • **hideous**
  • **repulsive**
4 *The weather was **horrible**.*
  • **awful**
  • **dreadful**
  • **terrible**
  • **appalling**

5 *I had a dream about a **horrible** monster.*
- **terrible**
- **frightening**
- **terrifying**

OPPOSITE pleasant

horrid adjective
*Everyone is being **horrid** to me!*
- **nasty**
- **unkind**
- **mean**
- **horrible**

OPPOSITE pleasant

horror noun
*The sight of the huge beast filled me with **horror**.*
- **fear**
- **terror**
- **dread**

horse noun
- **a pony**
- **a nag** (*an old horse*)
- **a mare** (*a female horse*)
- **a stallion** (*a male horse*)
- **a foal** (*a baby horse*)
- **a colt** (*a young horse*)

WORD WEB
some types of horse
- a carthorse
- a racehorse
- a Shetland pony
- a Shire horse

some words you might use to describe the colour of a horse
- black
- bay (*reddish brown*)
- chestnut
- dapple grey
- roan (*brown or black, with some white hairs*)
- piebald (*with patches of black and white*)
- skewbald (*with patches of white and another colour*)
- white

WRITING TIPS
Here are some useful words for writing about horses.
- The little pony **trotted** down the lane.
- The stallion **cantered** across the field.
- The racehorse **galloped** towards the finishing line.
- The foal **neighed** excitedly.

hot adjective
1 *The weather will be **hot** next week.*
- **warm**
- **boiling hot**
- **baking hot**
- **scorching hot**
- **sweltering**

Use **warm** when the weather is quite hot:
*It was a lovely **warm** spring morning.*
Use **boiling hot**, **baking hot**, and **scorching hot** when it is very hot:
*It was a **baking hot** summer's day.*
Use **sweltering** when it is too hot:
*We couldn't do anything in the afternoon because it was **sweltering**.*

OPPOSITE cold

2 *Be careful with that pan — it's **hot**.*
- **red hot**
- **burning hot**

Use **red hot** or **burning hot** for something that is very hot:
*The coals on the barbecue were **red hot**.*

OPPOSITE cold

3 *Don't spill that **hot** water over yourself*
- **boiling**
- **scalding** →

a
b
c
d
e
f
g
h
i
j
k
l
m
n
o
p
q
r
s
t
u
v
w
x
y
z

a
b
c
d
e
f
g
h
i
j
k
l
m
n
o
p
q
r
s
t
u
v
w
x
y
z

- **scalding hot**
- **piping hot**
Use **boiling** for a liquid that is hot enough to boil:
You make tea with **boiling** water.
Use **scalding** or **scalding hot** for a liquid that is hot enough to burn your skin:
Don't get into the bath yet – the water's **scalding hot**.
Use **piping hot** for food or drink that is nice and hot:
She brought us a bowl of **piping hot** soup.
OPPOSITE cold

4 We sat down in front of the **hot** fire.
- **warm**
- **blazing**
- **roaring**
OPPOSITE cold

5 We add spices to food to make it **hot**.
- **spicy**
- **peppery**
OPPOSITE mild

house noun
- **a home**

🕸 **WORD WEB**
some types of house
- a bungalow
- a castle
- a cottage
- a farmhouse
- a mansion
- a palace

---

hug verb
He **hugged** his mother.
- **to cuddle**
- **to hold**
- **to embrace**

huge adjective
The **huge** creature came after them.
- **great**
- **enormous**
- **gigantic**
- **massive**
OPPOSITE tiny

hungry adjective
1 I'm glad it's lunchtime, I'm **hungry**.
- **starving**
- **famished**
- **ravenous**
- **peckish**
Use **starving**, **famished**, or **ravenous** if you are very hungry:
I was absolutely **starving** after playing football.
Use **peckish** if you are slightly hungry:
It was getting close to lunch time and I was beginning to feel a bit **peckish**.
2 The people have no food, and their children are **hungry**.
- **starving**
- **underfed**
- **undernourished**

hunt verb
1 Lions **hunt** deer and other animals.
- **to chase**
- **to kill**
2 Will you help me **hunt** for my purse?
- **to look for**
- **to search for**

hurry verb
1 Come on, **hurry** up!
- **to be quick** Come on, be quick!
- **to get a move on** (informal) Come on, get a move on!
2 He **hurried** out of the room.
- **to rush**
- **to dash**

- to run
- to race

hurt verb

1 *You mustn't **hurt** animals.*
- to injure
- to harm

2 *I fell and **hurt** my leg.*
- to injure
- to cut
- to graze
- to bruise
- to sprain
- to twist
- to dislocate
- to break

3 *My head is **hurting**.*
- to be sore
- to be painful
- to ache
- to pound
- to throb
- to sting
- to smart

Use ***ache*** to describe a pain that continues for a long time:
*My poor head was **aching**.*
Use ***pound*** or ***throb*** to describe a banging pain:
*I had a toothache which was **throbbing** terribly.*
Use ***sting*** or ***smart*** to describe a sharp pain:
*The salt water made my eyes **sting**.*

hut noun
*We slept in a little **hut** in the wood.*
- a shack
- a cabin
- a shelter
- a shed

a
b
c
d
e
f
g
h
i
j
k
l
m
n
o
p
q
r
s
t
u
v
w
x
y
z

Ii

a
b
c
d
e
f
g
h
i
j
k
l
m
n
o
p
q
r
s
t
u
v
w
x
y
z

idea noun
1 *I've got an **idea**!*
  • **a suggestion**
  • **a plan**
  • **a thought**
  • **a brainwave**
    *A **brainwave** is a very good idea that you suddenly think of:*
    *We were wondering what to do, then Dora suddenly had a **brainwave**.*
2 *I don't always agree with your **ideas**.*
  • **an opinion**
  • **a belief**
3 *The film gave us an **idea** of what life was like in ancient Rome.*
  • **an impression**
  • **a picture**

ideal adjective
  *The weather was **ideal** for a picnic.*
  • **perfect**
  • **excellent**
  • **just right**

ignore verb
  *I said hello to them, but they **ignored** me.*
  • **to take no notice of** *They **took no notice of** me.*
  • **to pay no attention to** *They **paid no attention to** me.*

ill adjective
  *I felt too **ill** to go to school.*
  • **unwell**
  • **poorly**
  • **sick**
  • **queasy**

Use **queasy** when you feel as if you are going to be sick:
*I was feeling a bit **queasy** after eating all that chocolate.*
OPPOSITE healthy

illness noun
  *She is suffering from a nasty **illness**.*
  • **an ailment**
  • **a complaint**
  • **a disease**
  • **an infection**
  • **a bug**
    Use **ailment** or **complaint** for any illness:
    *Stomach ache is a very common **complaint**.*
    Use **disease** for a serious illness:
    *Cancer is a very serious **disease**.*
    Use **infection** or **bug** for an illness that you catch from other people:
    *I think I've caught a **bug** from someone at school.*

imaginary adjective
1 *Dragons are **imaginary** animals.*
  • **mythical**
  • **fictional**
  • **fictitious**
  • **legendary**
2 *We played on our **imaginary** island.*
  • **pretend**
  • **invented**
  • **made-up**
  OPPOSITE real

imagine verb
1 *I tried to **imagine** what life was like in Roman times.*
  • **to think about**
  • **to picture**
  • **to visualize**
  • **to envisage**

2 *It didn't really happen. You only **imagined** it.*
- **to dream**

immediately adverb
*Come here **immediately**!*
- **at once**
- **straight away**
- **this minute**
- **instantly**

important adjective
1 *There is one **important** thing you must remember.*
- **vital**
- **crucial**
- **essential**
2 *The World Cup is a very **important** sporting event.*
- **big**
- **major**
- **special**
- **significant**
3 *I was nervous about meeting such an **important** person.*
- **famous**
- **distinguished**
- **prominent**
- **high-ranking**
OPPOSITE unimportant

impossible adjective
*I can't do that — it's **impossible**!*
- **not possible**
- **not humanly possible**
- **not feasible**
OPPOSITE possible

improve verb
1 *Your maths is **improving**.*
- **to get better**
- **to come on**
2 *Try to **improve** your handwriting.*
- **to make progress with**

increase verb
1 *Our class has **increased** in size.*
- **to get bigger**
- **to grow**
- **to expand**
2 *The noise gradually **increased**.*
- **to get louder**
- **to build up**
3 *The price of tickets has **increased**.*
- **to go up**
- **to rise**
- **to double** (*to become twice as much*)
OPPOSITE decrease

incredible adjective
1 *It seems **incredible** that someone could survive for so long in the desert.*
- **unbelievable**
- **extraordinary**
- **unlikely**
- **unimaginable**
2 *It's an **incredible** film!*
- **great**
- **excellent**
- **brilliant**
- **wonderful**
- **fantastic**
- **amazing**

information noun
*We are collecting **information** about rainforests.*
- **facts**
- **details**
- **data**

injure verb
1 *He fell and **injured** his leg.*
- **to hurt**
- **to cut**
- **to bruise** →

a
b
c
d
e
f
g
h
i
j
k
l
m
n
o
p
q
r
s
t
u
v
w
x
y
z

- **to graze**
- **to gash**
  Use **graze** when you cut yourself not very badly:
  I **grazed** my arm slightly when I fell.
  Use **gash** when you cut yourself very badly:
  He **gashed** his leg on a sharp rock.

2 I landed on my wrist and **injured** it.
- **to sprain**
- **to twist**
- **to dislocate**
- **to break**

injury noun
The captain couldn't play because he had an **injury**.
- **a wound**
- **a cut**
- **a bruise**
- **a burn**
- **a graze** (a small cut)
- **a gash** (a big cut)

innocent adjective
The jury decided that he was **innocent**.
- **not guilty**
- **blameless**
OPPOSITE guilty

insect noun
Henry is fascinated by **insects**.
- **a bug**
- **a creepy-crawly**

🕷️ **WORD WEB**
some types of insect
- an ant
- a bee
- a beetle
- a bluebottle
- a bumble bee
- a butterfly
- a cricket
- a daddy-long-legs
- a dragonfly
- a fly
- a grasshopper
- a ladybird
- a locust
- a midge
- a mosquito
- a moth
- a stick insect
- a wasp
- a woodlouse

✏️ **WRITING TIPS**
Here are some useful words for writing about insects.
- The ladybird **flew** away.
- A wasp was **buzzing** around the kitchen.
- Bees come together and **swarm** when they are looking for a new hive.
- A fly **crawled** up my leg.
- The beetle **scuttled** away.
- Ants were **scurrying** around looking for food.

inspect verb
He **inspected** the cup to see if it was cracked.
- **to examine**
- **to check**
- **to look at**

instant adjective
The film was an **instant** success.
- **immediate**
- **instantaneous**

instruct verb
1 The judo teacher **instructs** us on move safety.
- **to coach**

- **to teach**
- **to train**

2 *The fire chief **instructed** everyone to leave the building.*
- **to order**
- **to command**
- **to tell**

instructions noun
*Read the **instructions** on the packet carefully.*
- **directions**
- **guidelines**

intelligent adjective
*He's a very **intelligent** boy.*
- **clever**
- **bright**
- **brainy**
- **quick**
- **sharp**
- **smart**
- **brilliant**
OPPOSITE stupid

intend verb
1 *I didn't **intend** to upset her.*
- **to mean**
- **to want**
- **to plan**
2 *We **intend** to set up a school football team next year.*
- **to plan**
- **to propose**
- **to aim**

interested adjective
*I'm very **interested** in old coins.*
- **fascinated** *I'm fascinated by old coins.*

interesting adjective
*This is a really **interesting** book.*

- **fascinating**
- **intriguing**
- **exciting**
OPPOSITE boring

interfere verb
*She's always **interfering**!*
- **to meddle**
- **to stick your nose in** *She's always sticking her nose in!*

interrupt verb
*Please don't **interrupt** when I'm talking.*
- **to butt in**
- **to barge in**

interval noun
*You can have an ice cream during the **interval**.*
- **a break**
- **an interlude**
- **an intermission**

invade verb
*The Romans **invaded** Britain.*
- **to attack**
- **to occupy**
- **to march into**

invent verb
*Who **invented** the first computer?*
- **to design**
- **to develop**
- **to create**
- **to devise**

investigate verb
*We had to **investigate** how the Romans lived for our homework.*
- **to explore**
- **to look into** →

a
b
c
d
e
f
g
h
i
j
k
l
m
n
o
p
q
r
s
t
u
v
w
x
y
z

a
b
c
d
e
f
g
h
i
j
k
l
m
n
o
p
q
r
s
t
u
v
w
x
y
z

• **to research**
• **to study**

invisible adjective
*Ivy had grown over the old door and made it **invisible**.*
• **hidden**
• **concealed**
OPPOSITE visible

invite verb
*I've **invited** all my friends to the party.*
• **to ask**

irritate verb
*My little brother keeps **irritating** me!*
• **to annoy**

• **to pester**
• **to bother**
• **to get on someone's nerves** (informal)
My little brother is getting on my nerves.

irritated adjective
*I was beginning to feel **irritated**.*
• **cross**
• **annoyed**
• **angry**
• **exasperated**

irritating adjective
*He has some very **irritating** habits.*
• **annoying**
• **infuriating**
• **maddening**

Jj

jab noun
The doctor gave me a jab.
- **an injection**

jail noun
He was locked up in jail.
- **prison**
- **a cell**
- **a dungeon**

jam verb
The door jammed and we couldn't open it.
- **to stick**
- **to get stuck**

jealous adjective
I felt a little bit jealous when I saw her new bike.
- **envious**
- **resentful**

jet noun
A jet of water spurted out of the pipe.
- **a stream**
- **a spray**
- **a fountain**

jewel noun
We found a box full of diamonds and other jewels.
- **a gem**
- **a precious stone**

WORD WEB
some types of jewel
- a diamond
- an emerald
- jet
- an opal
- a pearl
- a ruby
- a sapphire

some types of jewellery
- a bracelet
- a brooch
- a crown
- earrings
- a necklace
- a ring
- a tiara

job noun
1 *I want to have an interesting job.*
- **an occupation**
- **a profession**
- **work**
- **a career**
2 *I had to do a couple of jobs for my mum.*
- **a chore**
- **a task**

WORD WEB
some jobs people do
- an architect
- an artist
- a blacksmith
- a builder
- a carpenter
- a chef
- a cook
- a dentist
- a detective
- a doctor
- a dustman
- an electrician
- an engineer
- a farmer
- a firefighter
- a hairdresser
- a journalist
- a lawyer →

a
b
c
d
e
f
g
h
i
j
k
l
m
n
o
p
q
r
s
t
u
v
w
x
y
z

a
b
c
d
e
f
g
h
i
j
k
l
m
n
o
p
q
r
s
t
u
v
w
x
y
z

- a librarian
- a mechanic
- a musician
- a nurse
- an office worker
- an optician
- a photographer
- a pilot
- a plumber
- a policeman or policewoman
- a postman or postwoman
- a professor
- a reporter
- a sailor
- a scientist
- a secretary
- a shopkeeper
- a teacher
- a vet
- a waiter or waitress

join verb

1 *Join the two wires together.*
- **to fix**
- **to fasten**
- **to attach**
- **to connect**
- **to tie**
- **to stick**
- **to glue**

2 *Why don't you **join** your local drama group?*
- **to become a member of**

joke noun

1 *He told us some funny **jokes**.*
- **a funny story**
- **a gag** (informal)

2 *She hid my school bag as a **joke**.*
- **a trick**
- **a prank**

journey noun

*He set out on his **journey**.*

- **a trip**
- **an expedition**
- **a voyage**
- **a flight**
- **a drive**
- **a trek**
- **a hike**

An ***expedition*** *is a long journey:*
*They are planning an **expedition** to the North Pole.*
A ***voyage*** *is a journey by sea:*
*The **voyage** was long and very rough.*
A ***flight*** *is a journey by air:*
*Our **flight** took two hours.*
A ***drive*** *is a journey by car:*
*It's a long **drive** from London to Scotland.*
A ***trek*** *or **hike** is a long journey on foot:*
*The children were exhausted after their three-day **trek** through the mountains.*

jumble noun

1 *There was a **jumble** of books on her desk.*
- **a pile**
- **a heap**
- **a mass**

2 *Everything was in a complete jumble.*
- **a mess**
- **a muddle**

jump verb

1 *He **jumped** into the air and caught the ball.*
- **to leap**
- **to spring**

2 *The cat **jumped** on the mouse.*
- **to pounce**
- **to spring**

3 *The kangaroo **jumped** off into the distance.*
- **to hop**
- **to bound**

4 *She was **jumping** for joy.*
- **to leap about**
- **to prance about**
- **to skip about**

5 *Sammy **jumped** over the fence.*
- **to leap over**
- **to vault over**
- **to hurdle**
- **to clear**

Use **hurdle** when you jump over something while you are running:
*He ran towards the gate and **hurdled** it.*
Use **clear** when you jump over something easily, without touching it at all:
*The horse **cleared** the last fence and galloped towards the finishing line.*

6 *She **jumped** into the water.*
- **to leap**
- **to dive**
- **to plunge**

7 *The sudden noise made me **jump**.*
- **to start**
- **to flinch**

jungle noun
> *These animals live deep in the **jungle**.*
- **a forest**
- **a tropical forest**
- **a rainforest**

junk noun
> *The garage was full of old **junk**.*
- **rubbish**
- **odds and ends**

just adverb
1 *This is **just** what I wanted.*
- **exactly**
- **precisely**

2 *The classroom is **just** big enough for all the children.*
- **hardly**
- **barely**
- **scarcely**

a
b
c
d
e
f
g
h
i
j
k
l
m
n
o
p
q
r
s
t
u
v
w
x
y
z

a
b
c
d
e
f
g
h
i
j
k
l
m
n
o
p
q
r
s
t
u
v
w
x
y
z

Kk

keen adjective

1 *Most boys are **keen** on football.*
- **enthusiastic about**
- **fond of**

2 *She was **keen** to go with her sisters.*
- **eager**
- **anxious**

keep verb

1 *You don't have to give the book back to me. You can **keep** it.*
- **to have**
- **to hold on to**

2 *Keep still!*
- **to stay**
- **to remain**

3 *They **keep** chickens on their farm.*
- **to have**
- **to look after**

4 *I told him to be quiet, but he **kept** talking.*
- **to continue**
- **to carry on**

kill verb

1 *The knight **killed** the mighty dragon.*
- **to slay**

2 *Someone has threatened to **kill** him.*
- **to murder**
- **to assassinate**
- **to execute**
  Use **assassinate** when someone kills a very important person:
  Someone has **assassinated** the king!
  Use **execute** when people kill someone as a punishment:
  In some countries, they **execute** criminals instead of sending them to prison.

3 *The soldiers **killed** hundreds of innocent people.*
- **to slaughter**
- **to massacre**

4 *A butcher **kills** animals and sells their meat.*
- **to slaughter**

5 *Sometimes a vet has to **kill** an animal if it is badly injured.*
- **to destroy**
- **to put down**
- **to put to sleep**

kind adjective

1 *He's a very **kind** boy.*
- **gentle**
- **good-natured**
- **kind-hearted**
- **thoughtful**
- **considerate**
- **unselfish**

2 *It was very **kind** of you to give so much money to the school.*
- **generous**
OPPOSITE unkind

kind noun

1 *A dictionary is a **kind** of book.*
- **a type**
- **a sort**

2 *A terrier is a **kind** of dog.*
- **a breed**

3 *A ladybird is a **kind** of beetle.*
- **a species**

4 *What **kind** of trainers do you want to buy?*
- **a brand**
- **a make**

kneel verb

*I **knelt** down beside him.*
- **to bend**
- **to stoop**
- **to crouch**

knife noun

> **WORD WEB**
> **some types of knife**
> - a carving knife
> - a dagger
> - a kitchen knife
> - a penknife

knob noun

1 He turned the door **knob**.
   - **a handle**
2 She started fiddling with the **knobs** on the machine.
   - **a switch**
   - **a button**
   - **a control**

knock verb

1 I **knocked** on the door.
   - **to rap**
   - **to tap**
   - **to bang**
   - **to hammer**
   Use **rap** or **tap** when someone knocks not very loudly:
   She **rapped** lightly on the window.

Use **bang** or **hammer** when someone knocks loudly:
He **hammered** on the door with his fists.
2 I fell and **knocked** my head.
   - **to bang**
   - **to bump**
   - **to hit**
   - **to bash**

know verb

1 Do you **know** how a car works?
   - **to understand**
   - **to remember**
2 I didn't **know** the answer to that question.
   - **to be sure of**
   - **to be certain of** I wasn't certain of the answer.
3 I **knew** that someone was watching me.
   - **to sense**
   - **to be aware** I was aware that someone was watching me.
4 As soon as I saw the man, I **knew** who he was.
   - **to recognize**
   - **to identify**
5 Do you **know** my sister?
   - **to be acquainted with**
   Are you **acquainted** with my sister?

a
b
c
d
e
f
g
h
i
j
k
l
m
n
o
p
q
r
s
t
u
v
w
x
y
z

Ll

land noun

1 *This is good **land** for growing crops.*
- **ground**
- **earth**
- **soil**

2 *He has travelled to many **lands**.*
- **a country**
- **a nation**
- **a region**
- **a kingdom** (*a land with a king or queen*)

land verb

1 *The plane should **land** at seven o'clock.*
- **to touch down**
- **to come down**
- **to arrive**

2 *They rowed towards the island and **landed** on a small beach.*
- **to come ashore**
- **to go ashore**

3 *The bird **landed** on a small branch.*
- **to alight**
- **to fly down onto**
- **to come to rest on**

large adjective

1 *He was carrying a **large** box.*
- **big**
- **huge**
- **enormous**
- **massive**
- **gigantic**
  Use **huge** or **enormous** for something that is very large:
  *He came out with the most **enormous** sandwich I had ever seen.*
  Use **massive** or **gigantic** for something that is very large indeed:
  *Some dinosaurs were so **massive** that they couldn't run very fast.*

2 *There are some very **large** buildings in the city centre.*
- **big**
- **tall**
- **spacious**
- **grand**
- **magnificent**
  Use **spacious** for buildings that have plenty of space inside:
  *Our new flat is bright and **spacious**.*
  Use **grand** or **magnificent** for things that are very large and beautiful:
  *The prince lived in a **magnificent** palace.*

3 *She gave me a **large** portion of chips.*
- **big**
- **generous**
- **sizeable**
OPPOSITE small

last adjective
*Z is the **last** letter of the alphabet.*
- **final**
OPPOSITE first

last verb
*The film **lasted** for two hours.*
- **to continue**
- **to go on**

late adjective
*The bus was **late**.*
- **delayed**
- **overdue**
OPPOSITE early

a b c d e f g h i j k l m n o p q r s t u v w x y z

laugh verb

*All the children started **laughing**.*
- **to chuckle**
- **to giggle**
- **to titter**
- **to snigger**
- **to cackle**
- **to guffaw**
- **to roar with laughter**
- **to shriek with laughter**
- **to burst out laughing**

Use **chuckle** when someone laughs quietly to themselves:
*The professor read the letter and **chuckled** to himself.*
Use **giggle**, **titter**, or **snigger** when someone laughs in a slightly silly way:
*The girls **giggled** as he walked past.*
Use **cackle** when someone laughs in a nasty way:
*The old witch **cackled** with laughter.*
Use **guffaw**, **roar with laughter**, or **shriek with** laughter when someone laughs very loudly:
*He threw back his head and **guffawed** loudly.*
Use **burst out laughing** when someone suddenly starts to laugh:
*We all **burst out laughing** when we saw his new hat.*

law noun

*Everyone must obey the **laws** of the country.*
- **a rule**
- **a regulation**

lay verb

*I **laid** the clothes on my bed.*
- **to put**
- **to place**
- **to spread**

layer noun

1 *There was a thick **layer** of dust on the old books.*
   - **a coating**
   - **a covering**
   - **a film**
2 *The pond was covered in a **layer** of ice.*
   - **a sheet**

lazy adjective

*Get up! Don't be so **lazy**!*
- **idle**
- **indolent**

lead verb

1 *He **led** us to the secret cave.*
   - **to take**
   - **to guide**
2 *Who is going to **lead** the expedition?*
   - **to command**
   - **to be in charge of**
3 *Our team was **leading** at the end of the first round.*
   - **to be winning**
   - **to be in the lead** *Our team was in the lead.*

leader noun

*Who is the **leader** of your gang?*
- **the boss**
- **the chief**
- **the captain**

leak verb

*Water was **leaking** out of the pipe.*
- **to drip**
- **to trickle**
- **to seep**
- **to spill**

a
b
c
d
e
f
g
h
i
j
k
l
m
n
o
p
q
r
s
t
u
v
w
x
y
z

lean verb
1 *She **leaned** forward to look out of the window.*
- **to stretch**
- **to bend**
2 *The old building **leans** to one side.*
- **to slant**
- **to tilt**
3 *He was **leaning** against the wall.*
- **to recline**
4 *He **leaned** his bicycle against the wall.*
- **to prop**
- **to rest**

leap verb
1 *The cat **leaped** into the air.*
- **to jump**
- **to spring**
2 *She **leaped** over the fence.*
- **to jump over**
- **to vault over**
- **to hurdle**
  *She **hurdled** the fence.*
- **to clear**
  *She **cleared** the fence.*
3 *She **leaped** into the water.*
- **to jump**
- **to dive**
- **to plunge**

learn verb
*We are **learning** about the Vikings at school.*
- **to find out**
- **to discover**

leave verb
1 *What time does the train **leave**?*
- **to go**
- **to set off**
- **to depart**
  OPPOSITE *arrive*

2 *The ship **leaves** at nine o'clock.*
- **to sail**
- **to depart**
3 *The plane **leaves** at eleven thirty.*
- **to take off**
- **to depart**
4 *She **left** quietly when no one was looking.*
- **to sneak off**
- **to slip away**
- **to creep off**
5 *He **left** in a terrible temper.*
- **to go off**
- **to storm off**
- **to stomp off**
6 *Where did you **leave** your bag?*
- **to put**
7 *All my friends went away and **left** me!*
- **to desert**
- **to abandon**

lend verb
*Will you **lend** me your pen?*
- **to loan**
- **to let someone borrow**
  *Will you **let me borrow** your pen?*

let verb
*Will you **let** me ride your bike?*
- **to allow** *Will you **allow** me to ride your bike?*
- **to give someone permission** *Will you **give me permission** to ride your bike?*

level adjective
1 *You need a nice **level** surface to work on.*
- **flat**
- **even**
- **smooth**
- **horizontal**
  OPPOSITE *uneven*

a
b
c
d
e
f
g
h
i
j
k
l
m
n
o
p
q
r
s
t
u
v
w
x
y
z

2 *Their scores were **level** at half time.*
- **even**
- **equal**
- **the same**

OPPOSITE different

lid noun
*Put the **lid** back on the jar.*
- **a top**
- **a cap**
- **a cover**

lie noun
*Don't tell **lies**!*
- **a fib** (*informal*)
- **an untruth**

lie verb
1 *She was **lying** on the sofa.*
- **to rest**
- **to lounge**
- **to recline**
- **to sprawl**
- **to stretch out**
2 *I don't believe him — I think he's **lying**.*
- **to fib**
- **to tell lies**
- **to bluff**

lift noun
1 *We took the **lift** up to the fifth floor.*
- **an elevator**
2 *He gave us a **lift** in his new car.*
- **a ride**

lift verb
*She **lifted** the boy into the air.*
- **to raise**
- **to hoist**
- **to pick up**

light adjective
1 *My suitcase is quite **light**.*
- **not very heavy**

OPPOSITE heavy

2 *Our classroom is nice and **light**.*
- **bright**
- **well-lit**

OPPOSITE dim

3 *She was wearing **light** blue trousers.*
- **pale**
- **pastel**

OPPOSITE dark

light noun
1 *I couldn't see very well because there wasn't much **light**.*
- **daylight**
- **sunlight**
- **moonlight**
- **brightness**
2 *Please could you switch the **light** on?*
- **an electric light**
- **a lamp**

WORD WEB
some types of light
- floodlights (*lights at a sports ground*)
- lamp
- a headlight (*a light on a car*)
- a searchlight (*a powerful torch*)
- a spotlight (*a light on a stage*)
- a street light

WRITING TIPS
Here are some useful words for writing about light.
- I could see a light **shining** somewhere in the forest.
- A pale light began to **glow** beneath the water.
- The fairy lights **gleamed** and **glimmered** in the darkness.
- The water **glistened** and **sparkled** in the sunlight.
- Stars **twinkled** above us. →

a
b
c
d
e
f
g
h
i
j
k
l
m
n
o
p
q
r
s
t
u
v
w
x
y
z

- The light from the lighthouse **flashed** on and off.
- I could see the searchlights **flickering** in the distance.
- The headlights **glared** in the darkness.

like preposition

*Your pencil case is **like** mine.*
- **the same as**
- **similar to**
- **identical to**

like verb

1 *I **like** our new teacher.*
- **to get on well with**
- **to be fond of**
- **to love**
- **to idolize**
  Use **love**, **adore**, or **idolize** if you like someone a lot:
  *She **idolizes** her grandad!*
2 *Tom **likes** football.*
- **to be keen on**
- **to enjoy**
- **to love**
- **to adore**
- **to be mad about**
  Use **love**, **adore**, or **be mad about** if you like something a lot:
  *She **is mad about** ponies!*
3 *I think that boy **likes** you!*
- **to fancy**
OPPOSITE dislike

likely adjective

*It's quite **likely** that it will rain later.*
- **possible**
- **probable**
OPPOSITE unlikely

limp verb

*She was **limping** because her foot hurt.*
- **to hobble**

line noun

1 *Draw a **line** across the top of the page.*
- **a mark**
- **a stripe**
2 *Her old face was covered in **lines**.*
- **wrinkles**
3 *We all stood in a **line**.*
- **a row**
- **a queue**

listen verb

*Please **listen** to what I am going to say.*
- **to pay attention**

litter noun

*The playground was covered in **litter**.*
- **rubbish**
- **mess**

little adjective

1 *They live in a **little** house on the edge of the village.*
- **small**
- **tiny**
- **titchy** (informal)
- **cramped**
- **poky**
  Use **tiny** or **titchy** for something that is very small:
  *The mouse began to dig with its **tiny** paws.*
  Use **cramped** or **poky** for a house or room that is too small:
  *They lived in a **cramped** one-room flat.*
2 *He's only a **little** boy.*
- **young**
3 *It's only a **little** problem.*
- **small**
- **slight**
- **minor**
4 *We had a **little** chat.*
- **short**
- **brief**
OPPOSITE big

a b c d e f g h i j k **l** m n o p q r s t u v w x y z

live verb
1 *Plants cannot **live** without water.*
- **to exist**
- **to survive**
- **to remain alive**

2 *We live in London.*
- **to reside**

lively adjective
*The puppies were **lively**.*
- **active**
- **busy**
- **energetic**
- **boisterous**
- **playful**

OPPOSITE quiet

load verb
1 *We **loaded** the suitcases into the car.*
- **to put**
- **to lift**

2 *We **loaded** the trolley with food.*
- **to fill**
- **to pack**
- **to pile up**

lock noun
*We need to put a **lock** on the shed door.*
- **a bolt**
- **a padlock**

lock verb
*Don't forget to **lock** the door.*
- **to shut**
- **to fasten**
- **to bolt**
- **to secure**

lonely adjective
1 *I felt **lonely** when all my friends had left.*
- **alone**
- **isolated**
- **friendless**
- **forlorn**

2 *They live in a **lonely** part of the country.*
- **remote**
- **isolated**
- **secluded**
- **uninhabited**
  *Use **remote** or **isolated** for a place that is far away from towns and cities:*
  *On top of the hill is an **isolated** farmhouse.*
  *Use **secluded** for a place that people cannot see:*
  *Behind the house is a **secluded** garden.*
  *Use **uninhabited** for a place where no one lives:*
  *The northern side of the island is **uninhabited**.*

long adjective
1 *It's quite a **long** film.*
- **lengthy**

2 *We had to sit and listen to his **long** speech.*
- **endless**
- **interminable**
- **long-drawn-out**

OPPOSITE short

look verb

⚠️ **OVERUSED WORD**
Try to vary the words you use to mean *look*. Here are some other words you can use instead.

1 *I'm **looking** at a squirrel in the garden.*
- **to watch**
- **to observe**
- **to study**

2 *She **looked** at the picture.*
- **to glance**
- **to peep** →

a
b
c
d
e
f
g
h
i
j
k
l
m
n
o
p
q
r
s
t
u
v
w
x
y
z

a
b
c
d
e
f
g
h
i
j
k
l
m
n
o
p
q
r
s
t
u
v
w
x
y
z

- to stare
- to gaze
- to peer
- to squint
Use **glance** or **peep** when you look at something quickly:
I **glanced** at the clock to see what time it was.
Use **stare** or **gaze** when you look at something for a long time:
We **gazed** at the beautiful view.
Use **peer** or **squint** when you look at something carefully because you cannot see it very well:
We **peered** through the window into the dark room.

3 I could see that Lucy was **looking** at me.
- to stare
- to glare
- to glower
- to scowl
Use **stare** if you look at someone for a long time:
Why are you **staring** at me?
Use **glare**, **glower**, or **scowl** if you look at someone angrily:
Mum **glared** at me angrily.

4 That dog doesn't **look** very friendly.
- to seem
- to appear

look after verb
I have to **look after** my little brother.
- to take care of
- to care for
- to mind
- to keep an eye on (informal)

look for verb
I'll help you **look for** your purse.
- to search for
- to hunt for
- to try to find

loose adjective
1 One of my teeth is **loose**.
- wobbly
- shaky
OPPOSITE secure
2 The rope was a bit **loose**.
- slack
OPPOSITE tight
3 I like to wear **loose** clothes.
- baggy
- big
- oversized
OPPOSITE tight

lose verb
1 I've **lost** my watch.
- to mislay
- to misplace
OPPOSITE find
2 Our team **lost** the game.
- to be defeated
OPPOSITE win

lot noun
We ate a **lot** of sweets.
- lots
- loads

loud adjective
1 We heard a **loud** bang.
- noisy
- deafening
- ear-splitting
2 I don't like **loud** music.
- blaring
3 He spoke in a **loud** voice.
- booming
- thunderous
- shrill
- piercing
Use **booming** or **thunderous** for a deep voice:
'Come here!' he shouted in a **booming** voice.

Use **shrill** or **piercing** for a high voice:
*'Get away from me,' she shrieked in a **shrill** voice.*
OPPOSITE quiet

love verb

1 *Anita **loves** her sister.*
- **to be very fond of**
- **to adore**
- **to worship**
- **to idolize**
  Use **worship** or **idolize** if you love someone and admire them a lot:
  *He **idolizes** his older brother!*
2 *George **loves** football!*
- **to enjoy**
- **to be very keen on**
- **to be obsessed with**
- **to be mad about**
OPPOSITE hate

lovely adjective

1 *What a **lovely** picture!*
- **beautiful**
- **gorgeous**
- **delightful**
2 *You look **lovely** today.*
- **pretty**
- **beautiful**
- **attractive**
- **gorgeous**
- **stunning**
- **glamorous**
  Use **gorgeous** or **stunning** if someone is very lovely:
  *She looks absolutely **stunning** in that dress!*
  Use **glamorous** if someone looks lovely and rich:
  *The film stars all looked very **glamorous** in their evening dresses.*
3 *The food was **lovely**.*
- **delicious**
- **tasty**

4 *These flowers smell **lovely**.*
- **beautiful**
- **fragrant**
- **perfumed**
5 *He's a **lovely** boy.*
- **kind**
- **pleasant**
- **charming**
- **polite**
6 *It was a **lovely** day for sports day.*
- **beautiful**
- **warm**
- **sunny**
- **glorious**
- **wonderful**
7 *We had a **lovely** time on holiday.*
- **enjoyable**
- **wonderful**
- **fantastic**
OPPOSITE horrible

low adjective

1 *We sat on a **low** bench.*
- **small**
2 *Their prices are usually quite **low**.*
- **reasonable**
- **reduced**
3 *He spoke in a **low** voice.*
- **soft**
- **deep**
OPPOSITE high

loyal adjective

*He has many **loyal** supporters.*
- **devoted**
- **faithful**

luck noun

*It was just by **luck** that we arrived at the same time.*
- **chance**
- **accident**
- **coincidence**

a
b
c
d
e
f
g
h
i
j
k
l
m
n
o
p
q
r
s
t
u
v
w
x
y
z

lucky adjective

*We were **lucky** that we got home before the rain started.*
- **fortunate**

OPPOSITE unlucky

luggage noun

*We put all our **luggage** on the train.*
- **bags**
- **suitcases**
- **baggage**

lump noun

1 *She gave him some bread and a **lump** of cheese.*
   - **a piece**
   - **a chunk**
   - **a block**
   - **a wedge**
2 *I've got a **lump** on my head where I hit it.*
   - **a bump**
   - **a swelling**

a
b
c
d
e
f
g
h
i
j
k
l
m
n
o
p
q
r
s
t
u
v
w
x
y
z

Mm

machine noun
They have a special **machine** for cutting the metal.
- an appliance
- a contraption
- a tool
- a robot

mad adjective
1 I think you're **mad** if you go outside in this rain!
- crazy
- silly
- stupid
2 My mum was really **mad** with me.
- angry
- cross
- furious
- livid

magic noun
1 He says he can use **magic** to make it rain.
- sorcery
- witchcraft
- wizardry
2 The conjuror did some **magic**.
- conjuring
- tricks

magician noun
1 He was taken prisoner by an evil **magician**.
- a wizard
- a sorcerer
- an enchanter
2 The children watched the **magician** doing magic tricks.
- a conjuror

magnificent adjective
The king lived in a **magnificent** palace.
- grand
- splendid
- wonderful

mail noun
We didn't get any **mail** this morning.
- post
- letters
- parcels

main adjective
The **main** ingredient of bread is flour.
- most important
- principal
- chief
- essential

make verb
1 We managed to **make** a shelter out of some old pieces of wood.
- to build
- to form
- to construct
- to create
- to put together
2 They **make** cars in that factory.
- to produce
- to manufacture
- to assemble
3 The heat of the sun can be used to **make** electricity.
- to generate
- to produce
4 We **made** some cakes and biscuits for the party.
- to bake
- to cook
- to prepare
5 You can **make** this old dish into a bird bath.
- to change
- to turn
- to transform →

a
b
c
d
e
f
g
h
i
j
k
l
m
n
o
p
q
r
s
t
u
v
w
x
y
z

115

6 *Please don't **make** too much mess.*
- **to create**
- **to cause**

7 *They **made** me clean the floor.*
- **to force**
- **to order**
  *They **ordered** me to clean the floor.*

man noun
*I'll ask the **man** in the ticket office.*
- **a gentleman**
- **a bloke** (*informal*)
- **a guy** (*informal*)
- **a chap** (*informal*)
- **a bachelor** (*an unmarried man*)
- **a husband** (*a married man*)
- **a father** (*a man who has children*)
- **a widower** (*a man whose wife has died*)

manage verb
1 *I finally **managed** to open the door.*
- **to succeed in** *I finally succeeded in opening the door.*
2 *His father **manages** a shop.*
- **to run**
- **to be in charge of**

map noun
*He drew a **map** to show us how to get to the school.*
- **a plan**
- **a diagram**

mark noun
1 *His hands left dirty **marks** on the wall.*
- **a stain**
- **a spot**
- **a smear**
- **a smudge**
- **a streak**

2 *He had a red **mark** on his face.*
- **a spot**
- **a scar**
- **a bruise**
- **a birthmark**
- **footprints**
  *His feet had left deep **footprints** in the snow.*
- **tracks**

market noun
*You can buy all sorts of things at the **market**.*
- **a bazaar**
- **a street market**
- **a car boot sale**

marsh noun
*We began to sink into the **marsh**.*
- **a bog**
- **a swamp**

marvellous adjective
*We had a **marvellous** holiday.*
- **wonderful**
- **brilliant**
- **great**
- **fantastic**
- **perfect**

mash verb
*This machine will **mash** anything you put into it.*
- **to crush**
- **to squash**
- **to flatten**
- **to grind up**
- **to pulp**

mass noun
1 *There was a **mass** of rubbish to clear away.*
- **a heap**
- **a pile**

a b c d e f g h i j k l m n o p q r s t u v w x y z

- a mound
- a stack

2 There was a **mass** of people in front of the stage.
- a group
- a crowd
- a horde

massive adjective
They live in a **massive** house.
- **enormous**
- **huge**
- **gigantic**
- **colossal**
- **immense**
OPPOSITE tiny

match noun
1 We watched a football **match** on TV.
- a game
2 We went to see a boxing **match**.
- a contest
- a fight

material noun
1 Stone is a good building **material**.
- a substance
2 Her skirt was made of bright yellow **material**.
- cloth
- fabric

WORD WEB
some types of material
- corduroy
- cotton
- denim
- fleece
- linen
- lycra
- nylon
- polyester
- satin
- silk
- velvet
- wool

maths noun
I'm not very good at **maths**.
- **mathematics**
- **sums**
- **arithmetic**
- **addition**
- **subtraction**
- **multiplication**
- **division**

matter noun
We have an important **matter** to discuss.
- a subject
- a question
- an issue

maybe adverb
Maybe they'll come later.
- **perhaps**
- **possibly**
OPPOSITE definitely

meal noun

WORD WEB
some types of meal
- breakfast
- brunch
- dinner
- lunch
- tea
- supper
- a feast (a big meal)
- a snack (a small meal)
- a picnic (a meal outside)
- a barbecue (a meal that you cook outside)
- a buffet (a meal where people help themselves to food)

mean adjective
1 That was a really **mean** thing to do.
- unkind
- nasty →

a
b
c
d
e
f
g
h
i
j
k
l
m
n
o
p
q
r
s
t
u
v
w
x
y
z

- **selfish**
- **cruel**
- **vindictive**
OPPOSITE kind

2 *He's really* ***mean*** *with his money.*
- **stingy**
- **tight-fisted**
- **miserly**
OPPOSITE generous

mean verb
We ***meant*** *to be home by six.*
- **to intend**
- **to aim**
- **to plan**

measurement noun
We wrote down the ***measurements*** *of the room.*
- **the size**
- **the dimensions**
- **the length**
- **the width**
- **the breadth**
- **the height**
- **the depth**

meat noun

🕸 **WORD WEB**
some types of meat
- bacon
- beef
- chicken
- duck
- ham
- lamb
- pork
- turkey
- venison

---

medium adjective
I am ***medium*** *height for my age.*
- **average**

- **normal**
- **ordinary**

meet verb
1 *We'll* ***meet*** *at the swimming pool.*
- **to meet up**
- **to get together**
2 *Sara will* ***meet*** *us later.*
- **to join**
- **to see**
3 *As I was walking along the lane, I* ***met*** *a man.*
- **to encounter**
- **to see**
- **to bump into**
4 *I haven't* ***met*** *our new neighbours yet.*
- **to get to know**
- **to be introduced to** *I haven't been introduced to them yet.*
5 *Two rivers* ***meet*** *here.*
- **to join**
- **to come together**
- **to merge**
- **to converge**

meeting noun
The teachers are having a ***meeting*** *in the staff room.*
- **a gathering**
- **a discussion**
- **a conference**
- **a get-together**

melt verb
The ice ***melted*** *in the sun.*
- **to thaw**
- **to soften**
- **to unfreeze**

mend verb
1 *Do you think you can* ***mend*** *my CD player?*
- **to repair**
- **to fix**

2 *Dad likes **mending** old furniture.*
- **to do up**
- **to restore**
- **to renovate**

3 *I need to **mend** these jeans.*
- **to sew up**
- **to patch**

mention verb

1 *Nobody **mentioned** the stolen money.*
- **to talk about**
- **to refer to**
- **to allude to**

2 *She **mentioned** that the house looked very untidy.*
- **to say**
- **to remark**

mercy noun

*They begged the king to show **mercy**.*
- **pity**
- **kindness**
- **compassion**
- **forgiveness**

merry adjective

*They sang a **merry** song.*
- **happy**
- **cheerful**
- **joyful**
- **jolly**

OPPOSITE sad

mess noun

1 *Who's going to clear up all this **mess**?*
- **clutter**
- **untidiness**
- **litter**

2 *The papers were all in a terrible **mess**.*
- **a muddle**
- **a jumble**

message noun

*She sent me a **message** to say that she was ill.*
- **a letter**
- **a note**
- **an email**
- **a text message**

messy adjective

*The room was very **messy**.*
- **untidy**
- **cluttered**
- **dirty**
- **disorganized**

OPPOSITE neat

metal noun

> **WORD WEB**
> **some types of metal**
> - aluminium
> - brass
> - bronze
> - copper
> - gold
> - iron
> - silver
> - steel

middle noun

1 *There was a big puddle in the **middle** of the playground.*
- **the centre**

2 *They live right in the **middle** of London.*
- **the centre**
- **the heart**

3 *Is it possible to dig right through to the **middle** of the earth?*
- **the core**
- **the centre**

mild adjective

1 *The soup had a **mild** flavour.*
- **delicate** →

a
b
c
d
e
f
g
h
i
j
k
l
m
n
o
p
q
r
s
t
u
v
w
x
y
z

- **subtle**
- **bland**

2 *It was only a **mild** illness.*
- **slight**

3 *The weather was quite **mild**.*
- **warm**
- **calm**
- **pleasant**
- **balmy**

mind noun
*I don't know how he keeps all those facts in his **mind**.*
- **brain**
- **head**
- **memory**

mind verb
*I don't **mind** if you're a bit late.*
- **to object**
- **to care**
- **to be bothered**

minute noun
*Please could you wait a **minute**?*
- **a moment**
- **a second**

miserable adjective
*I felt really **miserable** when all my friends left.*
- **sad**
- **unhappy**
- **depressed**
- **gloomy**
- **wretched**
OPPOSITE cheerful

miss verb
1 *She stepped out into the road and a car just **missed** her.*
- **to avoid**

2 *I tried to catch the ball, but I **missed** it.*
- **to drop**

3 *Hurry, or you'll **miss** the bus.*
- **to be late for**

4 *I really **missed** my brother when he was away.*
- **to long for**
- **to pine for**

missing adjective
*Some of the money was still **missing**.*
- **lost**
- **nowhere to be found** *The money was nowhere to be found.*

mist noun
*They got lost in the **mist**.*
- **fog**
- **haze**

mistake noun
1 *I knew I had made a **mistake**.*
- **an error**
- **a blunder**
- **a slip-up**
- **an oversight**
  A **blunder** is a bad mistake: John knew that he had made a terrible **blunder**.
  A **slip-up** is a small mistake: She knew that if she made even one little **slip-up** she would be caught.
  An **oversight** is a mistake you make when you forget to do something: My name was missed off the list because of an **oversight**.

2 *There must be a **mistake** in your calculations.*
- **an error**
- **an inaccuracy**

3 The teacher corrected all the **mistakes** in my story.
- **a spelling mistake**
- **a misspelling**

mix verb

1 **Mix** red and yellow paint together to make orange.
- **to blend**
- **to combine**

2 **Mix** all the ingredients together in a bowl.
- **to stir**
- **to blend**
- **to beat**
- **to whisk**

mixture noun

1 She dipped her finger into the cake **mixture**.
- **a mix**

2 We made up a **mixture** of blue and yellow paint.
- **a blend**
- **a combination**

3 We had sausages with a **mixture** of different vegetables.
- **a variety**
- **an assortment**

moan verb

1 He **moaned** with pain.
- **to groan**
- **to wail**

2 I wish you would stop **moaning** about everything!
- **to complain**
- **to grumble**
- **to whinge**

model noun

They made a **model** of the Titanic.
- **a copy**
- **a replica**

modern adjective

1 She likes to wear very **modern** clothes.
- **fashionable**
- **trendy**
- **stylish**

2 The factory is full of very **modern** machinery.
- **new**
- **up-to-date**
- **futuristic**

OPPOSITE old-fashioned

modest adjective

1 She was very **modest** about all her achievements.
- **humble**
- **self-effacing**

OPPOSITE conceited

2 He was too **modest** to undress on the beach.
- **shy**
- **bashful**
- **coy**

moment noun

Could you just wait a **moment**?
- **a minute**
- **a second**
- **an instant**

money noun

1 I haven't got enough **money** to pay for the ice creams.
- **cash**
- **change**
- **coins**
- **silver**
- **coppers**
- **notes**
- **currency**

2 Some pop stars have got plenty of **money**.
- **wealth**
- **riches** →

a
b
c
d
e
f
g
h
i
j
k
l
m
n
o
p
q
r
s
t
u
v
w
x
y
z

3 *He earns **money** by working in a hospital.*
- **wages**
- **a salary**
- **an income**
- **pay**

4 *My parents give me **money** every week.*
- **pocket money**
- **an allowance**

5 *Have you got any **money** in the bank?*
- **savings**
- **funds**

monster noun
*A huge **monster** was coming towards them.*
- **a beast**
- **a creature**

🕸 **WORD WEB**

some types of monster
- a dragon
- a giant
- an ogre
- a troll
- a vampire
- a werewolf

✏ **WRITING TIPS**

Here are some useful words for writing about monsters.
- The **huge**, **ugly** giant was coming towards us.
- The ogre was **hideous**, with a **horrible**, **hairy** face.
- In the cave lived a **fierce** and **terrible** dragon.
- The **terrifying** dragon was **huge**, with green **scaly** skin.
- We had heard stories of a **fearsome** werewolf that lived in the forest.

---

mood noun
*Anita seems to be in a very good **mood** today.*
- **humour**
- **temper**

moody adjective
*Why are you so **moody** today?*
- **bad-tempered**
- **sulky**
- **grumpy**
- **irritable**
- **sullen**
OPPOSITE cheerful

more adjective
*We need some **more** money.*
- **extra**
- **additional**

mountain noun
*We could see the **mountains** in the distance.*
- **a hill**
- **a peak**
- **a mountain range** (*a group of mountains*)
- **a volcano**

move verb
1 *We **moved** the table into the corner of the room.*
- **to push**
- **to pull**
- **to carry**
- **to drag**
  Use **drag** when something is very heavy:
  They **dragged** the heavy crate outside.

2 *The train **moved** out of the station.*
  Use **to speed, to race, to hurtle, to whizz**, or **to zoom** when something moves very quickly:
  A sports car **zoomed** past us.
  Use **to crawl, to creep**, or **to trundle** when something moves very slowly:
  The train **crawled** along at 25 miles per hour.

Use **to glide, to slide, to float, or to drift** when something moves smoothly and gracefully:
The little boat **drifted** slowly through the water.
Use **to advance** or **to proceed** when something moves forwards:
Let us **proceed** to the castle.
Use **to retreat, to draw back,** or **to withdraw** when something moves backwards:
The army was losing the battle and had to **retreat**.
Use **to rise, to climb,** or **to ascend** when something moves upwards:
The rocket **ascended** into space.
Use **to fall, to descend, to drop,** or **to sink** when something moves downwards:
The hot-air balloon **sank** gently down to the ground.
Use **to stir, to sway, to wave, to flap,** or **to shake** when something moves about:
The huge trees **swayed** gently in the breeze.
Use **to spin, to turn, to rotate, to revolve, to twirl,** or **to whirl** when something moves round and round:
The dancers **whirled** round and round.
3 He sat in the corner and refused to **move**.
- **to budge**
- **to shift**
- **to change places**

mud noun
His boots were covered in **mud**.
- **dirt**
- **muck**
- **clay**
- **sludge**

muddle noun
My school books were in a terrible **muddle**.
- **a mess**
- **a jumble**

murder verb
A gunman **murdered** the president.
- **to kill**
- **to assassinate**

music noun

⟨WORD WEB⟩
some types of music
- blues
- classical
- country
- folk
- jazz
- opera
- pop
- rap
- reggae
- rock

musical instrument noun

⟨WORD WEB⟩
some stringed instruments
- a banjo
- a cello
- a double bass
- a guitar
- a harp
- a mandolin
- a sitar
- a viola
- a violin

some woodwind instruments
- a bassoon
- a clarinet
- a flute
- an oboe
- a piccolo
- a recorder →

a
b
c
d
e
f
g
h
i
j
k
l
m
n
o
p
q
r
s
t
u
v
w
x
y
z

some brass instruments
- a bugle
- a cornet
- a horn
- a saxophone
- a trombone
- a trumpet
- a tuba

some keyboard instruments
- an accordion
- a harpsichord
- a keyboard
- an organ
- a piano

some percussion instruments
- cymbals
- a drum
- a glockenspiel
- a tambourine
- a triangle
- a xylophone

musician noun
Would you like to be a professional ***musician****?*
- **a performer**
- **a player**
- **a singer**
- **a composer**

mysterious adjective
*She disappeared in a very **mysterious** way.*
- **strange**
- **weird**
- **puzzling**
- **baffling**
- **mystifying**

mystery noun
*The police finally solved the **mystery**.*
- **a puzzle**
- **a riddle**
- **a secret**

Nn

naked adjective
*The baby was **naked**.*
- **bare**
- **nude**
- **unclothed**
OPPOSITE dressed

name noun
*What is your **name**?*
- **a first name**
- **a surname**
- **a family name**
- **a nickname**

narrow adjective
*We walked along a **narrow** path.*
- **thin**
- **slim**
OPPOSITE broad

nasty adjective
1 *He's a very **nasty** boy.*
- **horrible**
- **unpleasant**
- **mean**
- **spiteful**
- **unkind**
- **obnoxious**
- **horrid**
2 *There was a **nasty** smell in the kitchen.*
- **horrible**
- **unpleasant**
- **revolting**
- **disgusting**
- **foul**
3 *She's got a **nasty** cut on her arm.*
- **bad**
- **awful**
- **terrible**

- **painful**
OPPOSITE nice

natural adjective
1 *This jumper is made of **natural** wool.*
- **real**
- **genuine**
- **pure**
OPPOSITE artificial
2 *It's **natural** to feel upset when your pet dies.*
- **normal**
- **ordinary**
- **usual**
OPPOSITE unnatural

naughty adjective
*Have you ever been **naughty**?*
- **bad**
- **badly behaved**
- **disobedient**
- **mischievous**
- **disruptive**
- **bad-mannered**
- **rude**
OPPOSITE well-behaved

near adjective
*Our house is **near** the school.*
- **close to**
- **next to**
- **beside**

nearly adverb
*I've **nearly** finished.*
- **almost**
- **virtually**
- **just about**
- **practically**

neat adjective
1 *Her bedroom is always very **neat**.*
- **tidy**
- **clean** →

a
b
c
d
e
f
g
h
i
j
k
l
m
n
o
p
q
r
s
t
u
v
w
x
y
z

- **orderly**
- **spick and span**

2 *He looked very **neat** in his new uniform.*
- **smart**
- **elegant**
- **well-turned-out**

OPPOSITE untidy

necessary adjective

*It is **necessary** to water plants in dry weather.*
- **important**
- **essential**
- **vital**

OPPOSITE unnecessary

need verb

1 *All plants and animals **need** water.*
- **to require**
- **to depend on**
- **to rely on**
- **to want**

2 *You **need** to finish your homework.*
- **to have to** *You have to finish your homework.*
- **should** *You should finish your homework.*

nervous adjective

1 *Are you **nervous** about starting your new school?*
- **worried**
- **anxious**
- **apprehensive**

2 *The horses seemed very **nervous**.*
- **jumpy**
- **agitated**
- **fearful**
- **panicky**
- **tense**

OPPOSITE calm

new adjective

1 *She was wearing a **new** dress.*
- **brand new**

2 *The hospital has got a lot of **new** equipment.*
- **modern**
- **up-to-date**
- **state-of-the-art**

3 *See if you can think of some **new** ideas.*
- **fresh**
- **different**
- **novel**
- **innovative**

OPPOSITE old

next adjective

1 *They live in the **next** street.*
- **nearest**
- **closest**
- **adjacent**

2 *They set off the **next** day.*
- **following**

nice adjective

⚠ **OVERUSED WORD**

Try to vary the words you use to mean *nice*. Here are some other words you can use instead.

1 *You look very **nice** with your hair short.*
- **pretty**
- **beautiful**
- **lovely**
- **handsome**
- **gorgeous**
- **glamorous**
- **stunning**

Use **pretty**, **beautiful** or **lovely** to describe a woman or girl. Use **handsome** to describe a boy or man. Use **gorgeous** or **stunning** for someone who looks very nice: *You look absolutely **stunning** in that dress.*

Use **glamorous** for someone who looks very rich:
All the pop stars were arriving for the ceremony looking very **glamorous**.

2 She likes wearing **nice** clothes.
- pretty
- lovely
- beautiful
- smart
- fashionable
- stylish

Use **fashionable** or **stylish** for clothes that look modern:
I saw a pair of really **stylish** shoes that I want to buy.

3 The food was very **nice**.
- delicious
- tasty

4 Some of the flowers smell very **nice**.
- pleasant
- fragrant
- perfumed

5 Did you have a **nice** holiday?
- pleasant
- lovely
- enjoyable
- wonderful
- fantastic

6 He's a very **nice** boy.
- friendly
- kind
- likeable
- pleasant
- helpful
- thoughtful
- charming
- polite

Use **helpful** or **thoughtful** for someone who thinks about other people or helps other people:
It was very **thoughtful** of you to unpack the shopping for me.

Use **charming** or **polite** for someone who behaves well and isn't rude to people:
Remember to be **polite** to your aunt and uncle.

7 I hope we have **nice** weather for our trip to the beach.
- fine
- lovely
- pleasant
- beautiful
- warm
- sunny
- glorious
- wonderful

Use **glorious** or **wonderful** for weather that is very nice:
It was a **glorious** hot summer's day.

OPPOSITE horrible

noise noun

1 Stop that terrible **noise**!
- din
- racket
- row
- rumpus
- uproar

2 I heard a sudden **noise**.
- a sound
- a bang
- a clatter
- a thud
- a thump
- a roar
- a rumble
- a clang
- a clank
- a scream
- a shout
- a screech
- a squeak

A **clatter** is the sound of things banging against each other: →

a
b
c
d
e
f
g
h
i
j
k
l
m
n
o
p
q
r
s
t
u
v
w
x
y
z

a
b
c
d
e
f
g
h
i
j
k
l
m
n
o
p
q
r
s
t
u
v
w
x
y
z

The plates fell to the floor with a
clatter.
A **thud** or **thump** is the sound of
something heavy falling to the floor:
The book fell to the floor with a **thud**.
A **roar** or **rumble** is a long, low
sound:
We heard a **rumble** of thunder in the
distance.
A **screech** is a loud scream:
She jumped out of the water with a loud
screech.
A **squeak** is a very high sound:
The gate opened with a **squeak**.

noisy adjective
1 The band's music was very **noisy**.
   • **loud**
   • **deafening**
   • **ear-splitting**
2 She asked the children not to be so
   noisy.
   • **loud**
   • **rowdy**
   • **boisterous**
   OPPOSITE quiet

nonsense noun
Don't talk **nonsense**!
   • **rubbish**
   • **drivel**

normal adjective
1 It's quite **normal** to feel tired at the end
   of the day.
   • **natural**
   • **common**
   • **usual**
2 It looked like a **normal** car.
   • **ordinary**
   • **standard**
   • **typical**
   • **average**
   • **everyday**
   OPPOSITE abnormal

normally adverb
I **normally** go to bed at eight o'clock.
   • **usually**
   • **generally**

nosy adjective
Don't be so **nosy**!
   • **inquisitive**
   • **curious**
   • **snooping**
   • **prying**
   Use **inquisitive** or **curious** when
   someone wants to know about
   something:
   I was **curious** to know why Oscar
   wasn't at school.
   Use **snooping** or **prying** when
   someone wants to know too much
   about something:
   I wish those **snooping** kids would
   mind their own business!

note noun
I found a **note** saying that he would be
home for tea.
   • **a letter**
   • **a message**
   • **a reminder**

notice noun
We put up a **notice** to tell people about
our play.
   • **a poster**
   • **a sign**
   • **an announcement**
   • **an advertisement**

notice verb
I **noticed** that there were no lights on in
the house.
   • **to observe**
   • **to see**
   • **to spot**

nuisance noun
> *The rain was a **nuisance**.*
> - **a problem**
> - **a pain**
> - **an inconvenience**
> - **a pest**
>
> Use **inconvenience** for something that causes you a lot of problems:
> *It can be a terrible **inconvenience** not having a car.*

Use **pest** for a person or animal that annoys you:
*My little sister is such a **pest**!*

number noun
> *Can you add up those **numbers**?*
> - **a figure**
> - **a digit**

a
b
c
d
e
f
g
h
i
j
k
l
m
n
o
p
q
r
s
t
u
v
w
x
y
z

a
b
c
d
e
f
g
h
i
j
k
l
m
n
o
p
q
r
s
t
u
v
w
x
y
z

Oo

obey verb
*You must **obey** the rules.*
- **to abide by** *You must abide by the rules.*
- **to not break** *You must not break the rules.*
OPPOSITE disobey

object noun
*We found some interesting **objects** in the cupboard.*
- **a thing**
- **an article**
- **an item**

obvious adjective
*It was **obvious** that he was lying.*
- **clear**
- **plain**
- **apparent**
- **evident**

occasionally adverb
*We **occasionally** go swimming.*
- **sometimes**
- **from time to time**
- **now and then**

odd adjective
*It seemed **odd** that the school was so quiet.*
- **strange**
- **funny**
- **peculiar**
- **curious**
- **weird**
OPPOSITE normal

offer verb
1 *She **offered** me a piece of cake.*
- **to give**
- **to hand**
2 *Tom **offered** to wash up.*
- **to volunteer**

often adverb
*We **often** go swimming on Saturdays.*
- **frequently**
- **regularly**
- **again and again**
- **time after time**
Use **again and again** or **time after time** for something that happens a number of times:
*I tried **again and again**, but I couldn't open the door.*

old adjective
1 *My grandmother is quite **old**.*
- **elderly**
- **aged**
OPPOSITE young
2 *Can we get a new TV? This one is too **old**!*
- **ancient**
- **old-fashioned**
- **out-of-date**
Use **ancient** for something that is very old:
*I found some **ancient** maps in the attic.*
Use **old-fashioned** or **out-of-date** for something that isn't very modern:
*There was an **old-fashioned** radio in the kitchen.*
OPPOSITE new
3 *My dad collects **old** coins.*
- **ancient**
- **antique**
Use **antique** for something that is old and valuable:
*My aunt told me off for putting my glass down on her **antique** table.*
OPPOSITE modern

4 *He was wearing some **old** jeans.*
- **tatty**
- **shabby**
- **scruffy**
- **worn-out**

OPPOSITE new

open adjective
*Someone had left the door **open**.*
- **ajar**
- **wide open**
- **unlocked**
- **unfastened**

OPPOSITE closed

open verb
1 *He **opened** the door.*
- **to unlock**
- **to push open**
- **to fling open**
- **to throw open**
- **to break down**

Use ***fling open*** or ***throw open*** when you open something suddenly or roughly:
*Jack **flung open** the door to the attic and cried, 'Go and see for yourselves!'*
Use ***break down*** when you open a door by breaking it:
*The police had to **break down** the door to get into the house.*

2 *The door **opened**.*
- **to swing open**
- **to burst open**
- **to fly open**

Use ***burst open*** or ***fly open*** when something opens suddenly or quickly:
*Suddenly, the door **burst open** and the teacher marched in.*

OPPOSITE close

opening noun
*We crawled through an **opening** in the fence.*

- **a gap**
- **a hole**
- **a space**
- **a crack**

opinion noun
*What's your **opinion** about what happened?*
- **an idea**
- **a belief**
- **a view**

opposite adjective
1 *They live on the **opposite** side of the road.*
- **facing**
2 *North is the **opposite** direction to south.*
- **different**
- **opposing**

order noun
*You must obey my **orders**.*
- **a command**
- **an instruction**

order verb
1 *He **ordered** us to stand still.*
- **to tell**
- **to command**
- **to instruct**
2 *We **ordered** some sandwiches and drinks.*
- **to ask for**
- **to request**
- **to send for**

ordinary adjective
1 *It was just an **ordinary** day.*
- **normal**
- **usual**
- **typical**
- **everyday** →

a
b
c
d
e
f
g
h
i
j
k
l
m
n
o
p
q
r
s
t
u
v
w
x
y
z

- **routine**
- **unexciting**

2 *It's just an **ordinary** house.*
- **normal**
- **standard**
- **average**

OPPOSITE special

organize verb
*Our teacher **organized** a trip to the zoo.*
- **to arrange**
- **to plan**
- **to set up**

original adjective
1 *Try to think of some **original** ideas.*
- **new**
- **fresh**
- **imaginative**

2 *The **original** version has been lost.*
- **first**
- **earliest**
- **initial**

outing noun
*We went on an **outing** to the country park.*
- **a trip**
- **an excursion**
- **an expedition**

overgrown adjective
*The garden was very **overgrown**.*
- **untidy**
- **weedy**
- **tangled**

own verb
*Do you **own** a bike?*
- **to have**
- **to possess**

own up verb
*He **owned up** to stealing the money.*
- **to admit** *He admitted stealing the money.*
- **to confess** *He confessed to stealing the money.*

a b c d e f g h i j k l m n o p q r s t u v w x y z

Pp

pack verb
> We **packed** everything into the car.
> • to put
> • to load
> • to stow
> • to cram

packed adjective
> The cinema was **packed** with people.
> • full
> • crowded
> • jam-packed

packet noun
> I bought a **packet** of cornflakes.
> • a box
> • a pack
> • a carton

page noun
> There's a lovely picture on the next **page**.
> • a sheet
> • a side

pain noun
> 1 I've got a **pain** in my stomach.
> • an ache
> • a twinge
> • a pang
> Use **ache** for a pain that continues for a long time:
> I could still feel an **ache** in my leg where the horse had kicked me.
> Use **twinge** or **pang** for a sudden sharp pain:
> I felt a sudden **twinge** in my leg as I was running.

> 2 She was in terrible **pain**.
> • agony

painful adjective
> Is your knee still **painful**?
> • sore
> • hurting
> • aching
> • tender

paint verb
> We're going to **paint** my bedroom during the holidays.
> • to decorate
> • to redecorate

pale adjective
> 1 She looked very tired and **pale**.
> • white
> • white-faced
> • pallid
> • pasty
> 2 He was wearing a **pale** blue shirt.
> • light
> • faded
> OPPOSITE bright

pant verb
> He was **panting** by the time he reached the top of the hill.
> • to gasp
> • to gasp for breath
> • to puff
> • to huff and puff

paper noun

 WORD WEB
some types of paper
• notepaper
• tissue paper
• wrapping paper
• writing paper

a
b
c
d
e
f
g
h
i
j
k
l
m
n
o
p
q
r
s
t
u
v
w
x
y
z

133

a
b
c
d
e
f
g
h
i
j
k
l
m
n
o
p
q
r
s
t
u
v
w
x
y
z

parcel noun

*There's a **parcel** for you!*
- **a package**
- **a packet**

part noun

1 *He kept a small **part** of the cake for himself.*
- **a bit**
- **a piece**
- **a portion**
- **a section**
2 *We have completed the first **part** of our journey.*
- **a stage**
- **a phase**
3 *This is a beautiful **part** of the country.*
- **an area**
- **a region**
4 *Which **part** of the city do you live in?*
- **an area**
- **a district**

particular adjective

1 *There was one **particular** dress that she liked.*
- **specific**
- **special**
2 *She has her own **particular** way of writing.*
- **individual**
- **personal**
- **special**
- **unique**

partner noun

*Choose a **partner** to work with.*
- **a friend**
- **a companion**
- **a colleague**
- **a helper**

party noun

*Are you having a **party**?*

- **a birthday party**
- **a celebration**
- **a gathering**
- **a disco**
- **a dance**

pass verb

1 *I **pass** this shop every day on my way to school.*
- **to go past**
- **to go by**
2 *We **passed** an old van on the motorway.*
- **to overtake**
3 *Could you **pass** me the salt, please?*
- **to hand**
- **to give**

passage noun

1 *We walked down a narrow **passage** to the kitchen.*
- **a corridor**
- **a passageway**
- **a walkway**
2 *They say there's a secret **passage** under the castle.*
- **a tunnel**

pat verb

*He **patted** the dog on the head.*
- **to touch**
- **to stroke**
- **to tap**

path noun

*We walked along the **path**.*
- **a footpath**
- **a track**
- **a bridleway** (*a path for horses*)

patient adjective

*It won't take very long, so please be **patient**.*

- **calm**
- **tolerant**
OPPOSITE impatient

pattern noun
*She was wearing a blue dress with a white **pattern**.*
- **a design**

pause verb
*He **paused** before opening the door.*
- **to stop**
- **to wait**
- **to hesitate**

pause noun
*Let's have a **pause** for lunch.*
- **a break**
- **an interval**
- **a rest**

pay noun
*You will get your **pay** at the end of the week.*
- **wages**
- **salary**

pay verb
1 *He **paid** a lot of money for that bike.*
- **to give**
- **to spend**
- **to fork out** (informal) *He forked out a lot of money on that bike.*
2 *If you let me have the video now, I'll **pay** you tomorrow.*
- **to repay**
- **to reimburse**

peace noun
1 *After the war ended there was **peace** between the two countries.*
- **friendliness**
- **an agreement**
- **a truce**
2 *We sat by the lake and enjoyed the **peace** of the evening.*
- **quiet**
- **silence**
- **peacefulness**
- **calmness**
- **stillness**

peaceful adjective
*It seemed very **peaceful** when the baby had gone to sleep.*
- **quiet**
- **calm**
- **tranquil**
OPPOSITE noisy

peculiar adjective
*This ice cream has a **peculiar** taste.*
- **strange**
- **funny**
- **odd**
- **curious**
- **bizarre**
OPPOSITE normal

pen noun

> **WORD WEB**
> **some types of pen**
> - a ballpoint pen
> - a Biro™
> - a felt-tip pen
> - a fountain pen
> - a quill (*an old-fashioned pen*)
> - a rollerball

people noun
1 *The streets were full of **people**.*
- **folk**
- **men and women** →

a b c d e f g h i j k l m n o **p** q r s t u v w x y z

135

2 *The president was elected by the **people** of his country.*
- **the public**
- **the population**
- **the citizens**

perfect adjective
1 *It's a **perfect** day for a picnic.*
- **ideal**
- **excellent**

2 *This is a **perfect** piece of work.*
- **excellent**
- **flawless**
- **faultless**

perform verb
1 *The children **performed** the play in front of their parents.*
- **to put on**
- **to present**

2 *I don't like **performing** in public.*
- **to act**
- **to dance**
- **to sing**
- **to be on stage**

perfume noun
*We bought Mum some **perfume** for her birthday.*
- **scent**

perhaps adverb
***Perhaps** we'll see you tomorrow.*
- **maybe**
- **possibly**

person noun
1 *I saw a **person** walking towards me.*
- **a man**
- **a woman**
- **an adult**
- **a grown-up**
- **a child**

- **a teenager**
- **a boy**
- **a girl**

2 *He's a very unpleasant **person**.*
- **an individual**
- **a character**
- **a human being**

personal adjective
*She's got her own **personal** mug.*
- **special**
- **individual**
- **private**

personality noun
*She's got a lovely **personality**.*
- **a character**
- **a nature**
- **a temperament**

persuade verb
1 *She **persuaded** her mum to take her swimming.*
- **to encourage**
- **to urge**
- **to talk someone into** *She talked her mum into taking her swimming.*

2 *The kitten was hiding under a chair, and I tried to **persuade** it to come out.*
- **to coax** *I tried to coax it out.*
- **to entice** *I tried to entice it out.*

pester verb
*My little brother kept **pestering** me.*
- **to annoy**
- **to bother**
- **to harass**
- **to hassle**
- **to nag**
  *Use **nag** when you keep reminding someone to do something:*
  *My mum keeps **nagging** me to do my homework.*

phone verb

*I **phoned** my grandma to ask how she was.*
- **to call**
- **to ring**
- **to telephone**
- **to give someone a ring** *I **gave** my grandma **a ring**.*

photograph noun

*I took a **photograph** of my sister.*
- **a photo**
- **a picture**
- **a shot**
- **a snapshot**

pick verb

1 *I didn't know which cake to **pick**.*
- **to choose**
- **to select**
- **to decide on**
2 *We **picked** some blackberries for tea.*
- **to gather**
- **to collect**
- **to harvest**
3 *She **picked** a flower from the bush.*
- **to pluck**
- **to cut**
4 *She **picked** the book up off the floor.*
- **to lift up**

picture noun

> 🕸 **WORD WEB**
> **some types of picture**
> - a caricature (*a funny picture of a real person*)
> - a cartoon
> - a drawing
> - an illustration (*a picture in a book*)
> - an image (*a picture in a film or on the computer*)
> - a painting
> - a photograph
> - a portrait (*a picture of a person*)
> - a sketch (*a rough drawing*)

piece noun

1 *She gave me a huge **piece** of cake.*
- **a bit**
- **a slice**
- **a sliver**
- **a wedge**
- **a square**
- **a lump**
- **a chunk**
- **a block**
- **a slab**

  A **sliver** is a thin piece:
  *She cut herself a tiny **sliver** of cake.*

  A **wedge** is a thick piece:
  *He was eating a huge **wedge** of chocolate cake.*

  A **square** is a small square piece:
  *Would you like a **square** of chocolate?*

  A **lump, chunk, block,** or **slab** is a big thick piece:
  *There was a big **slab** of concrete in the road.*

2 *We need another **piece** of wood.*
- **a bit**
- **a block**
- **a plank**
3 *She handed me a **piece** of paper.*
- **a bit**
- **a sheet**
- **a scrap**

  A **scrap** is a small piece of paper:
  *I wrote down his phone number on a small **scrap** of paper.*

4 *We need a new **piece** of glass for that window.*
- **a sheet**
- **a pane**
5 *There were **pieces** of broken cup all over the kitchen floor.*
- **a bit**
- **a chip**
- **a fragment**
  A **fragment** is a very small piece: →

a
b
c
d
e
f
g
h
i
j
k
l
m
n
o
p
q
r
s
t
u
v
w
x
y
z

*There were some tiny **fragments** of glass on the floor.*
6 *My dress was torn to **pieces**.*
   • **shreds** *My dress was torn to shreds.*

pierce verb
*The knight's sword **pierced** the dragon's thick skin.*
• **to prick**
• **to penetrate**
• **to go through**
• **to puncture**

pig noun
• **a hog**
• **a boar** (*a male pig*)
• **a sow** (*a female pig*)
• **a piglet** (*a baby pig*)

pile noun
*There was a **pile** of dirty clothes on the floor.*
• **a heap**
• **a mound**
• **a mass**
• **a stack**

pillar noun
*The roof was held up by large **pillars**.*
• **a column**
• **a post**
• **a support**

pipe noun
*There was water coming out of the **pipe**.*
• **a hose**
• **a tube**

pity noun
1 *She felt great **pity** for the hungry children.*

• **sympathy**
• **understanding**
2 *The soldiers showed no **pity** to their enemies.*
   • **mercy**
   • **kindness**
   • **compassion**
3 *It's a **pity** you can't come to the party.*
   • **a shame**

place noun
1 *A cross marks the **place** where the treasure is buried.*
   • **a spot**
   • **a position**
   • **a point**
   • **a location**
   • **a site**
2 *Our school is in a very nice **place**.*
   • **an area**
   • **a district**
   • **a neighbourhood**
   • **a town**
   • **a city**
   • **a village**
3 *Save me a **place** next to you.*
   • **a chair**
   • **a seat**

place verb, for other verbs, see **put**

plain adjective
*The food in the hotel was quite **plain**.*
• **ordinary**
• **simple**
• **basic**
• **not fancy**
• **dull**

plan noun
1 *He has a secret **plan** to get the money back.*
   • **an idea**

- a scheme
- a plot

2 *We drew a **plan** of the town to show where we all live.*
- a map
- a diagram
- a drawing
- a chart

3 *I made a **plan** for my story.*
- a framework
- a structure

plan verb

1 *When do you **plan** to leave?*
- to intend
- to aim

2 *He thinks they are **planning** to rob a bank.*
- to plot
- to scheme

3 *We need to **plan** this trip very carefully.*
- to organize
- to arrange
- to prepare for

plane noun, see aeroplane

plant noun

*The garden is full of beautiful **plants**.*

> **WORD WEB**
> **some types of plant**
> - a bulb
> - a bush
> - a cactus
> - a fern
> - a flower
> - a herb
> - a shrub
> - a tree
> - a vegetable
> - a weed

play noun

*The children are putting on a **play** at the end of term.*
- a show
- a performance
- a comedy (*a funny play*)
- a tragedy (*a sad play*)
- a pantomime
- a drama

play verb

1 *The children were playing on the beach.*
- to have fun
- to enjoy yourself *They were enjoying themselves.*
- to amuse yourself *They were amusing themselves.*

2 *Manchester United **play** Liverpool next week.*
- to take on
- to compete against

3 *She **played** a tune on the piano.*
- to perform

playful adjective

*Kittens can be **playful**.*
- lively
- mischievous
- frisky
- fun-loving
- cheeky

OPPOSITE serious

pleasant adjective

1 *We had a very **pleasant** day on the beach.*
- lovely
- enjoyable
- wonderful
- fantastic
- delightful

2 *He seems a very **pleasant** boy.*
- friendly
- kind
- likeable →

- **thoughtful**
- **charming**
- **polite**

Use **thoughtful** for someone who thinks about other people:

It was very **thoughtful** of you to buy me a present.

Use **charming** or **polite** for someone who behaves well and isn't rude to people:

Now remember you must be **polite** to all your relatives.

3 The weather was very **pleasant**.

- **lovely**
- **fine**
- **beautiful**
- **warm**
- **sunny**
- **glorious**
- **wonderful**

OPPOSITE unpleasant

pleased adjective

I was **pleased** that so many people came to my party.

- **happy**
- **glad**
- **delighted**
- **thrilled**
- **grateful**
- **thankful**

Use **delighted** or **thrilled** when you are very pleased about something:

I was **thrilled** when I won the first prize!

Use **grateful** or **thankful** when you are pleased because someone has been kind to you:

I'm very **grateful** for all your help.

OPPOSITE annoyed

pleasure noun

She smiled with **pleasure**.

- **happiness**
- **enjoyment**

- **contentment**
- **delight**
- **joy**

Use **delight** or **joy** for a feeling of great pleasure:

His face lit up with **delight** when he saw the huge pile of presents.

plot verb

I knew they were **plotting** to steal the jewels.

- **to plan**
- **to scheme**

plot noun

They had a secret **plot** to steal the money.

- **a plan**
- **a scheme**
- **a conspiracy**

plump adjective

The shopkeeper was a small, **plump** man.

- **fat**
- **tubby**
- **chubby**
- **podgy**
- **stout**
- **portly**
- **overweight**
- **obese**

Use **tubby**, **chubby**, or **podgy** for someone who is slightly fat in a nice way:

There was a **chubby** smiling baby in the buggy.

Use **stout** or **portly** for an older person who is quite fat:

Uncle Toby was a **portly** man with a round, smiling face.

Use **overweight** or **obese** for someone who is so fat that they are unhealthy:

It's important to exercise so you don't become **overweight**.
OPPOSITE thin

plunge verb
She **plunged** into the water.
- **to jump**
- **to leap**
- **to dive**

poem noun

> **WORD WEB**
> **some types of poem**
> - an acrostic
> - a calligram
> - a cinquain
> - a haiku
> - a limerick
> - a nursery rhyme
> - a rap
> - a sonnet

point noun
1 Be careful, that knife has got a very sharp **point**.
- **an end**
- **a tip**
2 We soon reached the **point** where the two roads met.
- **a place**
- **a spot**
3 At that **point** I did not know about the treasure.
- **a time**
- **a moment**
- **a stage**
4 What is the **point** of this game?
- **the purpose**
- **the aim**
- **the object**

point verb
1 He **pointed** towards the castle.

- **to indicate**
- **to gesture towards**
2 I **pointed** the hose at the paddling pool.
- **to aim**
- **to direct**

pointed adjective
He used a **pointed** stick to make a hole in the ground.
- **sharp**
- **sharpened**

poisonous adjective
1 Some toadstools are **poisonous**.
- **harmful**
- **toxic**
- **deadly**
- **lethal**
  Use **deadly** or **lethal** when something is so poisonous that it can kill you: Arsenic is a **deadly** poison.
2 She was bitten by a **poisonous** snake.
- **venomous**

poke verb
1 He **poked** the dead mouse with a stick.
- **to prod**
- **to push**
- **to jab**
2 She **poked** me in the back.
- **to nudge**
- **to dig**
- **to prod**
- **to elbow**

pole noun
We tied the flag to a **pole**.
- **a post**

policeman, policewoman noun
There was a **policeman** at the door.
- **a police officer**
- **an officer** →

a
b
c
d
e
f
g
h
i
j
k
l
m
n
o
p
q
r
s
t
u
v
w
x
y
z

- **a constable**
- **a sergeant**
- **an inspector**
- **a detective**

polite adjective
*He's a very **polite** boy.*
- **well-mannered**
- **well-behaved**
- **respectful**
- **courteous**
- **civil**
OPPOSITE rude

poor adjective
1 *His mother and father were very poor.*
- **hard up**
- **penniless**
- **broke** (*informal*)
- **needy**
- **poverty-stricken**
Use **hard up** for someone who doesn't have much money to spend:
*My dad's a bit **hard up** at the moment, so there's no point asking for a new bike.*
Use **penniless** or **broke** for someone who does not have any money to spend:
*I can't go to the fair because I'm absolutely **broke**!*
Use **needy** or **poverty-stricken** for someone who is very poor and doesn't have enough money for food:
*We collect money to help **poverty-stricken** families in poor countries.*
OPPOSITE rich
2 *This is very **poor** work.*
- **bad**
- **careless**
- **sloppy**
OPPOSITE good

poorly adjective
*I was **poorly** yesterday.*
- **ill**
- **unwell**
- **sick**
OPPOSITE well

popular adjective
*He is a **popular** TV presenter.*
- **famous**
- **well-known**
- **well-liked**
OPPOSITE unpopular

portion noun
1 *She gave me a huge **portion** of chips.*
- **a helping**
- **a serving**
2 *I only got a small **portion** of pie.*
- **a piece**
- **a slice**

positive adjective
*I am **positive** I saw him.*
- **certain**
- **sure**
- **convinced**

possessions noun
*We lost all our **possessions** in the fire.*
- **belongings**
- **property**
- **things**

possible adjective
*It is **possible** that it will rain later.*
- **likely**
- **conceivable**
- **feasible**
OPPOSITE impossible

a b c d e f g h i j k l m n o p q r s t u v w x y z

post noun

1 *The fence is supported by wooden **posts**.*
- **a pole**
- **a stake**

2 *Did you get any **post** this morning?*
- **mail**
- **letters**
- **parcels**

poster noun

*We put up a **poster** to tell people about our concert.*
- **a notice**
- **a sign**
- **an announcement**
- **an advertisement**

postpone verb

*We had to **postpone** the match because of the bad weather.*
- **to put off**
- **to cancel**
- **to delay**

pour verb

1 *I **poured** some orange juice into a glass.*
- **to tip**

2 *Water was **pouring** over the edge of the bath.*
- **to run**
- **to spill**
- **to splash**
- **to stream**
- **to gush**
   Use **splash** when water is pouring noisily:
   *Water from the roof was **splashing** down into the puddles below.*
   Use **stream** or **gush** when a lot of water is pouring:
   *A huge jet of water was **gushing** out of the burst pipe.*

3 *It was **pouring** with rain.*
- **to teem**
- **to pelt down**
- **to bucket down**

power noun

1 *The police have the **power** to arrest criminals.*
- **the right**
- **the authority**

2 *In stories, magicians have special **powers**.*
- **an ability**
- **a skill**
- **a talent**

3 *Many buildings were destroyed by the **power** of the waves.*
- **force**
- **strength**
- **might**
- **energy**

powerful adjective

1 *He was a rich and **powerful** king.*
- **mighty**
- **all-powerful**

2 *The lion crushed the bones with its **powerful** jaws.*
- **strong**
- **mighty**
- **great**
OPPOSITE **weak**

practise verb

1 *I need to **practise** my speech.*
- **to go through**
- **to run through**
- **to work on**
- **to rehearse**

2 *The football team meets once a week to **practise**.*
- **to train**

praise verb

*Our teacher **praised** us for working so hard.*
- **to congratulate** →

a
b
c
d
e
f
g
h
i
j
k
l
m
n
o
p
q
r
s
t
u
v
w
x
y
z

143

a
b
c
d
e
f
g
h
i
j
k
l
m
n
o
p
q
r
s
t
u
v
w
x
y
z

144

- **to commend**
- **to compliment**
OPPOSITE criticize

precious adjective
1 *The thieves stole a lot of **precious** jewellery.*
- **valuable**
- **expensive**
- **priceless**
2 *I have a special box for all my **precious** possessions.*
- **prized**
- **treasured**
- **cherished**
- **much-loved**

precise adjective
*Make sure you measure out the **precise** amount.*
- **exact**
- **correct**
- **right**
- **accurate**

prepare verb
1 *We are all busy **preparing** for the party.*
- **to get ready**
- **to make preparations**
- **to make arrangements**
- **to plan**
2 *I helped my mum **prepare** lunch.*
- **to make**
- **to cook**

present noun
*I got some lovely **presents** for my birthday.*
- **a gift**

present verb
1 *The head **presented** the prize to the winner.*
- **to give**

- **to hand**
- **to award**
2 *Who will **present** the show tonight?*
- **to introduce**
- **to host**

press verb
*Don't **press** any of the buttons.*
- **to push**
- **to touch**

pretend verb
1 *I thought she was hurt, but she was only **pretending**.*
- **to put it on**
- **to fake**
- **to play-act**
2 *Let's **pretend** we're pirates.*
- **to imagine**
- **to make believe**
- **to play**

pretty adjective
1 *You look **pretty** today.*
- **lovely**
- **beautiful**
- **attractive**
- **stunning**
- **gorgeous**
  Use **stunning** or **gorgeous** for someone who is very pretty:
  *My sister looked **stunning** in her wedding dress.*
2 *What a **pretty** little cottage!*
- **quaint**
- **charming**
- **delightful**
OPPOSITE ugly

prevent verb
1 *He tried to **prevent** us from leaving.*
- **to stop**

2 *We must act quickly to **prevent** an accident.*
- **to avoid**
- **to avert**

price noun
1 *What was the **price** of those trainers?*
- **the cost**

2 *What **price** do you have to pay to go into the museum?*
- **a charge**
- **a fee**

3 *What's the **price** for this bus journey?*
- **a fare**

prick verb
*I **pricked** my finger on a needle.*
- **to jab**
- **to stab**
- **to pierce**

prison noun
*The thief was sent to **prison** for ten years.*
- **jail**
- **a cell**
- **a dungeon**

prisoner noun
*The **prisoners** were only given bread and water.*
- **a convict**
- **an inmate**
- **a hostage** (*a person taken prisoner by a kidnapper*)
- **a captive**

private adjective
1 *They have their own **private** beach.*
- **personal**

2 *You mustn't read her **private** letters.*
- **confidential**
- **personal**
- **secret**

3 *We found a nice **private** spot for a picnic.*
- **hidden**
- **secluded**
- **quiet**
- **isolated**

prize noun
*I hope I win a **prize**.*
- **an award**
- **a trophy**
- **a cup**
- **a medal**

problem noun
1 *The lack of food was going to be a **problem**.*
- **a difficulty**
- **a worry**
- **trouble**

2 *We had some difficult maths **problems** to solve.*
- **a question**

3 *We solved the **problem** of the missing shoe.*
- **a mystery**
- **a riddle**
- **a puzzle**
- **an enigma**

prod verb
1 *She **prodded** the worm with a stick.*
- **to poke**
- **to push**
- **to jab**

2 *Someone **prodded** me in the back.*
- **to nudge**
- **to dig**
- **to poke**
- **to elbow**

a
b
c
d
e
f
g
h
i
j
k
l
m
n
o
p
q
r
s
t
u
v
w
x
y
z

produce verb
   1 This factory **produces** furniture.
   • **to make**
   • **to manufacture**
   • **to assemble**
   2 Farmers **produce** food for us.
   • **to grow**
   3 She **produced** a photo from her bag.
   • **to bring out**
   • **to take out**

promise verb
   Do you **promise** that you will be home
   by five o'clock?
   • **to give your word**
   • **to swear**
   • **to vow**
   • **to guarantee**

proof noun
   I think she took my pen, but I haven't
   got any **proof**.
   • **evidence**
   • **facts**
   • **information**

proper adjective
   1 Please put the book back in its **proper**
   place.
   • **correct**
   • **right**
   2 Can we have a ride in a **proper** boat?
   • **real**
   • **genuine**

protect verb
   1 The bird always **protects** its chicks.
   • **to defend**
   • **to guard**
   • **to look after**
   2 The hedge **protected** us from the wind.
   • **to shelter**
   • **to shield**

protest verb
   The children **protested** when
   the teacher said they had to stay
   indoors.
   • **to complain**
   • **to object**

proud adjective
   Her parents felt very **proud** when she
   went up to collect her prize.
   • **pleased**
   • **happy**
   • **delighted**
   • **honoured**
   OPPOSITE ashamed

prove verb
   Can you **prove** that you live here?
   • **to show**
   • **to establish**
   • **to demonstrate**

provide verb
   1 Our parents **provided** us with food for
   the trip.
   • **to supply**
   • **to give**
   2 You will need to **provide** your own
   towel.
   • **to bring**
   • **to take**

prowl verb
   The tiger **prowled** round the tree.
   • **to creep**
   • **to slink**

pry verb
   You shouldn't **pry** into other people's
   business
   • **to interfere**
   • **to meddle**
   • **to poke your nose in** (informal)

a b c d e f g h i j k l m n o **p** q r s t u v w x y z

public adjective
> This is a **public** beach, not a private one.
> - **open**
> - **communal**
> - **shared**
> OPPOSITE private

publish verb
> The school **publishes** a magazine once a term.
> - **to bring out**
> - **to produce**
> - **to issue**
> - **to print**

pudding noun
> Would you like some **pudding**?
> - **dessert**
> - **sweet**

puff verb
> I was **puffing** a bit by the time I got to the top of the hill.
> - **to pant**
> - **to huff and puff**
> - **to gasp**
> - **to gasp for breath**

pull verb
> 1 We **pulled** the heavy box across the floor.
> - **to drag**
> - **to haul**
> - **to lug**
> 2 I got hold of the handle and **pulled** hard.
> - **to tug**
> - **to yank**
> - **to heave**
> 3 The magician **pulled** a bunch of flowers out of a hat.
> - **to take**
> - **to lift**
> - **to draw**
> - **to produce**
> 4 I managed to **pull** the book out of her hands.
> - **to tear**
> - **to wrench**
> - **to drag**
> - **to rip**
> 5 The car was **pulling** a caravan.
> - **to tow**
> - **to draw**

pull off verb
> I **pulled** off the label.
> - **to rip off**
> - **to tear off**
> - **to break off**

punch verb
> That boy **punched** me!
> - **to hit**
> - **to thump**
> - **to wallop**
> - **to strike**

punish verb
> The teachers will **punish** you if you misbehave.
> - **to discipline**
> - **to make an example of**

pupil noun
> This school has about five hundred **pupils**.
> - **a schoolchild**
> - **a schoolboy**
> - **a schoolgirl**
> - **a student**

pure adjective
> 1 He was wearing a crown made of **pure** gold.
> - **real**
> - **solid** →

a
b
c
d
e
f
g
h
i
j
k
l
m
n
o
p
q
r
s
t
u
v
w
x
y
z

a
b
c
d
e
f
g
h
i
j
k
l
m
n
o
p
q
r
s
t
u
v
w
x
y
z

2 *We bought a carton of **pure** orange juice.*
  • **natural**
3 *The water here is lovely and **pure**.*
  • **clean**
  • **clear**
  • **fresh**
  • **unpolluted**

purse noun
  *Always keep your money in a **purse**.*
  • **a wallet**
  • **a bag**

push verb
1 *The door will open if you **push** harder.*
  • **to press**
  • **to shove**
  • **to apply pressure**
2 *I managed to **push** all the clothes into the bag.*
  • **to force**
  • **to stuff**
  • **to stick**
  • **to ram**
  • **to squeeze**
  • **to jam**
  • **to cram**
3 *We **pushed** the table into the corner of the room.*
  • **to move**
  • **to shove**
  • **to drag**
4 *We **pushed** the trolley towards the checkout.*
  • **to wheel**
  • **to trundle**
  • **to roll**
5 *Someone **pushed** me in the back.*
  • **to shove**
  • **to nudge**
  • **to prod**
  • **to poke**
  • **to elbow**

6 *The boy **pushed** past me.*
  • **to shove**
  • **to barge**
  • **to squeeze**
  • **to elbow your way**

put verb

⚠ **OVERUSED WORD**
Try to vary the words you use to mean *put*. Here are some other words you can use instead.
1 ***Put** all the pencils on my desk.*
  • **to place**
  • **to leave**
  • **to position**
  • **to arrange**
  • **to pop**
  • **to pile**
  • **to stack**
  • **to drop**
  • **to dump**
  • **to deposit**
  • **to plonk** (informal)
  *Use **position** when you put something carefully in a particular place:*
  *He **positioned** the clock so that he could see it from his bed.*
  *Use **arrange** when you put something in a place carefully so that it looks nice:*
  *He **arranged** the flowers in the vase.*
  *Use **pop** when you put something in a place quickly:*
  *Why don't you quickly **pop** your bike in the shed?*
  *Use **pile** or **stack** when you put things in a pile:*
  *I **stacked** the papers on my desk.*
  *Use **drop, dump, deposit,** or **plonk** when you put something in a place carelessly:*
  *She ran in and **dumped** her school bag on the floor.*

2 *I **put** a coin into the slot.*
- **to slide**
- **to insert**

3 *He **put** all the dirty clothes back into his bag.*
- **to shove**
- **to push**
- **to stick**
- **to bung**
- **to stuff**

4 *He **put** some sugar on his cereal.*
- **to sprinkle**
- **to scatter**

5 *Can you **put** some water on these plants?*
- **to spray**
- **to sprinkle**
- **to pour**

6 *I **put** some butter on my bread.*
- **to spread**

7 *We **put** all the pictures on the table so that we could see them.*
- **to lay**
- **to lay out**
- **to set out**
- **to spread out**
- **to arrange**

8 *She **put** her bike against the wall.*
- **to lean**
- **to rest**
- **to stand**
- **to prop**

9 *They have **put** some new lights on the outside of the school*
- **to fix**
- **to attach**

- **to install**
- **to fit**

10 *You can **put** your car in the car park.*
- **to park**
- **to leave**

put off verb
*The match has been **put off** until next week.*
- **to postpone**
- **to cancel**
- **to delay**

put up with verb
*How can you **put up** with this noise?*
- **to tolerate**
- **to endure**
- **to live with**

puzzle noun
1 *I like doing **puzzles**.*
- **a brainteaser**
- **a problem**
2 *The disappearance of the keys was still a **puzzle**.*
- **a mystery**
- **a riddle**
- **an enigma**

puzzled adjective
*I was **puzzled** when I found the door wide open.*
- **confused**
- **bewildered**
- **baffled**
- **mystified**

a
b
c
d
e
f
g
h
i
j
k
l
m
n
o
P
q
r
s
t
u
v
w
x
y
z

Qq

quake verb

*The children were **quaking** with fear.*
- **to shake**
- **to tremble**
- **to quiver**
- **to shiver**
- **to shudder**

quality noun

*The children have produced some work of very high **quality**.*
- **a standard**

quantity noun

*In hot weather the shop sells a large **quantity** of ice cream.*
- **an amount**

quarrel verb

*What are you two **quarrelling** about?*
- **to argue**
- **to disagree**
- **to squabble**
- **to fight**
- **to fall out**
- **to bicker**
  Use **fight** when people argue in a very angry or serious way:
  *The two brothers **fought** all the time and didn't get on at all.*
  Use **fall out** when people quarrel and stop being friends:
  *I've **fallen out** with my best friend.*
  Use **bicker** when people quarrel about little things:
  *The two girls were **bickering** over how many sweets they had.*

quarrel noun

*She had a **quarrel** with her brother.*
- **an argument**
- **a disagreement**
- **a squabble**
- **a row**
- **a fight**
  A **row** is a loud quarrel:
  *I had a big **row** with my parents.*
  A **fight** is an angry, serious quarrel:
  *We had a really big **fight** about who should have the main part in the play.*

question noun

*There was no one who could answer my **question**.*
- **a query**
- **an enquiry**

queue noun

1 *There was a long **queue** of people waiting for ice creams.*
- **a line**
2 *There was a long **queue** of traffic on the motorway.*
- **a line**
- **a tailback**

quick adjective

1 *It was quite a **quick** journey.*
- **fast**
- **speedy**
- **swift**
- **rapid**
2 *He made a **quick** recovery from his illness.*
- **rapid**
- **speedy**
- **instant**
- **immediate**
  Use **instant** or **immediate** for something that happens very quickly:
  *The programme was an **instant** success.*

3 *He was walking at a **quick** pace.*
- **brisk**
- **fast**
- **swift**

4 *We had a **quick** lunch and then left.*
- **hasty**
- **hurried**
- **brief**

5 *They only came for a **quick** visit.*
- **short**
- **brief**
- **fleeting**

quiet adjective

1 *Our teacher told us to be **quiet**.*
- **silent**
- **hushed**

OPPOSITE noisy

2 *We found a **quiet** place for our picnic.*
- **peaceful**
- **calm**
- **isolated**

- **tranquil**

OPPOSITE crowded

3 *She's a very **quiet** girl.*
- **reserved**
- **placid**
- **shy**
- **timid**

OPPOSITE noisy

4 *I listened to some **quiet** music.*
- **low**
- **soft**

OPPOSITE loud

quite adverb

1 *The water's **quite** warm.*
- **fairly**
- **pretty**
- **reasonably**
- **rather**

2 *I'm not **quite** sure.*
- **completely**
- **totally**
- **absolutely**
- **fully**

a
b
c
d
e
f
g
h
i
j
k
l
m
n
o
p
q
r
s
t
u
v
w
x
y
z

a
b
c
d
e
f
g
h
i
j
k
l
m
n
o
p
q
r
s
t
u
v
w
x
y
z

Rr

rain noun
> There could be some **rain** later.
- **a shower**
- **drizzle**
- **a downpour**
- **a storm**
> **Drizzle** is very light rain:
> The rain had slowed down to just a light **drizzle**.
> A **downpour** is a heavy shower of rain:
> We got soaked when we got caught in a **downpour**.
> A **storm** is heavy rain with thunder:
> That night there was a terrible **storm**.

 WRITING TIPS
Here are some useful words for writing about the rain.
- A **fine**, **light** rain was **falling** outside.
- There was **steady** rain all day.
- There were strong winds and **heavy** rain during the night.
- **Torrential** rain can cause flooding.
- The rain **poured down** all day.
- I could hear rain **pattering** on the window.

rain verb
> It's still **raining**.
- **to drizzle**
- **to spit**
- **to pour**
> Use **drizzle** or **spit** when it is not raining very hard:
> It was only **spitting** so we decided to carry on with our walk.
> Use **pour** when it is raining a lot:
> We can't go outside! It's **pouring**!

raise verb
1 A crane **raised** the car out of the ditch.
- **to lift**
- **to hoist**
2 Our school is trying to **raise** money for charity.
- **to make**
- **to get**
- **to collect**

rare adjective
> Pandas are very **rare** animals.
- **uncommon**
- **unusual**
- **scarce**
OPPOSITE common

rather adverb
> The water's **rather** cold.
- **quite**
- **fairly**
- **pretty**

ration noun
> Each person was given a daily **ration** of food.
- **a share**
- **an allowance**
- **a quota**
- **a measure**

ray noun
> A **ray** of light shone through the crack in the door.
- **a beam**
- **a shaft**

reach verb
1 I **reached** out my hand to pick up the packet.
- **to stretch**
2 Can you **reach** the biscuit tin?
- **to touch**
- **to grasp**
- **to get hold of**

3 *It was dark when we **reached** London.*
- **to arrive at/in** *It was dark when we arrived in London.*

read verb
*I **read** a magazine while I was waiting.*
- **to look at**
- **to flick through**
- **to browse through**
- **to read through**
- **to study**
- **to pore over**
  Use **look at**, **flick through**, and **browse through** when you read something quickly:
  *I **flicked through** the address book until I found her address.*
  Use **read through** when you read all of something:
  *Make sure you **read through** the instructions.*
  Use **study** or **pore over** when you read something very carefully:
  *He spent hours **poring over** the documents.*

ready adjective
1 *Are you **ready** to leave?*
- **prepared**
- **all set**
- **waiting**
2 *Your goods are now **ready** for you to collect.*
- **available**
3 *Is lunch **ready**?*
- **prepared**
- **cooked**

real adjective
1 *Is that a **real** diamond?*
- **genuine**
- **authentic**
OPPOSITE artificial

2 *Is Tiny your **real** name?*
- **actual**
- **proper**
OPPOSITE false
3 *She had never felt **real** sadness before.*
- **true**
- **sincere**

realistic adjective
*We used fake blood, but it looked quite **realistic**.*
- **lifelike**
- **natural**
- **authentic**
OPPOSITE unrealistic

realize verb
*I suddenly **realized** that I had made a terrible mistake.*
- **to know**
- **to understand**
- **to become aware**
- **to notice**
- **to see**

really adverb
1 *The water's **really** cold!*
- **very**
- **extremely**
2 *Tom apologized, but I don't think he's **really** sorry.*
- **truly**
- **honestly**
- **genuinely**
3 *Is your dad **really** a spy?*
- **actually**

reason noun
1 *There must be a **reason** why this plant has died.*
- **a cause**
- **an explanation** →

a
b
c
d
e
f
g
h
i
j
k
l
m
n
o
p
q
r
s
t
u
v
w
x
y
z

2 *What was your **reason** for telling us these lies?*
- **a motive**

reasonable adjective
1 *It is **reasonable** to expect you to help with the work.*
- **fair**
- **right**
OPPOSITE unreasonable
2 *Let's try and discuss this in a **reasonable** way.*
- **sensible**
- **rational**
- **mature**
OPPOSITE irrational
3 *You can earn a **reasonable** amount of money.*
- **fair**
- **quite good**
- **respectable**

rebel verb
*The soldiers **rebelled**.*
- **to revolt**
- **to rise up**
- **to mutiny**
- **to disobey orders**

receive verb
1 *I **received** some lovely presents.*
- **to get**
- **to be given** (*I was given some lovely presents.*)
2 *How much money do you **receive** each week for doing the paper round?*
- **to get**
- **to earn**
OPPOSITE give

recent adjective
*Her **recent** film is not as good as the others.*
- **new**
- **latest**

- **current**
- **up-to-date**

reckon verb
*I **reckon** our side will win.*
- **to think**
- **to believe**
- **to feel sure**

recognize verb
*Would you **recognize** that man if you saw him again?*
- **to remember**
- **to know**
- **to identify**

recommend verb
1 *A lot of people have **recommended** this book to me.*
- **to suggest**
- **to speak highly of** *A lot of people have spoken highly of this book.*
2 *I **recommend** that you should see a doctor.*
- **to suggest**
- **to advise** *I advise you to see a doctor.*

record noun
*We kept a **record** of the birds we saw on holiday.*
- **an account**
- **a diary**
- **a list**
- **a journal**
- **a log**

recover verb
*Have you **recovered** from your illness?*
- **to get better**
- **to get well**
- **to recuperate**

red adjective
1 *She was wearing a **red** dress.*
- **crimson**
- **scarlet**
- **maroon**
2 *Her cheeks were **red**.*
- **rosy**
- **glowing**
- **flushed**

reduce verb
1 *She **reduced** her speed when she saw the police car.*
- **to decrease**
2 *We want to **reduce** the amount of litter in the playground.*
- **to lessen**
- **to cut down**
3 *The school shop has **reduced** some of its prices.*
- **to lower**
- **to cut**
- **to slash**
- **to halve**
  Use **slash** when a price is reduced a lot:
  *That shop is closing down, so all the prices have been **slashed**.*
  Use **halve** when something is reduced by half:
  The price was halved from £10 to £5.
  OPPOSITE increase

refer to verb
*He **referred to** the story he had read.*
- **to mention**
- **to comment on**
- **to talk about**

refreshed adjective
*I felt **refreshed** after my rest.*
- **invigorated**
- **restored**
- **revived**

refreshing adjective
1 *I had a lovely **refreshing** shower.*
- **invigorating**
2 *I need a **refreshing** drink.*
- **cooling**
- **thirst-quenching**

refuse verb
*I offered to take him to the party, but he **refused**.*
- **to say no** *He said no.*
- **to decline** *He declined.*
- **to be unwilling** *He was unwilling.*
OPPOSITE accept

region noun
*These animals only live in hot **regions**.*
- **an area**
- **a place**
- **a zone**

regular adjective
1 *You should take **regular** exercise.*
- **frequent**
- **daily**
- **weekly**
2 *The postman was on his **regular** delivery round.*
- **normal**
- **usual**
- **customary**
3 *The drummer kept a **regular** rhythm.*
- **even**
- **steady**
OPPOSITE irregular

rehearse verb
1 *We **rehearsed** for the concert all afternoon.*
- **to practise**
- **to prepare** →

a
b
c
d
e
f
g
h
i
j
k
l
m
n
o
p
q
r
s
t
u
v
w
x
y
z

155

2 *I think you should **rehearse** your speech.*
- **to go through**
- **to run through**

relation noun
*She is a **relation** of mine.*
- **a relative**

relax verb
1 *I like to **relax** after school.*
- **to rest**
- **to unwind**
- **to take it easy**
2 ***Relax**, there's nothing to worry about.*
- **to calm down**
- **to not panic** *Don't panic!*

release verb
*They **released** the animals from the cage.*
- **to free**
- **to liberate**
- **to set free** *They set the animals free.*
- **to turn loose** *They turned the animals loose.*

reliable adjective
*I'm surprised that Joshua is late, he's usually so **reliable**.*
- **dependable**
- **responsible**
- **trustworthy**
OPPOSITE unreliable

relieved adjective
*I was very **relieved** when I heard that no one was hurt.*
- **happy**
- **glad**
- **thankful**

religion noun
*Different people follow different **religions**.*
- **a belief**
- **a faith**
- **a creed**

> WORD WEB
> **some different religions**
> - Buddhism
> - Christianity
> - Hinduism
> - Islam
> - Judaism
> - Sikhism

religious adjective
*They got married in a special **religious** ceremony.*
- **holy**
- **sacred**

reluctant adjective
*I was **reluctant** to walk home because it was raining.*
- **unwilling**
- **unhappy**
- **not keen**
- **hesitant**
OPPOSITE keen

rely on verb
1 *the young chicks **rely on** their mother for food.*
- **to depend on**
- **to need**
2 *We know we can always **rely on** you to help us.*
- **to trust**
- **to count on**

remain verb
*Please **remain** in your seats.*
- **to stay**
- **to wait**

remains noun

1 *We visited the **remains** of a Roman castle.*
- **ruins**
- **remnants**

2 *We gave the **remains** of the food to the dog.*
- **the leftovers**
- **the rest**

remark verb
*I **remarked** that it was a nice day.*
- **to comment**
- **to mention**
- **to observe**
- **to point out**

remarkable adjective
*This was a **remarkable** achievement.*
- **extraordinary**
- **amazing**
- **astonishing**
- **incredible**
OPPOSITE ordinary

remember verb

1 *I can't **remember** his name.*
- **to recall**
- **to recollect**

2 *I'm going to give you my phone number, and you must **remember** it.*
- **to learn**
- **to memorize**
- **to make a mental note of**
OPPOSITE forget

remind verb
*Seeing her with her swimming kit **reminded** me that I needed mine.*
- **to jog someone's memory** *Seeing her with her swimming kit jogged my memory.*

remove verb

1 *Please **remove** this rubbish.*
- **to move**
- **to take away**
- **to get rid of**

2 *He opened the drawer and **removed** some of the papers.*
- **to take out**
- **to lift out**
- **to extract**

3 *She carefully **removed** the stamp from the envelope.*
- **to take off**
- **to tear off**
- **to cut off**
- **to detach**

4 *Someone had **removed** the door handle.*
- **to take off**
- **to break off**
- **to snap off**

5 *He walked into the house and **removed** his shoes.*
- **to take off**
- **to kick off**
- **to slip off**

6 *We scrubbed the walls to **remove** the dirt.*
- **to wipe off**
- **to scrape off**
- **to scratch off**
- **to rub off**

7 *I **removed** her name from the list.*
- **to cross out**
- **to rub out**
- **to erase**
- **to delete**

8 *I accidentally **removed** some files from my computer.*
- **to delete**
- **to wipe**

9 *The police **removed** him from the building.*
- **to evict**
- **to throw out**

a
b
c
d
e
f
g
h
i
j
k
l
m
n
o
p
q
r
s
t
u
v
w
x
y
z

157

a
b
c
d
e
f
g
h
i
j
k
l
m
n
o
p
q
r
s
t
u
v
w
x
y
z

repair verb
*She managed to **repair** the TV.*
- **to mend**
- **to fix**

repeat verb
*Could you **repeat** that, please?*
- **to say again** *Could you say that again, please?*
- **reiterate** *Mum reiterated that we must be home by seven o'clock.*

reply noun
*I called her name, but there was no **reply**.*
- **an answer**
- **a response**

reply verb
*I asked him another question, but he didn't **reply**.*
- **to answer**
- **to respond**

report noun
1 *We had to write a **report** of what had happened.*
- **an account**
- **a description**
2 *There was a **report** about our school in the local newspaper.*
- **an article**
- **a story**

rescue verb
1 *They **rescued** the prisoners from the dungeon.*
- **to free**
- **to release**
- **to liberate**
- **to set free** *He **set** the prisoners **free**.*
2 *A lifeboat was sent out to **rescue** the men on the sinking boat.*
- **to save**

reserve noun
*Each team is allowed three **reserves**.*
- **a substitute**

reserve verb
*We **reserved** our seats on the train.*
- **to book**

resign verb
*Our teacher **resigned** at the end of last term.*
- **to leave**
- **to quit**

respect verb
*I **respect** my grandparents.*
- **to look up to**
- **to admire**
- **to think highly of**

respect noun
*You should always treat other people with **respect**.*
- **consideration**
- **thoughtfulness**
- **courtesy**
- **politeness**

responsible adjective
1 *You are **responsible** for feeding the fish.*
- **in charge of** *You are in charge of feeding the fish.*
2 *Who is **responsible** for breaking this window?*
- **to blame for** *Who is to blame for breaking this window?*
- **guilty of** *Who is guilty of breaking this window?*
3 *We need a **responsible** person to look after the money.*
- **sensible**

- **reliable**
- **trustworthy**

OPPOSITE irresponsible

rest noun

1 *I need a **rest**!*
   - **a break**
   - **a pause**
   - **a sit-down**
   - **a lie-down**
   - **a breather**
     A **breather** is a short rest to get your breath back:
     *We stopped for a **breather** before continuing up the mountain.*
2 *The doctor says that I need plenty of **rest**.*
   - **sleep**
   - **relaxation**
3 *If you have finished, the dog will eat the **rest**.*
   - **the remainder**
   - **the leftovers**

rest verb

*We'll **rest** for half an hour before we continue.*
   - **to relax**
   - **to take it easy**
   - **to sit down**
   - **to lie down**
   - **to sleep**
   - **to have a nap**

result noun

1 *As a **result** of our good behaviour we got extra playtime.*
   - **a consequence**
   - **an outcome**
2 *I didn't see the match, but I know the **result**.*
   - **a score**

retreat verb

*The soldiers **retreated** towards the fort.*
   - **to go back**
   - **to move back**
   - **to withdraw**
   - **to flee**

return verb

1 *We decided to **return** to the cave.*
   - **to go back**
2 *He left, and we didn't know if he would ever **return**.*
   - **to come back**
   - **to reappear**

reveal verb

1 *He opened the door and **revealed** a secret room.*
   - **to expose**
   - **to show**
2 *She drew back the curtain and **revealed** a statue of a man.*
   - **to uncover**
   - **to unveil**
3 *Don't ever **reveal** our secret!*
   - **to tell**
   - **to disclose**
   - **to let out** *Don't ever let this secret out.*
   - **to make known** *Don't ever make this secret known.*

revenge noun

*He wanted **revenge** for the death of his father.*
   - **vengeance**
   - **retribution**

review noun

*I wrote a **review** of the book.*
   - **an evaluation**
   - **a judgement**

a
b
c
d
e
f
g
h
i
j
k
l
m
n
o
p
q
r
s
t
u
v
w
x
y
z

revolting adjective

1 *The food was **revolting**.*
- **horrible**
- **disgusting**
- **tasteless**
- **inedible**

2 *What a **revolting** dress!*
- **horrible**
- **vile**
- **hideous**
- **repulsive**

OPPOSITE pleasant

rich adjective

*She dreamed of being **rich** and famous.*
- **wealthy**
- **well-off**
- **prosperous**

OPPOSITE poor

get rid of verb

*We need to **get rid of** all this rubbish.*
- **to remove**
- **to throw away**
- **to throw out**
- **to dispose of**
- **to destroy**

ridiculous adjective

*That's a **ridiculous** thing to say!*
- **silly**
- **absurd**
- **foolish**
- **stupid**
- **ludicrous**
- **preposterous**
- **crazy**

OPPOSITE sensible

right adjective

1 *All my answers were **right**.*
- **correct**
- **accurate**
- **spot-on**
   Use **spot-on** when something is exactly right:
   *I guessed he weighed 24 kilos, and I was **spot-on**.*

2 *Is that the **right** time?*
- **exact**
- **precise**

3 *I haven't got the **right** books.*
- **appropriate**
- **suitable**
- **proper**

4 *It's **right** to own up when you've been naughty.*
- **honest**
- **fair**
- **good**
- **sensible**
- **honourable**

OPPOSITE wrong

ring noun

*We all stood in a **ring**.*
- **a circle**

ring verb

1 *I could hear bells **ringing**.*
- **to sound**
- **to chime**
- **to peal**
- **to tinkle**
- **to jingle**
   Use **chime** or **peal** to describe the sound of large bells:
   *The church bells **chimed**.*
   Use **tinkle** or **jingle**, to describe the sound of small bells:
   *The bells around the horse's neck **jingled** as it trotted along.*

2 *I'll **ring** you later.*
- **to call**
- **to phone**
- **to telephone**

riot noun

*There was a **riot** in the street.*
- **a disturbance**
- **a commotion**

rip verb

*I **ripped** my jeans.*
- **to tear**
- **to split**

rise verb

1 *I watched the balloon **rise** into the sky.*
- **to climb**
- **to ascend**
- **to soar**
  Use **soar** when something rises very high:
  *The eagle **soared** high into the sky.*
  OPPOSITE descend
2 *The sun was **rising** when we got up.*
- **to come up**
  OPPOSITE set
3 *Bus fares are going to **rise** next week.*
- **to increase**
- **to go up**
  OPPOSITE fall

risk noun

*There is a **risk** that you might fall.*
- **a danger**
- **a chance**
- **a possibility**

rival noun

*On Saturday we're playing against our old **rivals**.*
- **an opponent**
- **an adversary**
- **an enemy**

river noun

*We walked along next to the **river**.*
- **a stream**
- **a brook**
- **a canal**
  *A **stream** or **brook** is a small river:*
  *There was a little **stream** at the bottom of the garden.*
  *A **canal** is a man-made river:*
  *In the past, goods were transported along **canals**.*

WRITING TIPS

Here are some useful words for writing about rivers.
- They sailed along the **wide**, **meandering** river.
- The river here is **broad** and **slow-moving**.
- They came to the edge of a **deep**, **fast-moving** river.
- The **mighty** river **flows** towards the sea.
- A river **winds** through the field.
- A **shallow** river **runs** through the middle of the forest.
- We watched the river **rushing** past.

---

road noun

1 *This is the **road** where I live.*
- **a street**
- **an avenue**
- **a close**
2 *There is a narrow **road** between the two farms.*
- **a track**
- **a path**
- **a lane**
- **an alley**
3 *We drove along the **road** between Birmingham and London.*
- **a main road**
- **a motorway**

roar verb

*The crowd **roared**.*
- **to bellow**
- **to shout** →

a
b
c
d
e
f
g
h
i
j
k
l
m
n
o
p
q
r
s
t
u
v
w
x
y
z

- **to cry**
- **to yell**

robber noun

The **robbers** managed to escape.
- **a burglar**
- **a thief**
- **a crook**
- **a pickpocket**
- **a shoplifter**

rock noun

He picked up a **rock** and hurled it into the sea.
- **a stone**
- **a boulder**
  A **boulder** is a very big rock:
  We had to climb over some huge
  boulders.

rock verb

1 The little boat **rocked** gently in the breeze.
- **to sway**
- **to swing**
2 The ship **rocked** violently in the storm.
- **to roll**
- **to toss**
- **to pitch**

roll verb

The logs **rolled** down the hill.
- **to spin**
- **to tumble**
- **to slide**

room noun

Is there enough **room** for me to sit down?
- **space**

rope noun

The boat was tied up with a strong **rope**.

- **a cable**
- **a line**
- **a cord**

rotten adjective

1 The wood was old and **rotten**.
- **decayed**
- **decomposed**
OPPOSITE sound
2 We couldn't eat the meat because it was **rotten**.
- **bad**
- **mouldy**
- **off**
  Use **mouldy** for cheese:
  There was some **mouldy** old cheese in the fridge.
  Use **off** for meat and fish:
  We can't eat this meat. It's gone **off**.
OPPOSITE fresh
3 That was a **rotten** thing to do!
- **nasty**
- **unkind**
- **mean**
- **horrible**
OPPOSITE good

rough adjective

1 We jolted along the **rough** road.
- **bumpy**
- **uneven**
- **stony**
- **rocky**
OPPOSITE even
2 Sandpaper feels **rough**.
- **coarse**
- **scratchy**
- **prickly**
OPPOSITE smooth
3 He spoke in a **rough** voice.
- **gruff**
- **husky**
- **hoarse**
OPPOSITE soft

a b c d e f g h i j k l m n o p q r s t u v w x y z

4 *The sea was very **rough**.*
- **stormy**
- **choppy**

OPPOSITE calm

5 *I don't like **rough** games.*
- **boisterous**
- **rowdy**

OPPOSITE gentle

6 *Don't be so **rough** with your little brother.*
- **violent**
- **aggressive**

OPPOSITE gentle

7 *At a **rough** guess, I would say there were fifty people there.*
- **approximate**
- **estimated**

OPPOSITE exact

round adjective
*He was wearing a **round** badge.*
- **circular**

row (*rhymes with* cow) noun

1 *I had a **row** with my sister.*
- **an argument**
- **a quarrel**
- **a squabble**
- **a disagreement**
- **a fight**

2 *What's that terrible **row**?*
- **noise**
- **din**
- **racket**
- **rumpus**
- **uproar**

row (*rhymes with* toe) noun
*We stood in a straight **row**.*
- **a line**
- **a queue**

rub verb

1 *He **rubbed** the paint to see if it would come off.*
- **to scratch**
- **to scrape**

2 *He **rubbed** the old coin to make it shine.*
- **to clean**
- **to polish**

rub out verb
*She **rubbed** out what she had just written.*
- **to erase**
- **to remove**
- **to delete**

rubbish noun

1 *The **rubbish** is collected from people's homes once a week.*
- **refuse**
- **waste**
- **garbage** (*American*)
- **trash** (*American*)

2 *There was **rubbish** all over the playground.*
- **litter**

3 *The garage is full of old **rubbish**.*
- **junk**

4 *You're talking **rubbish**!*
- **nonsense**
- **balderdash**
- **drivel**

rude adjective

1 *Don't be **rude** to your teacher.*
- **cheeky**
- **impertinent**
- **impudent**
- **insolent**
- **disrespectful**

2 *It's **rude** to interrupt when someone is talking.*
- **bad-mannered**
- **impolite**

a b c d e f g h i j k l m n o p q r s t u v w x y z

3 *They got told off for telling **rude** jokes.*
- **indecent**
- **dirty**
- **vulgar**

OPPOSITE polite

ruin verb
1 *The storm **ruined** the farmers' crops.*
- **to spoil**
- **to damage**
- **to destroy**
- **to wreck**

2 *The bad weather **ruined** our holiday.*
- **to spoil**
- **to mess up**

rule noun
*It is a school **rule** that all children must wear school uniform.*
- **a regulation**
- **a law**

rule verb
*In the old days, the king used to **rule** the country.*
- **to govern**
- **to control**
- **to run**

ruler noun
*Who is the **ruler** of this country?*
- **a king**
- **a queen**
- **a monarch**
- **a king or queen**
- **a sovereign**
- **a king or queen**
- **an emperor**
- **an empress**
- **a president**

run verb

⚠ **OVERUSED WORD**
Try to vary the words you use to mean *run*. Here are some other words you can use instead.

1 *We **ran** across the field.*
- **to jog**
- **to sprint**
- **to race**
- **to tear**
- **to charge**
- **to fly**
- **to rush**
- **to dash**
- **to hurry**
- **to career**

Use ***jog*** if you run quite slowly: *I sometimes go **jogging** with my dad.*
Use ***sprint**, **race**, **tear**, **charge**,* or ***fly*** if you run as fast as you can: *I **raced** home as fast as I could.*
Use ***rush**, **dash**,* or ***hurry*** if you are running because you are in a hurry: *I **dashed** back home to pick up my PE kit.*
Use ***career*** if you are running fast and out of control: *The two boys came **careering** into the kitchen and knocked over a vase of flowers.*

2 *The dog **ran** towards us.*
- **to bound**
- **to scamper**

3 *The horses **ran** across the field.*
- **to trot**
- **to canter**
- **to gallop**

4 *The little mouse **ran** into its hole.*
- **to scurry**
- **to scuttle**
- **to scamper**

> **5** Our English teacher **runs** a drama club after school.
> • **to be in charge of**
> • **to manage**

run away verb

I chased them but they **ran away**.
• **to escape**
• **to get away**
• **to flee**

runny adjective

The jelly hasn't set yet — it's still **runny**.
• **watery**
• **sloppy**
• **liquid**

rush verb

I **rushed** to the bus stop.
• **to dash**
• **to hurry**
• **to run**
• **to race**

a
b
c
d
e
f
g
h
i
j
k
l
m
n
o
p
q
r
s
t
u
v
w
x
y
z

a
b
c
d
e
f
g
h
i
j
k
l
m
n
o
p
q
r
s
t
u
v
w
x
y
z

Ss

sacred adjective

*The Bible and the Koran are **sacred** books.*
- **holy**
- **religious**

sad adjective

1 *The little boy looked very **sad**.*
- **unhappy**
- **upset**
- **miserable**
- **fed up**
- **dejected**
- **despondent**
- **depressed**
- **gloomy**
- **glum**
- **down in the dumps** (*informal*)
- **disappointed**
- **tearful**
- **heartbroken**

Use **disappointed** if someone is sad because something has gone wrong: *I was really **disappointed** when we lost in the final.*
Use **tearful** if someone is sad and almost crying: *Amy was very **tearful** when her kitten died.*
Use **heartbroken** when someone is extremely sad: *I was **heartbroken** when my best friend moved to another town.*

2 *This is very **sad** news.*
- **upsetting**
- **tragic**
- **depressing**
- **distressing**
- **disappointing**
OPPOSITE happy

safe adjective

1 *Once we reached the house I knew that we were **safe**.*
- **secure**
- **out of danger**
- **out of harm's way**
- **sheltered**
- **protected**
OPPOSITE in danger

2 *The building was destroyed, but all the people were **safe**.*
- **safe and sound**
- **unharmed**
- **unhurt**
- **in one piece**
OPPOSITE hurt

3 *Castles were very **safe** places.*
- **secure**
- **well-protected**
- **well-defended**
- **impregnable**
OPPOSITE dangerous

4 *Is this ladder **safe**?*
- **firm**
- **secure**
- **strong enough**
OPPOSITE dangerous

5 *Tigers are wild animals and are never completely **safe**.*
- **harmless**
- **tame**
OPPOSITE dangerous

sail verb

1 *We're **sailing** to France tomorrow.*
- **to set sail**
- **to go by ship**

2 *We watched the yachts **sailing** on the lake.*
- **to float**
- **to glide**
- **to drift**
- **to bob**

3 *The huge ship **sailed** out of the harbour.*
- **to steam**
- **to chug**

same adjective
*The houses look the **same**.*
- **identical**
- **similar**
- **alike**
OPPOSITE **different**

satisfactory adjective
*Your work is **satisfactory**, but I think you could do better.*
- **all right**
- **OK**
- **acceptable**
- **fair**
- **adequate**
OPPOSITE **unsatisfactory**

satisfied adjective
*The teacher was **satisfied** with the children's behaviour.*
- **pleased**
- **happy**
OPPOSITE **dissatisfied**

save verb
1 *A firefighter climbed into the burning building to **save** her.*
- **to rescue**
- **to free**
- **to release**
- **to liberate**
   Use **rescue** when you save someone from danger:
   *A lifeboat was sent out to **rescue** the men on the boat.*
   Use **free**, **release**, or **liberate** when you save someone who is a prisoner:
   *She opened the cage and **liberated** the birds.*
2 *I'm going to **save** this money.*
- **to keep**
- **to put aside** *I'm going to put this money aside.*

say verb

⚠ **OVERUSED WORD**
Try to vary the words you use to mean *say*. Here are some other words you can use instead.
*'It's time to leave,' she **said**.*
Use **add** when someone says something more:
*'I've got some money,' he said. 'About £5,' he **added**.*
Use **ask** or **enquire** when someone asks a question:
*'How old are you?' the policeman **asked**.*
Use **complain** or **moan** when someone is not happy about something:
*'You didn't wait for me,' she **moaned**.*
Use **confess** or **admit** when someone admits they have done something wrong:
*'I'm afraid I've spent all your money,' George **confessed**.*
Use **suggest** when someone makes a suggestion:
*'Let's go and find something to eat,' Dora **suggested**.*
Use **announce** or **declare** when someone says something important:
*'We must leave tomorrow,' he **announced**.*
Use **answer**, **reply**, or **respond** when someone is giving an answer:
*George thought about the question, then **answered**, 'No.'*
Use **shout**, **cry**, **yell**, **scream**, or **shriek** when someone says something very loudly:
*'You idiot!' **yelled** Matt.*
Use **mutter**, **mumble**, **murmur**, or **whisper** when someone says something very quietly: →

a
b
c
d
e
f
g
h
i
j
k
l
m
n
o
p
q
r
s
t
u
v
w
x
y
z

*'I'm sorry,' she **muttered** quietly.*
Use **snap**, **growl**, or **snarl** when someone says something angrily:
*'Be quiet!' **snapped** Katie.*
Use **stutter**, **stammer**, or **splutter** when someone has difficulty saying the words:
*'I d-d-don't know,' she **stammered**.*
Use **laugh** if someone is laughing while they speak:
*'That's so funny!' he **laughed**.*
Use **sneer**, **scoff**, or **jeer** if someone is making fun of another person:
*'You'll never win the race on that old bike,' Tim **scoffed**.*
Use **chorus** when a lot of people say something together:
*'Yes, Miss Edwards,' **chorused** the girls.*

saying noun
*Do you know that **saying** about too many cooks?*
- **a proverb**
- **an expression**
- **a phrase**

scare verb
*Some of the scenes in the film really **scared** me.*
- **to frighten**
- **to terrify**
- **to startle**
- **to give someone a fright**
- **to make someone jump**
Use **terrify** when something scares you a lot:
*The thought of starting a new school **terrified** me.*
Use **startle** or **make someone jump** when something suddenly scares you:
*The phone rang suddenly, which **made me jump**.*

scared adjective
*Are you **scared** of mice?*
- **frightened**
- **afraid**
- **terrified**
- **petrified**
Use **terrified** or **petrified** when you are very scared:
*I was absolutely **terrified** when I saw the giant.*

scary adjective
*The woods were **scary** at night.*
- **frightening**
- **eerie**
- **spooky**
- **terrifying**
Use **eerie** or **spooky** when you think there might be ghosts:
*It was really **eerie** being in the old castle at night.*
Use **terrifying** when something is very scary:
*In front of us stood a **terrifying** monster.*

scramble verb
*We **scrambled** over the rocks.*
- **to climb**
- **to clamber**
- **to crawl**

scrape verb
*We **scraped** the mud off our shoes.*
- **to rub**
- **to clean**
- **to scrub**

scratch verb
1 *Mind you don't **scratch** the paint on the car.*
- **to damage**
- **to scrape**
- **to mark**

2 *His head was itching so he **scratched** it.*
- **to rub**

scream verb
1 *Everyone **screamed** when the ride went faster and faster.*
- **to cry out**
- **to shriek**
- **to squeal**
2 *'Go away!' she **screamed**.*
- **to cry**
- **to shout**
- **to call**
- **to yell**
- **to shriek**
- **to screech**

sea noun
*They sailed across the **sea**.*
- **the ocean**
- **the water**
- **the waves**
- **the deep**

search verb
*I was **searching** for my watch.*
- **to look for**
- **to hunt for**
- **to try to find**

seaside noun
*We **spent** the day at the seaside.*
- **the beach**
- **the coast**

seat noun
*I sat down on a **seat** by the door.*
- **a chair**

🕷 **WORD WEB**
some types of seat
- an armchair
- a bench
- a high chair (*a child's seat*)
- a rocking chair
- a settee
- a sofa
- a stool

secret adjective
1 *She wrote everything down in her **secret** diary.*
- **personal**
- **private**
2 *There is a **secret** garden behind the house.*
- **hidden**
- **concealed**
- **secluded**

see verb
1 *I **saw** a horse in the field.*
- **to notice**
- **to observe**
- **to watch**
- **to spot**
- **to spy**
- **to catch sight of**
- **to glimpse**
- **to catch a glimpse of**
- **to witness**

Use **observe** or **watch** when you look at something for quite a long time:
*You can **observe** birds in your garden.*
Use **spot** or **spy** when you see something that is difficult to see:
*We **spotted** a tiny ship on the horizon.*
Use **catch sight of**, **glimpse**, or **catch a glimpse of** when you see something very quickly and then it disappears:
*I **caught a glimpse of** a deer as it ran through the forest.*
Use **witness** when you see a crime or accident:
*Did anyone **witness** this accident?*
2 *I'm going to **see** my grandma tomorrow.*
- **to visit** →

a b c d e f g h i j k l m n o p q r s t u v w x y z

- **to pay a visit to**
- **to call on**

3 I **see** what you mean.
- **to understand**
- **to know**

seem verb
Everyone **seems** very happy today.
- **to appear**
- **to look**
- **to sound**

seize verb
1 I **seized** the end of the rope.
- **to grab**
- **to take hold of**
- **to clutch**
- **to grasp**
2 The thief **seized** my bag and ran off.
- **to grab**
- **to snatch**
3 The police **seized** the two men.
- **to arrest**
- **to catch**
- **to capture**

select verb
She opened the box and **selected** a chocolate.
- **to choose**
- **to pick**

selfish adjective
You shouldn't be so **selfish**.
- **mean**
- **self-centred**
- **thoughtless**
opposite unselfish

sell verb
1 This shop **sells** exotic tropical fish.
- **to deal in**
- **to stock**

2 I **sold** my old bike to one of my friends.
- **to flog** (informal)

send verb
1 I **sent** a birthday card to my cousin.
- **to post**
2 The teacher **sent** her out of the room.
- **to order**

sense noun
That child has got no **sense**!
- **common sense**
- **intelligence**
- **brains**

sensible adjective
1 She is usually a very **sensible** girl.
- **careful**
- **thoughtful**
- **level-headed**
- **responsible**
- **mature**
- **wise**
2 I think that would be the **sensible** thing to do.
- **logical**
- **prudent**
- **wise**
opposite stupid

sensitive adjective
1 Tom is a very **sensitive** boy.
- **easily hurt**
- **easily upset**
- **touchy**
opposite insensitive
2 You shouldn't use this suncream if you have **sensitive** skin.
- **delicate**

separate adjective
1 We need to keep the two piles **separate**.
- **apart**

2 *The two brothers sleep in **separate** bedrooms.*
- **different**
OPPOSITE together

separate verb
1 *It's a good idea to **separate** the foreign stamps from the British ones.*
- **to divide**
- **to split**
- **to remove**
2 *The two girls wouldn't stop talking, so the teacher **separated** them.*
- **to move**
- **to split up** *The teacher split them up.*
- **to break up** *The teacher broke them up.*

series noun
*There has been a **series** of accidents in the playground.*
- **a succession**
- **a string**

serious adjective
1 *The old man was looking very **serious**.*
- **sad**
- **solemn**
- **grave**
- **thoughtful**
OPPOSITE cheerful
2 *Are you **serious** about wanting to help?*
- **sincere**
- **genuine**
OPPOSITE insincere
3 *This is a very **serious** problem.*
- **important**
- **significant**
- **difficult**
OPPOSITE unimportant
4 *Several people were hurt in the **serious** accident.*
- **bad**
- **terrible**

- **awful**
- **dreadful**
OPPOSITE minor
5 *She has a very **serious** illness.*
- **bad**
- **dangerous**
- **life-threatening**
OPPOSITE minor

set noun
*I need to get one more card, then I'll have the whole **set**.*
- **a collection**
- **a series**

set verb
1 *The teacher forgot to **set** us any homework.*
- **to give**
2 *We'll camp for the night when the sun **sets**.*
- **to go down**
3 *Has the glue **set** yet?*
- **to harden**
- **to solidify**

set off verb
*We'll **set off** early tomorrow morning.*
- **to leave**
- **to depart**
- **to set out**

settle down verb
*She **settled down** to watch a film.*
- **to sit down**
- **to sit back**
- **to make yourself comfortable** *She made herself comfortable.*

shade noun
*Stay in the **shade** if it's very hot.*
- **the shadow**

a
b
c
d
e
f
g
h
i
j
k
l
m
n
o
p
q
r
s
t
u
v
w
x
y
z

shadow noun
> We sat in the **shadow** of a big tree.
> • **the shade**

shady adjective
> We found a **shady** place to eat our lunch.
> • **cool**
> • **shaded**
> OPPOSITE sunny

shake verb
> **1** I picked up the money box and **shook** it.
> • **to rattle**
> **2** The man **shook** his fist at me.
> • **to wave**
> • **to waggle**
> **3** The whole house seemed to **shake**.
> • **to move**
> • **to rock**
> • **to sway**
> • **to wobble**
> • **to vibrate**
> • **to shudder**
> **4** The old truck **shook** as it drove along the bumpy lane.
> • **to judder**
> • **to jolt**
> • **to rattle**
> **5** I was **shaking** with fear.
> • **to tremble**
> • **to quake**
> • **to quiver**
> • **to shiver**
> • **to shudder**

shame noun
> **1** His face was red with **shame**.
> • **embarrassment**
> • **guilt**
> • **humiliation**
> • **disgrace**
> **2** It's a **shame** you can't come to the party.
> • **a pity**

shape noun
> **1** In the darkness I could just see the **shape** of a building.
> • **the outline**
> **2** He's a powerful magician who can take on any **shape** he chooses.
> • **a form**

WORD WEB
some different shapes
• a circle
• a heptagon
• a hexagon
• an octagon
• an oval
• a pentagon
• a polygon
• a quadrilateral
• a square
• a rectangle
• a triangle

some 3D shapes
• a cone
• a cube
• a cuboid
• a cylinder
• a prism
• a pyramid
• a sphere

---

share noun
> Don't worry, you will get your **share** of the money.
> • **a part**
> • **a portion**

share verb
> We **shared** the food between us.
> • **to divide**
> • **to split**

sharp adjective
> **1** Be careful, that knife is **sharp**.
> • **razor-sharp**
> OPPOSITE blunt

2 It hurt our feet walking over the **sharp** rocks.
- **pointed**
- **jagged**

OPPOSITE smooth

3 A hedgehog's body is covered in **sharp** spines.
- **prickly**
- **spiky**

OPPOSITE smooth

4 There was a **sharp** bend in the road.
- **sudden**
- **tight**

OPPOSITE gradual

5 He's a very **sharp** boy.
- **clever**
- **intelligent**
- **bright**
- **brainy**
- **quick**
- **smart**

OPPOSITE stupid

shed noun

There's a **shed** at the bottom of the garden.
- **a hut**
- **an outhouse**
- **a shack**

shed verb

1 Some trees **shed** their leaves in the winter.
- **to drop**
- **to lose**

2 Snakes **shed** their old skin each year.
- **to cast off**

sheet noun

Have you got a spare **sheet** of paper?
- **a piece**
- **a page**

shelter noun

The trees gave us some **shelter** from the rain.
- **protection**
- **refuge**
- **cover**

shelter verb

1 We **sheltered** from the storm in an old barn.
- **to hide**
- **to stay safe**

2 The hedge **sheltered** us from the wind.
- **to protect**
- **to shield**

shine verb

1 The sun **shone** all day.
- **to be out** The sun was out all day.
- **to blaze down**
- **to beat down**

2 I saw a light **shining** in the distance.
- **to glow**
- **to glimmer**
- **to gleam**
- **to shimmer**
- **to flash**
- **to flicker**
- **to twinkle**
- **to sparkle**
- **to glint**
- **to glitter**

Use **glow**, **glimmer**, **gleam**, or **glimmer** when something shines gently:
The light from the fire **glowed** softly in the darkness.

Use **flash** when a light shines on and off:
The light from the lighthouse **flashed** in the darkness.

Use **flicker**, **twinkle**, or **sparkle** when a light shines in an unsteady way, like a star:
The lights on the Christmas tree **flickered** and **sparkled**.

Use **glint** or **glitter** when something made of metal or glass shines:
His sword **glinted** in the moonlight.

a b c d e f g h i j k l m n o p q r s t u v w x y z

a
b
c
d
e
f
g
h
i
j
k
l
m
n
o
p
q
r
s
t
u
v
w
x
y
z

shiny adjective
1 *We found a **shiny** new coin.*
  • **bright**
  • **gleaming**
2 *He was wearing **shiny** shoes.*
  • **polished**
3 *We printed our designs on **shiny** paper.*
  • **glossy**
  OPPOSITE dull

shiver verb
1 *I was **shivering** with cold.*
  • **to shake**
2 *She was **shivering** with fear.*
  • **to shake**
  • **to tremble**
  • **to quake**
  • **to quiver**
  • **to shudder**

shock verb
1 *The explosion **shocked** everyone.*
  • **to frighten**
  • **to alarm**
  • **to shake**
2 *News of the terrible accident **shocked** us all.*
  • **to upset**
  • **to distress**
3 *The swearing in the film **shocked** us.*
  • **to offend**
  • **to disgust**
  • **to horrify**

shocked adjective
1 *I felt quite **shocked** when I realized I had won.*
  • **surprised**
  • **astonished**
  • **astounded**
  • **staggered**
2 *Everyone was **shocked** by the terrible accident.*
  • **upset**
  • **distressed**
  • **traumatized**
3 *I was **shocked** when I heard the children swearing.*
  • **disgusted**
  • **appalled**
  • **horrified**

shoe noun

WORD WEB
some types of shoe
• boots
• plimsolls
• pumps
• sandals
• slippers
• trainers
• wellingtons

shoot verb
  *Try to **shoot** straight.*
  • **to fire**
  • **to aim**

shop noun
  *You can buy sweets in the **shop** on the corner.*
  • **a store**

WORD WEB
some big shops
• a department store
• a hypermarket
• a supermarket

some other types of shop
• a baker
• a book shop
• a boutique
• a butcher
• a chemist
• a clothes shop
• a delicatessen
• a fishmonger
• a florist
• a gift shop

• a grocer
• an ironmonger
• a jeweller
• a music shop
• a newsagent
• a post office
• a shoe shop
• a toy shop

short adjective

1 I'm quite **short** for my age.
• **small**
• **little**
OPPOSITE tall

2 It was a strange animal, with a long body and **short** legs.
• **stumpy**
• **stubby**
OPPOSITE long

3 It was just a **short** visit.
• **brief**
• **fleeting**
• **quick**

shout verb

'You're here at last!' he **shouted**.
• **to yell**
• **to cry**
• **to call**
• **to bawl**
• **to bellow**
• **to scream**
• **to shriek**
• **to cheer**
• **to jeer**
Use **scream** or **shriek** when someone is very frightened or excited:
'Help!' she **screamed**.
Use **cheer** when people are happy about something:
'Hooray!' they **cheered**.
Use **jeer** when people are making fun of someone:
'You're useless!' they **jeered**.
OPPOSITE whisper

show noun

We're putting on a school **show** at the end of term.
• **a performance**
• **a production**
• **a play**
• **a concert**

show verb

1 Shall I **show** you my new bike?
• **to let someone see** I'll let you see my new bike.

2 He **showed** me the place where the accident happened.
• **to point to**
• **to indicate** He indicated the place where the accident happened.

3 We **showed** our work to the visitors.
• **to display**
• **to exhibit**

4 She **showed** me how to use the computer.
• **to tell**
• **to teach**
• **to explain** She explained to me how to use the computer.

show off verb

Stop **showing off**!
• **to boast**
• **to brag**
• **to gloat**

shrivel verb

The plants **shrivelled** in the heat.
• **to dry up**
• **to wither**

shut verb

She went out of the room and **shut** the door.
• **to close**
• **to fasten** →

a
b
c
d
e
f
g
h
i
j
k
l
m
n
o
p
q
r
s
t
u
v
w
x
y
z

- **to pull shut**
- **to push shut**
- **to lock**
- **to bolt**
- **to slam**
- **to bang**
  Use **lock** or **bolt** when you shut something and lock it:
  He **bolted** the door securely when he left.
  Use **slam** or **bang** when you shut something noisily:
  She ran out and **slammed** the door angrily.
  OPPOSITE open

shut up verb
  The boy told us to **shut up**.
- **to be quiet**
- **to keep quiet**
- **to be silent**

shy adjective
  He was too **shy** to say that he knew the answer.
- **nervous**
- **timid**
- **bashful**
- **modest**

sick adjective
1 I stayed off school because I was **sick**.
- **ill**
- **unwell**
- **poorly**
2 After eating all that chocolate I felt really **sick**.
- **queasy**

side noun
1 Some people were standing at one **side** of the field.
- **an edge**

2 We waited at the **side** of the road.
- **the edge**
- **the verge**

sight noun
  She is quite old and doesn't have very good **sight**.
- **eyesight**
- **vision**

sign noun
1 The **sign** for a dollar is $.
- **a symbol**
- **a logo**
2 There was a **sign** telling people to keep off the grass.
- **a notice**
- **a signpost**
3 I'll give you a **sign** when I'm ready for you to start.
- **a signal**
- **a gesture**

signal noun
  Don't move until I give the **signal**.
- **a sign**
- **a gesture**

silent adjective
1 The hall was empty and **silent**.
- **quiet**
- **peaceful**
- **noiseless**
  OPPOSITE noisy
2 The teacher told us to be **silent**.
- **quiet**
  OPPOSITE talkative
3 I asked him some questions, but he remained **silent**.
- **tight-lipped**

silly adjective
1 It's **silly** to go out in the rain.
- **daft**
- **foolish**

- **stupid**
- **unwise**

2 *Please stop this **silly** behaviour.*
- **childish**
- **immature**

3 *Why are you wearing such **silly** clothes?*
- **ridiculous**
- **peculiar**
- **odd**
- **unsuitable**

similar adjective
*The two girls look quite **similar**.*
- **alike**
- **identical**
- **the same**
OPPOSITE different

simple adjective
1 *That's a **simple** question.*
- **easy**
- **straightforward**
- **clear**
- **obvious**
OPPOSITE difficult

2 *We used quite a **simple** design for our poster.*
- **plain**
- **not fancy**
OPPOSITE elaborate

sing verb
1 *He was **singing** quietly to himself.*
- **to hum**
2 *The birds were **singing** in the trees.*
- **to chirp**
- **to cheep**
- **to twitter**
- **to warble**

sink verb
*The ship **sank** in a storm.*
- **to go down**

- **to founder**
- **to be submerged** *The ship was submerged.*

site noun
*This would be a very good **site** for the new school.*
- **a place**
- **a spot**
- **a position**
- **a location**

situation noun
1 *This is a terrible **situation**.*
- **a state of affairs**
2 *I wouldn't like to be in your **situation**.*
- **a position**

size noun
*What is the **size** of this room?*
- **the measurements**
- **the dimensions**
- **the length**
- **the width**
- **the breadth**
- **the height**

skate verb
*He **skated** gracefully over the ice.*
- **to glide**
- **to slide**
- **to float**

skilful adjective
*He is a **skilful** player.*
- **talented**
- **clever**
- **competent**

skill noun
*Everyone admired her **skill**.*
- **ability** →

a
b
c
d
e
f
g
h
i
j
k
l
m
n
o
p
q
r
s
t
u
v
w
x
y
z

a
b
c
d
e
f
g
h
i
j
k
l
m
n
o
p
q
r
s
t
u
v
w
x
y
z

• **talent**
• **expertise**

skin noun
1 Their clothes were made of animal **skins**.
• **a hide**
• **a fur**
• **a pelt**
2 You can eat the **skin** on some fruits but not others.
• **the rind**
• **the peel**

skip verb
1 She **skipped** happily down the road.
• **to dance**
• **to prance**
• **to trip**
• **to trot**
2 The lambs were **skipping** about in the fields.
• **to jump**
• **to leap**
• **to frisk**
• **to prance**

sledge noun
The children were playing on **sledges**.
• **a toboggan**
• **a sleigh** (a big sledge that is pulled by animals)

sleep verb
1 He was **sleeping** in front of the fire.
• **to be asleep**
• **to fall asleep**
• **to doze**
• **to snooze**
• **to slumber**
• **to snore**
• **to have a nap**
• **to nod off**

2 Some animals **sleep** all winter.
• **to hibernate**

sleepy adjective
I was **sleepy** so I went to bed.
• **tired**
• **drowsy**
• **weary**
OPPOSITE wide awake

slide verb
1 The sledge **slid** across the ice.
• **to glide**
• **to skim**
• **to slither**
2 The car **slid** on the icy road.
• **to skid**
• **to slip**

slight adjective
We've got a **slight** problem.
• **small**
• **little**
• **minor**
• **unimportant**

slim adjective
She was tall and **slim**.
• **thin**
• **slender**

slip verb
1 Sam **slipped** and fell over.
• **to trip**
• **to stumble**
• **to lose your balance** He lost his balance.
2 The wheels kept **slipping** on the wet road.
• **to slide**
• **to skid**

slippery adjective
*Take care: the floor is **slippery**.*
- slippy
- greasy
- oily
- slimy
- icy
- slithery

slope noun
*We climbed up the steep **slope** to the castle.*
- a hill
- a bank
- a rise

slope verb
1 *The beach **slopes** down to the sea.*
- to drop
- to dip
- to fall
2 *The field **slopes** gently upwards towards a wood.*
- to rise
3 *The floor **slopes** to one side.*
- to tilt
- to slant
- to lean

sloppy adjective
1 *The mixture was still too **sloppy**.*
- wet
- runny
- watery
2 *This is a very **sloppy** piece of work!*
- careless
- messy
- untidy
- shoddy

slot noun
*I put a coin in the **slot**.*
- a slit
- an opening
- a groove

slow adjective
1 *They were walking at a **slow** pace.*
- steady
- leisurely
- unhurried
- dawdling
2 *We got stuck behind a **slow** lorry on the main road.*
- slow-moving
3 *He made a **slow** recovery from his illness.*
- steady
- gradual
OPPOSITE quick

sly adjective
*They say the fox is a **sly** animal.*
- clever
- crafty
- cunning
- wily
- devious

smack verb
*Don't **smack** your little brother!*
- to slap
- to hit
- to spank

small adjective
1 *He handed me a **small** box.*
- little
- tiny
- titchy (*informal*)
- minute
  Use **tiny**, **titchy**, or **minute** for something that is very small:
  *She was riding a strange-looking bike with **tiny** wheels.*
2 *They live in a **small** flat.*
- little
- tiny →

a
b
c
d
e
f
g
h
i
j
k
l
m
n
o
p
q
r
s
t
u
v
w
x
y
z

- **cramped**
- **poky**
  Use **cramped** or **poky** for a room or building that is too small:
  Our classroom would feel very **cramped** with 50 children in it.
3 I'm quite **small** for my age.
  - **short**
  - **slight**
  - **petite**
4 She gave us **small** helpings.
  - **mean**
  - **measly**
  - **stingy**
5 This dress is too **small** for me.
  - **tight**
  - **short**
6 It's only a **small** problem.
  - **little**
  - **slight**
  - **minor**
  OPPOSITE big

smart adjective
1 You look very **smart** in your new clothes.
  - **neat**
  - **elegant**
  - **stylish**
  - **well-dressed**
  - **chic**
  OPPOSITE scruffy
2 He's a **smart** boy.
  - **clever**
  - **intelligent**
  - **bright**
  - **sharp**
  OPPOSITE stupid

smear verb
The baby had **smeared** jam all over the walls.
  - **to wipe**
  - **to rub**

- **to spread**
- **to daub**

smell noun
What's that **smell**?
  - **a scent**
  - **a perfume**
  - **a fragrance**
  - **an aroma**
  - **a stink**
  - **a stench**
  - **an odour**
  A **scent**, **perfume**, or **fragrance** is a nice smell, like the smell of perfume or flowers:
  These roses have a lovely **scent**.
  An **aroma** is a nice smell of food cooking:
  A delicious **aroma** of fresh bread was coming from the kitchen.
  A **stink**, **stench**, or **odour** is a nasty smell:
  There was a horrible **stink** of sweaty socks!

smell verb
Your feet **smell**!
  - **to stink**
  - **to reek**
  - **to pong**

smile verb
She looked up and **smiled** at me.
  - **to grin**
  - **to beam**
  - **to smirk**
  Use **grin** or **beam** when someone smiles because they are happy:
  The children **beamed** when they saw the presents.
  Use **smirk** when someone smiles in an annoying way:
  Henry **smirked** at me when I got told off.

smoke noun

*The room was full of black **smoke**.*
- **fumes**

smooth adjective

1 *Roll out the dough on a **smooth** surface.*
- **level**
- **even**
- **flat**

OPPOSITE uneven

2 *I stroked the cat's lovely **smooth** fur.*
- **soft**
- **silky**
- **velvety**
- **sleek**

OPPOSITE rough

3 *We rowed across the **smooth** surface of the lake.*
- **calm**
- **flat**
- **still**

OPPOSITE rough

snatch verb

*The dog **snatched** the sandwich out of my hand.*
- **to grab**
- **to take**
- **to pull**
- **to seize**

sneak verb

*She **sneaked** out of the room when no one was looking.*
- **to creep**
- **to slip**
- **to steal**

soft adjective

1 *Work the clay with your hands until it is nice and **soft**.*
- **doughy**
- **squashy**
- **malleable**

OPPOSITE hard

2 *The bed was warm and **soft**.*
- **springy**

OPPOSITE hard

3 *The kitten's coat was lovely and **soft**.*
- **smooth**
- **fluffy**
- **furry**
- **silky**
- **velvety**

OPPOSITE rough

4 *Our feet sank into the **soft** ground.*
- **boggy**
- **marshy**
- **spongy**
- **squashy**

OPPOSITE hard

5 *There was **soft** music playing in the background.*
- **quiet**
- **gentle**
- **low**
- **soothing**
- **restful**

OPPOSITE loud

soil noun

*You plant seeds in the **soil**.*
- **earth**
- **ground**

soldier noun

*They have sent **soldiers** to fight the terrorists.*
- **troops** *They have sent troops.*
- **the army** *They have sent the army.*

solid adjective

1 *The walls are **solid**.*
- **dense**
- **rigid**
- **strong**

OPPOSITE hollow

a
b
c
d
e
f
g
h
i
j
k
l
m
n
o
p
q
r
s
t
u
v
w
x
y
z

a
b
c
d
e
f
g
h
i
j
k
l
m
n
o
p
q
r
s
t
u
v
w
x
y
z

2 *Water becomes **solid** when it freezes.*
- **hard**
- **firm**

OPPOSITE soft

solve verb
*Have you **solved** the mystery yet?*
- **to work out**
- **to figure out**
- **to get to the bottom of**

song noun
*As he walked along he sang a little **song**.*
- **a tune**
- **a ditty**

WORD WEB
some types of song
- an anthem
- a ballad
- a carol (*a Christmas song*)
- a folk song
- a hymn (*a religious song*)
- a lullaby (*a song to send a baby to sleep*)
- a nursery rhyme
- a pop song
- a rap

---

sore adjective
*My knee is **sore**.*
- **hurting**
- **painful**
- **aching**
- **throbbing**
- **bruised**
- **tender**
  Use **aching** if something is sore for a long time:
  *I sat down to rest my **aching** feet.*
  Use **throbbing** if something is sore with a banging pain:

*My knee was still **throbbing**.*
Use **bruised** if something has a bruise on it:
*Mum gently bathed my **bruised** knee.*
Use **tender** if something is sore when you touch it:
*I can walk around now, but my leg is still a bit **tender**.*

sorry adjective
1 *He was **sorry** when he saw the damage he had done.*
- **apologetic**
- **ashamed**
- **upset**
- **remorseful**

OPPOSITE unrepentant
2 *I feel **sorry** for the little girl.*
- **sympathetic** *I feel sympathetic towards the little girl.*

OPPOSITE unsympathetic

sort noun
1 *What **sort** of sandwich do you want?*
- **a type**
- **a kind**
- **a variety**
2 *A terrier is a **sort** of dog.*
- **a breed**
3 *A ladybird is a **sort** of beetle.*
- **a species**
4 *What **sort** of trainers do you want to buy?*
- **a brand**
- **a make**

sort verb
*We **sorted** the books into three different piles.*
- **to arrange**
- **to group**
- **to organize**

sound noun

*I heard a strange **sound** coming from the kitchen.*
- **a noise**

> **WORD WEB**
>
> **some loud sounds**
> - bang
> - boom
> - buzz
> - clang
> - clank
> - clatter
> - crash
> - pop
> - rattle
> - ring
> - roar
> - rumble
> - thud
> - thump
> - whistle
>
> **some gentle sounds**
> - bleep
> - click
> - drip
> - fizz
> - hum
> - plop
> - splash
> - tick
> - whirr

sour adjective

*Lemon has a **sour** taste.*
- **bitter**
- **sharp**
- **acid**
- **tart**

OPPOSITE sweet

space noun

1 *Is there enough **space** for me there?*
- **room**
2 *We squeezed through a **space** between the two rocks.*
- a gap
- a hole
- an opening

spacecraft noun

*I would love to go in a **spacecraft**.*
- **a spaceship**
- **a rocket**
- **a space shuttle**

spare adjective

*Remember to take a **spare** pair of shoes.*
- **extra**
- **additional**

sparkle verb

*The sea **sparkled** in the sunlight.*
- **to shine**
- **to glisten**
- **to shimmer**
- **to glint**

speak verb

*Everyone started to **speak** at once.*
- **to talk**
- **to say something**
- **to start a conversation**

special adjective

1 *Your birthday is a very **special** day.*
- **important**
- **significant**
- **unusual**
- **extraordinary**
2 *I've got my own **special** mug.*
- **personal**
- **individual**
- **particular**

OPPOSITE ordinary

spectacular adjective

*We watched a **spectacular** fireworks display.*
- **exciting**
- **impressive** →

a b c d e f g h i j k l m n o p q r s t u v w x y z

- **magnificent**
- **wonderful**

speech noun
The winner had to give a **speech**.
- **a talk**
- **a lecture**

speed noun
1 We were walking at a fairly average **speed**.
- **a pace**
2 The pilot told us the height and **speed** of the aeroplane.
- **velocity**
3 They worked with amazing **speed**.
- **quickness**
- **swiftness**
- **haste**

speed verb
A sports car **sped** past us.
- **to shoot**
- **to zoom**
- **to whizz**
- **to flash**

spell noun
She was under a magic **spell**.
- **an enchantment**
- **a charm**

spend verb
I've already **spent** all my pocket money.
- **to use**
- **to pay out** I paid out a lot of money for that jacket.

spill verb
1 Mind you don't **spill** your drink.
- **to drop**

- **to knock over**
- **to upset**
2 She **spilt** milk all over the kitchen floor.
- **to drop**
- **to pour**
- **to tip**
- **to slop**
3 Some water had **spilt** on to the floor.
- **to drip**
- **to leak**
- **to splash**
4 Water was **spilling** over the edge of the bath.
- **to pour**
- **to run**
- **to stream**
- **to gush**
- **to splash**

spin verb
1 I **spun** round when I heard his voice.
- **to turn**
- **to whirl**
- **to swivel**
2 We watched the dancers **spinning** across the floor.
- **to twirl**
- **to pirouette**
3 The back wheel of my bike was still **spinning**.
- **to turn**
- **to revolve**
- **to rotate**
- **to go round**

spirit noun
The house is supposed to be haunted by evil **spirits**.
- **a ghost**
- **a phantom**

spiteful adjective
> *That was a very **spiteful** thing to do.*
> - **nasty**
> - **unkind**
> - **horrible**
> - **mean**
> OPPOSITE kind

splash verb
> 1 *They **splashed** us with water.*
> - **to shower**
> - **to spray**
> - **to squirt**
> - **to spatter**
> 2 *They **splashed** water all over the floor.*
> - **to spill**
> - **to slop**
> - **to slosh**

split verb
> 1 *He **split** the log with an axe.*
> - **to cut**
> - **to chop**
> 2 *The bag **split** open and all the shopping fell out.*
> - **to break**
> - **to tear**
> - **to rip**
> 3 *We **split** the chocolate between us.*
> - **to share**
> - **to divide**

spoil verb
> 1 *The water had **spoilt** some of the books.*
> - **to damage**
> - **to ruin**
> 2 *The bad weather **spoilt** our holiday.*
> - **to ruin**
> - **to mess up**

sport noun
> *Do you enjoy **sport**?*
> - **exercise**
> - **games**

WORD WEB
some team sports
- baseball
- basketball
- cricket
- football
- hockey
- ice hockey
- netball
- rounders
- rugby
- volleyball

some individual sports
- athletics
- badminton
- canoeing
- cycling
- fishing
- golf
- gymnastics
- ice skating
- jogging
- judo
- karate
- kick-boxing
- skiing
- snooker
- snowboarding
- swimming
- table tennis
- tae kwondo
- tennis
- trampolining

spot noun
> 1 *Leopards have dark **spots** on their bodies.*
> - **a mark**
> - **a dot**
> - **a blotch**
> - **a patch**
> 2 *Oh, no! I've got a **spot** on my nose!*
> - **a pimple**
> - **acne**
> - **a rash**
> **Acne** *is a lot of spots on your face:*
> *Some teenagers get very bad **acne**.* →

a
b
c
d
e
f
g
h
i
j
k
l
m
n
o
p
q
r
s
t
u
v
w
x
y
z

a
b
c
d
e
f
g
h
i
j
k
l
m
n
o
p
q
r
s
t
u
v
w
x
y
z

A rash is a lot of spots you get when you are ill:
Chickenpox gives you a rash.

3 *There were a few spots of paint on the floor.*
- **a mark**
- **a dot**
- **a drop**
- **a blob**
- **a smear**
- **a smudge**

4 *We found a lovely spot for a picnic.*
- **a place**
- **a site**
- **a location**

spray verb

1 *He sprayed some water on to the plants.*
- **to splash**
- **to sprinkle**
- **to squirt**

2 *She sprayed us with water.*
- **to splash**
- **to shower**
- **to squirt**
- **to spatter**

spread verb

1 *The bird spread its wings and flew away.*
- **to open**
- **to stretch out**

2 *We spread a cloth on the ground.*
- **to lay out**
- **to unfold**
- **to open out**
- **to arrange**

3 *I spread some jam on to the bread.*
- **to put**
- **to smear**

spring verb

The cat crouched, ready to spring on the mouse.
- **to jump**
- **to leap**
- **to pounce**

squabble verb

Those children are always squabbling.
- **to argue**
- **to quarrel**
- **to disagree**
- **to fall out**
- **to fight**
- **to bicker**

squash verb

1 *Mind you don't squash those flowers.*
- **to crush**
- **to flatten**
- **to damage**
- **to break**

2 *We all squashed into the back of the car.*
- **to squeeze**
- **to crowd**

3 *I squashed everything into the suitcase.*
- **to push**
- **to shove**
- **to cram**
- **to squeeze**
- **to jam**

squeeze verb

1 *We all squeezed into the tiny room.*
- **to squash**
- **to crowd**

2 *I squeezed everything into the box.*
- **to push**
- **to shove**
- **to squash**
- **to cram**
- **to jam**

squirt verb
  1 *Water **squirted** out of the hole.*
  • **to spurt**
  • **to gush**
  • **to spray**
  2 *She **squirted** water at me.*
  • **to spray**
  • **to splash**

stable adjective
  *Be careful, the ladder's not very **stable**.*
  • **steady**
  • **firm**
  • **secure**

stack noun
  *I've got a whole **stack** of books to read.*
  • **a heap**
  • **a pile**
  • **a mound**

stage noun
  *We have finished the first **stage** of our journey.*
  • **a part**
  • **a phase**

stain noun
  *Her shirt was covered in **stains**.*
  • **a mark**
  • **a spot**
  • **a smudge**
  • **a smear**

stairs noun
  *She ran down the **stairs**.*
  • **steps**

stale adjective
  *All we had to eat was water and **stale** bread.*
  • **old**
  • **dry**
  • **mouldy**
  OPPOSITE fresh

stand verb
  1 *We all **stood** when the visitors arrived.*
  • **to get up**
  • **to get to your feet** *We all got to our feet.*
  • **to rise** *We all rose.*
  2 *I can't **stand** this noise!*
  • **to bear**
  • **to put up with**
  • **to tolerate**

standard noun
  *The **standard** of your work has improved this term.*
  • **level**
  • **quality**

stare verb
  *Why is that boy **staring** at me?*
  • **to look**
  • **to gaze**
  • **to gape**
  • **to glare**
    *Use **gape** if you stare at someone in a surprised way:*
    *My friends all **gaped** at me as I climbed into the stretch limousine.*
    *Use **glare** if you stare at someone in an angry way:*
    *My aunt **glared** at me angrily, so I knew I had to behave.*

start verb
  1 *What time does the film **start**?*
  • **to begin**
  • **to commence**
  OPPOSITE finish
  2 *We're going to **start** a chess club.*
  • **to set up**
  • **to create**
  • **to establish**
  3 *She **started** the engine.*
  • **to switch on**
  • **to turn on**

a
b
c
d
e
f
g
h
i
j
k
l
m
n
o
p
q
r
s
t
u
v
w
x
y
z

start noun
> When is the **start** of the football season?
> • **the beginning**
> OPPOSITE end

statue noun
> In the main hall is a **statue** of a woman.
> • **a carving**
> • **a sculpture**
> • **a bust** (a statue of someone's head and shoulders)

stay verb
> 1 **Stay** here until I come back.
> • **to remain**
> • **to wait**
> • **to hang around**
> 2 **Stay** on this path until you reach the river.
> • **to continue**
> • **to carry on**
> 3 I'm going to **stay** with my grandma.
> • **to visit**
> 4 I hope it **stays** dry this afternoon.
> • **to remain**

steady adjective
> 1 Make sure the ladder is **steady**.
> • **firm**
> • **stable**
> • **secure**
> OPPOSITE wobbly
> 2 The music had a **steady** rhythm.
> • **even**
> • **regular**
> • **constant**
> OPPOSITE irregular

steal verb
> Someone's **stolen** my purse.
> • **to take**
> • **to pinch**
> • **to nick**

steep adjective
> There was a **steep** drop down to the river.
> • **sharp**
> • **vertical**
> • **sheer**
> OPPOSITE gradual

step noun
> 1 He took a **step** forwards.
> • **a pace**
> • **a stride**
> 2 I climbed up the **steps**.
> • **stairs**

stick noun
> 1 We collected some **sticks** to make a fire.
> • **a twig**
> • **a branch**
> 2 He was holding a long **stick**.
> • **a pole**
> • **a rod**
> • **a cane**
> • **a baton**
> • **a truncheon**
> • **a club**
> • **a walking stick**
> • **a crutch**
>> A **baton** is a stick you use to conduct an orchestra, or in a relay race. A **truncheon** is a stick that a policeman carries. A **club** is a stick you use as a weapon. A **walking stick** or **crutch** is a stick you use to help you walk.

stick verb
> 1 I **stuck** the pictures in my book.
> • **to glue**
> • **to fix**
> 2 Sometimes the door **sticks** a bit.
> • **to jam**
> • **to get stuck**

a b c d e f g h i j k l m n o p q r **s** t u v w x y z

3 She **stuck** a pin into my arm.
- **to jab**
- **to stab**

sticky adjective
She picked up some of the **sticky** mixture.
- **gooey**
- **tacky**
- **gluey**

stiff adjective
1 Use a piece of **stiff** cardboard for the base of the model.
- **hard**
- **rigid**
OPPOSITE soft
2 Mix the ingredients together to make a **stiff** paste.
- **thick**
- **firm**
OPPOSITE soft
3 The door handle was a bit **stiff**.
- **stuck**
- **jammed**
- **difficult to move**
4 I woke up with a **stiff** neck.
- **sore**
- **painful**

still adjective
1 It was a very **still** evening.
- **quiet**
- **calm**
- **peaceful**
2 We all stood perfectly **still**.
- **motionless**

stir verb
She **stirred** the mixture with a spoon.
- **to mix**
- **to beat**
- **to whisk**

stomach noun
I've got a pain in my **stomach**.
- **tummy**
- **belly**

stone noun
He threw a **stone** into the water.
- **a pebble**
- **a rock**
- **a boulder**
A **pebble** is a small round stone: We found some pretty **pebbles** on the beach.
A **rock** is a big stone: We climbed over the **rocks** and down to the sea.
A **boulder** is a very big heavy stone: Huge **boulders** came tumbling down the mountainside.

stop verb
1 The policeman **stopped** the traffic.
- **to halt**
- **to hold up**
2 The bus **stopped** outside the school.
- **to pull up**
- **to draw up**
- **to park**
- **to come to a halt**
- **to grind to a halt**
- **to come to a standstill**
3 He **stopped** for a moment.
- **to hesitate**
- **to pause**
- **to wait**
4 Shall we **stop** for lunch?
- **to break off**
- **to knock off**
5 I wish you would **stop** teasing your little brother!
- **to finish**
- **to quit**
- **to give up** →

a
b
c
d
e
f
g
h
i
j
k
l
m
n
o
p
q
r
s
t
u
v
w
x
y
z

a
b
c
d
e
f
g
h
i
j
k
l
m
n
o
p
q
r
s
t
u
v
w
x
y
z

6 *This silly behaviour has got to stop.*
- **to end**
- **to finish**
- **to come to an end**
- **to cease**

7 *It is time to stop this nonsense.*
- **to end**
- **to put an end to**
- **to put a stop to**

8 *We must stop him from getting away.*
- **to prevent**

store verb
We can store all these boxes in the garage.
- **to keep**
- **to put away**

storm noun
That night there was a terrible storm.
- **a thunderstorm**
- **a blizzard**
- **a gale**
- **a hurricane**
- **a tornado**
   A thunderstorm is a storm with thunder. A blizzard is a storm with snow:
   The blizzard had left huge snowdrifts the next morning.
   A gale, hurricane, or tornado is a storm with a very strong wind:
   A lot of buildings were damaged by the hurricane.

story noun
He told us a story about a fox.
- **a tale**
- **a yarn**

WORD WEB
some types of story
- **an adventure story**
- **a fable**
- **a fairy tale**
- **a fantasy story**
- **a folk tale**
- **a legend**
- **a myth**
- **a parable**
- **a science fiction story**
- **a traditional tale**

straight adjective
That picture isn't straight.
- **level**
- **upright**
OPPOSITE crooked

strain verb
1 *I had to strain to reach the handle.*
- **to struggle**
- **to try hard**
- **to make an effort**

2 *I strained a muscle when I was running.*
- **to hurt**
- **to injure**
- **to damage**

strange adjective
1 *What a strange animal!*
- **funny**
- **peculiar**
- **odd**
- **curious**
- **unusual**
- **extraordinary**
- **remarkable**
OPPOSITE normal

2 *When I woke up I was in a strange place.*
- **different**
- **new**

• **unfamiliar**
• **unknown**
OPPOSITE familiar

stream noun
We paddled across the **stream**.
• **a brook**
• **a river**

street noun
That boy lives in the same **street** as me.
• **a road**
• **an avenue**

strength noun
I had to use all my **strength** to open the door.
• **force**
• **might**
• **power**
• **energy**

stretch verb
You can **stretch** elastic.
• **to pull out**
• **to lengthen**
• **to extend**

strict adjective
Our teacher is quite **strict**.
• **harsh**
• **severe**
• **stern**
• **firm**

string noun
We tied the parcel up with **string**.
• **cord**
• **rope**
• **twine**
• **ribbon**

strip verb
He **stripped** and got into the bath.
• **to undress**
• **to take your clothes off**

stripe noun
She was wearing a blue dress with white **stripes**.
• **a line**
• **a band**

strong adjective
1 You have to be very **strong** to be a weightlifter.
  • **tough**
  • **powerful**
  • **muscular**
  • **brawny**
  • **strapping**
    Use **muscular**, **brawny**, or **strapping** for someone who has big muscles:
    The lifeguard was tall and **muscular**.
2 She's been very ill, and she's not **strong** enough to go outside yet.
  • **well**
  • **fit**
  • **healthy**
3 The rope wasn't **strong** enough to hold my weight.
  • **tough**
  • **thick**
4 The roof must be made of a **strong** material.
  • **tough**
  • **solid**
  • **hard-wearing**
  • **heavy-duty**
  • **durable**
  • **unbreakable**
  • **indestructible**
5 The shelter they had built was quite **strong**.
  • **well-made** →

a
b
c
d
e
f
g
h
i
j
k
l
m
n
o
p
q
r
s
t
u
v
w
x
y
z

a
b
c
d
e
f
g
h
i
j
k
l
m
n
o
p
q
r
s
t
u
v
w
x
y
z

- **well-built**
- **sturdy**

6 *This orange squash is too **strong**.*
- **concentrated**
OPPOSITE weak

struggle verb
1 *The thief **struggled** to get away.*
- **to fight**
- **to wrestle**
2 *We were **struggling** to carry all the boxes.*
- **to try hard**
- **to work hard**

stubborn adjective
*He was **stubborn** and refused to come with us.*
- **obstinate**
- **defiant**
- **wilful**
- **pig-headed**
- **disobedient**

study verb
1 *We're **studying** the Romans at school.*
- **to learn about**
- **to read about**
- **to research**
- **to investigate**
2 *He **studied** the map carefully.*
- **to look at**
- **to examine**

stuff noun
1 *There was some sticky **stuff** on the floor.*
- **a substance** There was a sticky substance on the floor.
2 *We cleared all the old **stuff** out of the cupboards.*
- **things**
- **odds and ends**
- **bits and pieces**

3 *Don't forget to take all your **stuff** with you.*
- **things**
- **belongings**
- **possessions**
- **kit**

stuffy adjective
*The room was **stuffy**.*
- **warm**
- **airless**
OPPOSITE airy

stumble verb
*I **stumbled** over a big stone.*
- **to trip**
- **to slip**
- **to lose your balance**

stupid adjective
1 *That was a **stupid** thing to do!*
- **silly**
- **daft**
- **foolish**
- **unwise**
- **idiotic**
2 *You must be **stupid** if you believe that!*
- **daft**
- **dim**
- **dense**
- **brainless**
- **thick** (informal)
OPPOSITE intelligent

subject noun
*I want to choose an interesting **subject** for my project.*
- **a topic**
- **a theme**

subtract verb
*Can you **subtract** 6 from 9?*
- **to take away**

- **to deduct**
- **to find the difference between**
  Can you find the difference between 6 and 9?

succeed verb
1 *She wants to become a pilot, but I don't know if she'll **succeed**.*
- **to manage**
- **to be successful**
2 *All children should try to **succeed** at school.*
- **to do well**
3 *Did your plan **succeed**?*
- **to work**
- **to be successful** *Was your plan **successful**?*
OPPOSITE fail

success noun
*The concert was a great **success**.*
- **a triumph**
- **a hit**
OPPOSITE failure

sudden adjective
1 *There was a **sudden** change in the weather.*
- **unexpected**
- **abrupt**
2 *He made a **sudden** dash for the door.*
- **quick**
- **swift**
- **hasty**
- **hurried**

suddenly
1 *I realized **suddenly** that I was lost.*
- **all of a sudden**
2 *A man appeared **suddenly** from behind the door.*
- **unexpectedly**
- **without warning**

suffer verb
*I hate to see animals **suffering**.*
- **to be in pain** *I hate to see animals in pain.*

suggest verb
*I **suggested** that we should go back home.*
- **to propose**
- **to advise**
- **to recommend**

suggestion noun
*What do you think we should do? What's your **suggestion**?*
- **an idea**
- **a proposal**
- **a plan**

suit verb
*That dress really **suits** you.*
- **to look nice on** *That dress looks nice on you.*
- **to look right on** *That dress looks right on you.*

suitable adjective
*Is this dress **suitable** for a wedding?*
- **appropriate**
- **right**
OPPOSITE unsuitable

sulk verb
Is Tom still sulking?
- **to be in a mood** *Is Tom still in a mood?*

sulky adjective
*He's been **sulky** all afternoon.*
- **moody**
- **sullen**
- **bad-tempered**
- **grumpy**

a
b
c
d
e
f
g
h
i
j
k
l
m
n
o
p
q
r
s
t
u
v
w
x
y
z

a
b
c
d
e
f
g
h
i
j
k
l
m
n
o
p
q
r
s
t
u
v
w
x
y
z

sunny adjective
*It was a lovely **sunny** day.*
- **bright**
- **fine**
- **clear**
- **cloudless**
OPPOSITE cloudy

super adjective
*That's a **super** painting!*
- **wonderful**
- **marvellous**
- **brilliant**
- **fabulous**
- **fantastic**
- **superb**

supply noun
*There's a **supply** of paper in the cupboard.*
- **a store**
- **a stock**
- **a reserve**

support verb
1 *Those pillars **support** the roof.*
- **to hold up**
- **to prop up**
- **to reinforce**
2 *You should **support** your friends when they are in trouble.*
- **to help**
- **to defend**
- **to stand up for**
- **to stick up for**
3 *We went to **support** our team.*
- **to encourage**
- **to cheer on**

suppose verb
1 *I **suppose** we ought to go home now.*
- **to think**

- **to guess**
- **to reckon**
2 *I **suppose** she must be the new teacher.*
- **to assume**
- **to presume**

sure adjective
1 *I'm **sure** she lives somewhere round here.*
- **certain**
- **positive**
- **convinced**
- **confident**
2 *He's **sure** to remember.*
- **bound**
OPPOSITE unsure

surprise noun
1 *Winning the competition was a complete **surprise**.*
- **a shock**
- **a bombshell**
- **a bolt from the blue**
2 *He looked at me in **surprise**.*
- **amazement**
- **astonishment**
- **wonder**

surprise verb
*It **surprised** everyone when our team won the game.*
- **to amaze**
- **to astonish**
- **to astound**
- **to shock**

surprised adjective
*I was really **surprised** when I saw all the presents.*
- **amazed**
- **astonished**
- **astounded**

- **staggered**
- **flabbergasted**
- **shocked**

surrender verb

After a long fight, the army
surrendered.
- **to give in**
- **to capitulate**
- **to yield**

survive verb

The plane crashed, but all the
passengers survived.
- **to live**
- **to stay alive**

suspect verb

I suspect that he is not telling the truth.
- **to think**
- **to believe**
- **to guess**
- **to have a feeling** *I have a feeling*
  that he is not telling the truth.
- **to have a hunch** *I have a hunch*
  that he is not telling the truth.

swamp noun

We didn't want to get lost in the
swamp.
- **a bog**
- **a marsh**

swear verb

1 *He swore he would never do it again.*
- **to promise**
- **to vow**
- **to give your word** *He gave his*
  word that he would never do it again.
2 *The teacher told him off because he*
swore.
- **to use bad language**
- **to curse**

sweep verb

I swept the floor.
- **to brush**
- **to clean**

sweet adjective

1 *This orange juice is too*
sweet.
- **sugary**
OPPOSITE bitter
2 *That little dog is really sweet!*
- **lovely**
- **lovable**
- **cute**
- **adorable**
OPPOSITE ugly

swim verb

We swam in the river.
- **to bathe**
- **to go swimming**

swing verb

1 *The loose rope was swinging*
backwards and forwards.
- **to sway**
- **to wave**
2 *The monkey was swinging from a*
branch.
- **to hang**
- **to dangle**

switch noun

Don't touch any of those
switches.
- **a button**
- **a knob**
- **a control**

switch verb

I switched the light on.
- **to turn**

a
b
c
d
e
f
g
h
i
j
k
l
m
n
o
p
q
r
s
t
u
v
w
x
y
z

swoop verb

*The owl **swooped** down on its prey.*

- **to dive**
- **to drop**
- **to descend** *The owl descended on its prey.*

sympathy noun

*Everyone gave me a lot of **sympathy** when I was ill.*

- **compassion**
- **understanding**
- **pity**

Tt

take verb

1 *I offered him a sweet and he **took** one.*
- to pick up
- to take hold of
- to grab
- to snatch
- to grasp
  Use **grab**, **snatch**, or **grasp** if someone takes something roughly: *Sara rudely **snatched** the book out of my hands.*

2 *Don't forget to **take** your lunch.*
- to carry
- to bring

3 *The nurse **took** us to the ward.*
- to lead
- to accompany
- to guide

4 *Dad **took** us to the station in his car.*
- to drive
- to transport
- to give someone a lift. *Dad gave us a lift in his car.*

5 *The burglar **took** the jewels.*
- to steal
- to pinch
- to seize
- to run off with

take off verb

*I **took** off my coat.*
- to remove
- to slip off

take out verb

*The dentist **took** out one of my teeth.*
- to remove
- to pull out
- to extract

talent noun

*He's a young tennis player with a lot of **talent**.*
- ability
- skill
- flair
- aptitude

talented adjective

*He is a very **talented** musician.*
- clever
- gifted
- skilful
- able

talk noun

1 *I had a **talk** with my teacher.*
- a chat
- a conversation
- a discussion

2 *Mr Rose gave us a **talk** on owls.*
- a speech
- a lecture

talk verb

1 *We **talked** about our hobbies.*
- to chat
- to converse
- to have a conversation
- to have a discussion

2 *The teacher told us to stop **talking**.*
- to chat
- to chatter
- to natter
- to gossip

tall adjective

1 *She is quite **tall** for her age.*
- big
- lanky
OPPOSITE short →

a
b
c
d
e
f
g
h
i
j
k
l
m
n
o
p
q
r
s
t
u
v
w
x
y
z

2 *There are some very **tall** buildings in the city centre.*
- **big**
- **high**
- **lofty**
- **towering**

OPPOSITE low

tame adjective
*The animals in the zoo are all very **tame**.*
- **gentle**
- **docile**
- **safe**
- **obedient**

OPPOSITE wild

tangled adjective
*The string was all **tangled**.*
- **knotted**
- **twisted**

tap verb
*She **tapped** on the door.*
- **to knock**
- **to rap**

taste noun
1 *The ice cream had a lovely creamy **taste**.*
- **a flavour**
2 *Can I have a **taste** of your chocolate?*
- **a bit**
- **a bite**
- **a piece**
- **a mouthful**
- **a nibble**
3 *He let me have a **taste** of his orange juice.*
- **a sip**
- **a mouthful**

taste verb
*Would you like to **taste** my drink?*
- **to try**
- **to sample**

teach verb
1 *A teacher's job is to **teach** children.*
- **to educate**
2 *My brother **taught** me how to use the computer.*
- **to show**
- **to tell**
- **to train** *He trained us to use the computer.*

tear verb
*Be careful you don't **tear** your dress.*
- **to rip**
- **to split**

tease verb
*Sometimes my friends **tease** me.*
- **to make fun of**
- **to laugh at**
- **to torment**
- **to taunt**

telephone verb
*I'll **telephone** you later.*
- **to phone**
- **to call**
- **to ring**
- **to give someone a ring** (*informal*) *I'll give you a ring later.*

tell verb
1 *He **told** me he'd be home for tea.*
- **to say** *He said he'd be home for tea.*
- **to promise** *He promised he'd be home for tea.*
2 *My dad **told** me how to use a calculator.*
- **to show**

a
b
c
d
e
f
g
h
i
j
k
l
m
n
o
p
q
r
s
t
u
v
w
x
y
z

- **to teach**
- **to explain** *He explained to me how to use a calculator.*

3 *You should **tell** the police if you see anything unusual.*
- **to inform**
- **to notify**

4 *She finally **told** me the secret.*
- **to reveal** *She revealed the secret to me.*

5 *My dad **told** us a story.*
- **to relate** *He related a story.*
- **to narrate** *He narrated a story to us.*

6 *Can you **tell** us what happened?*
- **to describe** *Can you describe what happened?*
- **to recount** *Can you recount what happened?*

7 *Mum **told** us to stop shouting.*
- **to order**
- **to instruct**
- **to command**

tell off verb
*The teacher **told** us **off**.*
- **to scold**
- **to reprimand**
- **to rebuke**

temper noun
1 *You seem to be in a very good **temper** today.*
- **mood**
- **humour**

2 *The man was in a terrible **temper**!*
- **a rage**
- **a fury**

terrible adjective
1 *The weather was **terrible**!*
- **awful**
- **dreadful**
- **appalling**

- **horrible**
- **ghastly**

2 *This is **terrible** news!*
- **bad**
- **sad**
- **awful**
- **shocking**
- **upsetting**

3 *I'm a **terrible** tennis player.*
- **hopeless**
- **useless**

terrific adjective
*I think that's a **terrific** idea!*
- **wonderful**
- **brilliant**
- **excellent**
- **fantastic**

terrified adjective
*I was absolutely **terrified**!*
- **petrified**

terrify verb
*The thought of singing in front of all those people would **terrify** me.*
- **to frighten**
- **to scare**
- **to petrify**

terror noun
*People ran away from the fire in **terror**.*
- **fear**
- **fright**
- **panic**

test noun
*We've got a spelling **test** tomorrow.*
- **an exam**
- **an examination**

a
b
c
d
e
f
g
h
i
j
k
l
m
n
o
p
q
r
s
t
u
v
w
x
y
z

test verb

*Now we must **test** the machine to see if it works.*
- **to try**
- **to try out**
- **to use**

thank verb

*I **thanked** them for their present.*
- **to say thank you**
- **to express your gratitude** *I expressed my gratitude.*
- **to show your appreciation** *I showed my appreciation.*

thaw verb

1 *The snow has started to **thaw**.*
- **to melt**
2 *I took the meat out of the freezer so that it would **thaw**.*
- **to defrost**
- **to warm up**

thick adjective

1 *He drew a **thick** line.*
- **wide**
- **broad**
2 *The castle had **thick** stone walls.*
- **solid**
- **strong**
3 *She cut herself a **thick** slice of cake.*
- **big**
- **large**
- **fat**
4 *We had to walk through **thick** mud.*
- **deep**
5 *He was wearing a **thick** coat.*
- **heavy**
- **warm**
OPPOSITE thin

thief noun

*The money was stolen by a **thief**.*
- **a robber**
- **a burglar**
- **a pickpocket**
- **a mugger**
- **a shoplifter**
A **burglar** goes into a person's house to steal things:
*Always lock your windows so that **burglars** can't get in.*
A **pickpocket** steals things from a person's pocket:
*Be careful, there are **pickpockets** about on the streets.*
A **mugger** attacks someone in the street and steals things from them:
*The old lady was attacked by a **mugger**.*
A **shoplifter** steals things from shops:
*In some shops there are security men to catch **shoplifters**.*

thin adjective

1 *She drew a **thin** line.*
- **fine**
- **narrow**
OPPOSITE thick
2 *My sister is very **thin**.*
- **slim**
- **slender**
- **skinny**
- **scrawny**
- **bony**
Use **skinny**, **scrawny**, or **bony** for someone who is too thin:
*The evil witch had horrible **bony** hands.*
OPPOSITE fat
3 *This paint is too **thin**.*
- **watery**
- **weak**
- **runny**
- **diluted**
OPPOSITE thick

4 *She was only wearing a **thin** cotton dress.*
- **light**
- **flimsy**

OPPOSITE thick

thing noun
1 *We found some very interesting **things** in the attic.*
- **an object**
- **an article**
- **an item**

2 *Don't forget to take all your **things** with you when you leave.*
- **belongings**
- **possessions**
- **stuff**

3 *A corkscrew is a **thing** for opening bottles.*
- **a tool**
- **a device**
- **a gadget**
- **a machine**

4 *A very strange **thing** happened to me today.*
- **an event**
- **an incident**

5 *We had to do some very difficult **things**.*
- **an action**
- **an act**
- **a job**
- **a task**

think verb
1 ***Think** before you act.*
- **to concentrate**
- **to use your mind**

2 *He was sitting in a chair just **thinking**.*
- **to meditate**
- **to muse**
- **to daydream**

3 *I was **thinking** about all the things that had happened the day before.*
- **to reflect on** *I reflected on what had happened.*
- **to mull over** *I mulled over what had happened.*
- **to ponder** *I pondered over what had happened.*

4 *He was still **thinking** about what to do next.*
- **to consider** *He was considering what to do next.*
- **to plan** *He was planning what he would do next.*

5 *I **think** that you are right.*
- **to believe**
- **to reckon**
- **to suppose**

thoroughly adverb
1 *Make sure you clean everything **thoroughly**.*
- **carefully**
- **properly**

2 *I was **thoroughly** exhausted.*
- **completely**
- **totally**
- **utterly**
- **absolutely**

thought noun
*I've just had an interesting **thought**.*
- **an idea**
- **a brainwave**

thoughtful adjective
1 *He was sitting on his own, looking **thoughtful**.*
- **serious**
- **pensive**
- **reflective**

2 *You should try to be more **thoughtful**.*
- **considerate**
- **kind**
- **caring** →

a
b
c
d
e
f
g
h
i
j
k
l
m
n
o
p
q
r
s
t
u
v
w
x
y
z

a
b
c
d
e
f
g
h
i
j
k
l
m
n
o
p
q
r
s
t
u
v
w
x
y
z

- **helpful**
- **unselfish**

OPPOSITE thoughtless

thrilling adjective
*Going on the big rides was a **thrilling** experience.*
- **exciting**
- **electrifying**

throw verb
1 *She **threw** a stone and broke the glass.*
- **to fling**
- **to hurl**
- **to sling** (*informal*)
- **to toss**
- **to chuck** (*informal*)
- **to lob** (*informal*)
Use ***fling*** or ***hurl*** *when you throw something with a lot of force:*
*Someone had **hurled** a brick through the window.*
Use ***sling**, **toss**,* or ***chuck*** *when you throw something carelessly:*
*She **tossed** the letter into the bin.*
Use ***lob*** *when you throw something high into the air:*
*I **lobbed** the ball over the fence.*
2 *He threw the ball towards the batsman.*
- **to bowl**

throw away verb
*My old shoes didn't fit me any more so I **threw** them **away**.*
- **to throw out**
- **to get rid of**
- **to dispose of**
- **to discard**
- **to dump**

tidy adjective
1 *My aunt's house is always very **tidy**.*

- **neat**
- **shipshape**
- **orderly**
- **uncluttered**
- **spick and span**
2 *The children all looked **tidy**.*
- **neat**
- **smart**
- **well-groomed**
3 *Are you a **tidy** person?*
- **neat**
- **organized**
- **house-proud**
OPPOSITE untidy

tie verb
1 *I can't **tie** my shoelaces.*
- **to do up**
- **to fasten**
2 *Why don't you **tie** the two bits together?*
- **to fasten**
- **to join**
- **to fix**
- **to knot**
3 *They **tied** the boat to a post.*
- **to fasten**
- **to secure**
- **to moor**
4 *He **tied** the animal to the fence.*
- **to tether**

tight adjective
1 *My trousers are a bit **tight**.*
- **small**
- **tight-fitting**
- **close-fitting**
2 *Make sure the jar has a **tight** lid.*
- **firm**
- **secure**
3 *Pull the rope until it is **tight**.*
- **stretched**
- **taut**
OPPOSITE loose

time noun
1 *He sat in silence for a long **time**.*
- **a while**
- **a period**
2 *The 1950s was a very interesting **time**.*
- **a period**
- **an era**
- **an age**
3 *I thought this was a good **time** to ask for more pocket money.*
- **a moment**
- **an opportunity**

tiny adjective
*Some insects are **tiny**.*
- **minute**
- **minuscule**
- **microscopic**
OPPOSITE big

tip noun
1 *She stood up on the **tips** of her toes.*
- **the end**
- **the point**
2 *We could only see the **tip** of the iceberg.*
- **the top**

tip verb
1 *I could feel the bench beginning to **tip** back.*
- **to lean**
- **to tilt**
2 *She **tipped** water all over the floor.*
- **to pour**
- **to spill**
- **to slop**

tip over verb
*The boat **tipped over** in the rough sea.*
- **to capsize**
- **to overturn**

tired adjective
1 *We were **tired** after our walk.*
- **weary**
- **exhausted**
- **worn out**
- **sleepy**
  Use **exhausted** or **worn out** when you are very tired:
  *I was **exhausted** after our long day.*
  Use **sleepy** when you are tired and want to sleep:
  *Sitting by the warm fire was making me **sleepy**.*
2 *I'm tired of this game.*
- **fed up** *I'm fed up with this game.*
- **bored** *I'm bored with this game.*

toilet noun
*Can I use your **toilet**, please?*
- **a lavatory**
- **a WC**
- **a loo**

tool noun
*You can use a special **tool** to get the lid off.*
- **a device**
- **a gadget**
- **an implement**

WORD WEB
some tools for woodwork
- a drill
- a hammer
- a plane
- pliers
- a screwdriver
- a spanner

some tools you use in the garden
- a fork
- a hoe
- a rake
- shears
- a spade
- a trowel
- a watering can

---

a
b
c
d
e
f
g
h
i
j
k
l
m
n
o
p
q
r
s
t
u
v
w
x
y
z

top noun
1 *We climbed to the **top** of the mountain.*
- **the summit**
2 *We could see the **tops** of the mountains in the distance.*
- **a peak**
- **a tip**
3 *We drove over the **top** of the hill.*
- **the crest**
4 *Put the **top** back on the jar.*
- **a lid**
- **a cover**
- **a cap**
OPPOSITE bottom

topic noun
*The **topic** we are studying this term is food.*
- **a subject**
- **a theme**

torment verb
*Stop **tormenting** your brother!*
- **to tease**
- **to bully**
- **to annoy**

total adjective
1 *What will the **total** cost be?*
- **full**
- **whole**
2 *Because it rained, the picnic was a **total** disaster.*
- **complete**
- **absolute**

totally adverb
*My new bike was **totally** ruined!*
- **completely**
- **absolutely**
- **utterly**

touch verb
1 *He **touched** my arm.*
- **to pat**
- **to tap**
- **to stroke**
- **to brush**
2 *You mustn't **touch** the things on display in the museum.*
- **to handle**
- **to hold**
- **to feel**
3 *Please don't **touch** the controls.*
- **to fiddle with**
- **to mess about with** (*informal*)
- **to play with**

tough adjective
1 *The rope is made of very **tough** nylon.*
- **strong**
- **hard-wearing**
- **unbreakable**
2 *He thinks he's a really **tough** guy.*
- **strong**
- **hard**
- **rough**
- **violent**
OPPOSITE weak

tradition noun
*Having a cake on your birthday is a **tradition**.*
- **a custom**

traffic noun
*There was a lot of **traffic** on the road.*
- **cars**
- **lorries**
- **buses**
- **coaches**
- **vans**
- **vehicles**

tragedy noun
*The plane crash was a terrible **tragedy**.*
- **a disaster**

a
b
c
d
e
f
g
h
i
j
k
l
m
n
o
p
q
r
s
t
u
v
w
x
y
z

• a catastrophe
• a calamity

train verb
 1 Mr Grout **trains** our football team.
   • **to coach**
   • **to instruct**
   • **to teach**
 2 Our team **trains** every Thursday.
   • **to practise**

trap noun
   The poor rabbit got caught in a **trap**.
   • **a snare**

trap verb
   We **trapped** the smugglers in the cave.
   • **to catch**
   • **to corner**

travel verb
   We **travelled** all around the world.
   • **to go**
   • **to journey**
   • **to tour**
   • **to drive**
   • **to sail**
   • **to fly**
   • **to walk**
   • **to ride**
   • **to cycle**
   • **to hitch-hike**

tread verb
   Mind you don't **tread** on the flowers.
   • **to step**
   • **to walk**
   • **to stand**
   • **to trample**
   • **to stamp**

treasure noun
   We found a box of buried **treasure**.

• gold
• silver
• jewels
• riches

tree noun

> **WORD WEB**
> **some types of deciduous tree**
> • ash
> • beech
> • birch
> • elm
> • hawthorn
> • hazel
> • horse chestnut
> • larch
> • maple
> • oak
> • poplar
> • sycamore
> • willow
>
> **some types of evergreen tree**
> • fir
> • holly
> • palm
> • pine
> • yew
>
> **some types of trees around the world**
> • baobab
> • buffalo thorn
> • jacaranda
> • mango
> • marula
> • mopane
> • palm

tremble verb
   I was **trembling** with fear.
   • **to shake**
   • **to quake**
   • **to quiver**
   • **to shiver**
   • **to shudder**

a
b
c
d
e
f
g
h
i
j
k
l
m
n
o
p
q
r
s
t
u
v
w
x
y
z

a
b
c
d
e
f
g
h
i
j
k
l
m
n
o
p
q
r
s
t
u
v
w
x
y
z

tremendous adjective
1 *The machines make a **tremendous** noise.*
- **great**
- **huge**
- **terrific**
2 *We had a **tremendous** time.*
- **great**
- **wonderful**
- **fantastic**
- **excellent**

trick noun
1 *We played a **trick** on our friends.*
- **a joke**
- **a prank**
- **a hoax**
2 *The dolphins did some amazing **tricks**.*
- **a stunt**

trick verb
*He **tricked** us into giving him our money.*
- **to cheat**
- **to fool**
- **to deceive**
- **to swindle**
- **to con**

trickle verb
*Water **trickled** out of the tap.*
- **to drip**
- **to dribble**
- **to leak**
- **to seep**

trip noun
*We went on a **trip** to the seaside.*
- **an outing**
- **an excursion**
- **a journey**
- **a visit**
- **a day out**

trip verb
*I **tripped** and fell.*
- **to stumble**
- **to slip**
- **to lose your balance** *I lost my balance.*

trouble noun
1 *She's had a lot of **troubles** recently.*
- **difficulties**
- **problems**
- **cares**
- **worries**
- **suffering**
2 *There was some **trouble** in the playground at lunchtime.*
- **bother**
- **fighting**
- **hassle**

true adjective
1 *The film is based on a **true** story.*
- **real**
- **genuine**
- **actual**
2 *What he said isn't **true**.*
- **correct**
- **accurate**
- **right**
OPPOSITE made-up

trust verb
1 *I don't **trust** that man.*
- **to have confidence in**
2 *Can I **trust** you to get on with your work while I am away?*
- **to rely on**
- **to depend on**
- **to count on**

try verb
1 *I **tried** to climb over the wall.*
- **to attempt**

- **to make an effort**
- **to strive**

2 *Can I **try** the cake?*
- **to taste**
- **to sample**

3 *Would you like to **try** my new bike?*
- **to try out**
- **to test**
- **to have a go** (*informal*) *Would you like to have a go on my new bike?*

tune noun
*Do you know the words to this **tune**?*
- **a melody**

tunnel noun
*There is a secret **tunnel** leading to the castle.*
- **a passage**
- **an underpass** (*a tunnel under a road*)

turn verb

1 *I **turned** round to see who was behind me.*
- **to spin**
- **to whirl**
- **to swivel**

2 *I **turned** the key in the lock.*
- **to rotate**

3 *The wheel began to **turn**.*
- **to revolve**
- **to rotate**
- **to spin**

4 *In the autumn some leaves **turn** red.*
- **to become**
- **to go**

5 *Tadpoles **turn** into frogs.*
- **to become**
- **to change into**

6 *I **turned** the light on.*
- **to switch**

7 *We **turned** the attic into a playroom.*
- **to change**

- **to convert**
- **to transform**

turn noun
*Be patient — it will be your **turn** in a minute.*
- **a go**
- **a chance**
- **an opportunity**

twinkle verb
*The lights **twinkled** in the distance.*
- **to shine**
- **to sparkle**

twist verb

1 *I **twisted** the wire round the pole.*
- **to wind**
- **to loop**
- **to coil**

2 *She **twisted** the ribbons together.*
- **to plait**
- **to wind**

type noun

1 *What **type** of music do you like?*
- **a kind**
- **a sort**

2 *A collie is a **type** of dog.*
- **a breed**

3 *A ladybird is a **type** of beetle.*
- **a species**

4 *I don't like that **type** of trainers.*
- **a brand**
- **a make**

typical adjective
*It was a **typical** winter's day.*
- **normal**
- **ordinary**
- **average**
- **standard**
OPPOSITE unusual

a
b
c
d
e
f
g
h
i
j
k
l
m
n
o
p
q
r
s
t
u
v
w
x
y
z

Uu

ugly adjective

1 We screamed when we saw the **ugly** monster.
- **horrible**
- **hideous**
- **frightful**
- **repulsive**
- **grotesque**

2 Cinderella was beautiful, but her two sisters were **ugly**.
- **plain**
- **unattractive**

OPPOSITE beautiful

uncomfortable adjective

The bed was very **uncomfortable**.
- **hard**
- **lumpy**

OPPOSITE comfortable

unconscious adjective

The blow knocked him **unconscious**.
- **out cold**
- **senseless**

OPPOSITE conscious

understand verb

Do you **understand** what I'm saying?
- **to follow**
- **to grasp**
- **to see**

undo verb

She **undid** her shoelaces.
- **to untie**
- **to unfasten**

unemployed adjective

My uncle is **unemployed**.
- **out of work**
- **on the dole** (informal)
- **jobless**

OPPOSITE employed

uneven adjective

The road was very **uneven**.
- **bumpy**
- **rough**

OPPOSITE smooth

unfair adjective

1 It's **unfair** if she gets more than me.
- **wrong**
- **unjust**
- **unreasonable**

2 We complained that the referee was **unfair**.
- **biased**

OPPOSITE fair

unfriendly adjective

The other children were very **unfriendly**.
- **unkind**
- **nasty**
- **hostile**
- **rude**
- **mean**
- **unwelcoming**

OPPOSITE friendly

unhappy adjective

I was **unhappy** at my last school.
- **sad**
- **miserable**
- **depressed**
- **glum**
- **dejected**
- **down in the dumps** (informal)
- **gloomy**
- **despondent**

- **upset**
- **heartbroken**
- **fed up**
  Use **gloomy** or **despondent** if you think something bad is going to happen:
  *My dad was quite **gloomy** because he thought he was going to lose his job.*
  Use **upset** or **heartbroken** if something sad has happened:
  *I was really **upset** when I fell out with my friends.*
  Use **fed up** if you are unhappy and bored:
  *Max was **fed up** because all his friends were away on holiday.*
  OPPOSITE happy

unkind adjective
  *Jo hates to see people being **unkind** to animals.*
- **horrible**
- **nasty**
- **mean**
- **cruel**
- **spiteful**
  OPPOSITE kind

unlucky adjective
  *We were **unlucky** to miss the bus.*
- **unfortunate**
  OPPOSITE lucky

unpleasant adjective
1 *He said some **unpleasant** things to me.*
- **horrible**
- **nasty**
- **mean**
- **unkind**
- **rude**
- **unfriendly**
- **upsetting**
2 *The meat had an **unpleasant** taste.*
- **horrible**
- **nasty**

- **disgusting**
- **revolting**
- **terrible**
  OPPOSITE pleasant

untidy adjective
1 *The bedroom is always **untidy**.*
- **messy**
- **chaotic**
- **jumbled**
- **muddled**
- **scruffy**
  Use **jumbled** or **muddled** if a lot of things are mixed together in an untidy way:
  *There was a huge **jumbled** pile of clothes on the floor.*
  Use **scruffy** to describe someone's clothes or appearance:
  *George never looks smart — he always looks **scruffy**!*
2 *This work is very **untidy**!*
- **messy**
- **careless**
- **sloppy**
  OPPOSITE tidy

unusual adjective
  *It's **unusual** to have snow in May.*
- **extraordinary**
- **odd**
- **peculiar**
- **strange**
- **surprising**
- **uncommon**
  OPPOSITE ordinary

upset adjective
  Sita was crying and looked very upset.
- **sad**
- **distressed**
- **hurt** →

a
b
c
d
e
f
g
h
i
j
k
l
m
n
o
p
q
r
s
t
u
v
w
x
y
z

a
b
c
d
e
f
g
h
i
j
k
l
m
n
o
p
q
r
s
t
u
v
w
x
y
z

Use **hurt** if you are upset by something unkind that someone has done:
*I felt **hurt** that I wasn't invited to the party.*

upset verb
1 *Seeing the pictures of the war on TV* ***upset** me.*
- **to distress**
- **to sadden**
- **to frighten**
- **to scare**
- **to worry**
2 *Some of the nasty things he said really **upset** me.*
- **to hurt**
- **to hurt someone's feelings** *Some of the things he said hurt my feelings.*

urge noun
*I had a sudden **urge** to giggle.*
- **a desire**
- **a wish**
- **a need**

use verb
1 *They **used** machines to dig the tunnel.*
- **to employ**
- **to make use of**
2 *Do you know how to **use** this tool?*
- **to handle**
- **to manipulate**
3 *He taught me how to **use** the machine.*
- **to work**
- **to operate**
4 *Have we **used** all the paint?*
- **to finish**

useful adjective
1 *Mobile phones are very **useful**.*
- **handy**
- **practical**
- **convenient**
2 *She gave us some very **useful** advice.*
- **helpful**
- **valuable**
OPPOSITE useless

useless adjective
1 *This old bicycle is **useless**!*
- **unusable**
- **worthless**
OPPOSITE useful
2 *I was a **useless** goalkeeper.*
- **hopeless**
- **terrible**
- **incompetent**
OPPOSITE good

usual adjective
1 *I went to bed at my **usual** time of eight o'clock.*
- **normal**
- **ordinary**
2 *The **usual** answer is no.*
- **normal**
- **typical**

usually adverb
*I **usually** get up at seven o'clock.*
- **normally**
- **generally**

Vv

vague adjective
*He only gave a **vague** description of the thief.*
- **general**
- **unclear**
- **confused**
- **not very detailed**

OPPOSITE exact

vain adjective
*He's so **vain** that he's always looking in the mirror.*
- **conceited**
- **arrogant**
- **big-headed**

OPPOSITE modest

valuable adjective
*Some of the coins in my collection are quite **valuable**.*
- **expensive**
- **precious**
- **priceless**
  Use **precious** if something is valuable and important to you:
  *The jewellery my grandmother gave me is very **precious** to me.*
  Use **priceless** if something is so valuable you can't say how much it is worth:
  *These old paintings are **priceless**.*

OPPOSITE worthless

value noun
*No one knows the exact **value** of these jewels.*
- **the worth**
- **the price**

variety noun
1 *There is a **variety** of colours to choose from.*
- **an assortment**
- **a choice**
- **a mixture**
- **a range**

2 *They sell ten different **varieties** of ice cream.*
- **a type**
- **a sort**
- **a kind**

various adjective
*There were **various** things to eat.*
- **different**
- **assorted**

vary verb
*The date of Easter **varies** each year.*
- **to change**
- **to be different** *The date is different each year.*

vegetable noun

WORD WEB
some types of vegetable
- asparagus
- aubergines
- beans
- beetroot
- broccoli
- cabbage
- carrots
- cauliflower
- celery
- courgettes
- leeks
- mangetout
- marrows
- okra
- onions
- parsnips
- peas
- plantain →

a b c d e f g h i j k l m n o p q r s t u **v** w x y z

211

- potatoes
- pumpkins
- spinach
- sprouts
- sweetcorn
- turnips
- yams

vibrate verb
*The whole house **vibrates** when a lorry goes past.*
- **to shake**
- **to wobble**
- **to rattle**
- **to shudder**

victory noun
*We celebrated our team's **victory**.*
- **a win**
- **a success**
- **a triumph**
OPPOSITE defeat

villain noun
*The police caught the **villain** in the end.*
- **a criminal**
- **a crook**
- **a baddy**

violent adjective
1 *Sometimes he is quite **violent** towards other children.*
- **aggressive**
- **rough**
- **ferocious**
- **savage**

*Use **ferocious** or **savage** if someone is very violent:*
*She was the victim of a **ferocious** attack.*
2 *That night there was a **violent** storm.*
- **severe**
- **fierce**
- **raging**

visible adjective
*Stars are only **visible** at night.*
- **noticeable**
- **obvious**
OPPOSITE invisible

visit verb
*I'm going to **visit** my grandma next week.*
- **to see**
- **to call on**
- **to stay with**

visitor noun
*Are you expecting a **visitor**?*
- **a guest**
- **a caller**
- **company** *Are you expecting company?*

volume noun
*Please could you turn down the **volume** on the TV?*
- **the sound**
- **the loudness**

vote for verb
*Who did you **vote** for?*
- **to choose**
- **to pick**
- **to select**

Ww

wait verb

1 *Wait here until I get back.*
- **to stay**
- **to remain**
- **to hang on**
- **to hold on**
 Use **hang on** or **hold on** when you wait only a short time:
 Hang on for just a minute. I won't be long.

2 *She waited for a while before she opened the door.*
- **to pause**
- **to hesitate**

wake up verb

I wake up at seven o'clock.
- **to awaken**
- **to get up**
- **to rise**

walk verb

⚠ **OVERUSED WORD**
Try to vary the words you use to mean *walk*. Here are some other words you can use instead.
 They **walked** along the street.
 Use **stride** or **march** when someone walks with big steps:
 The professor came striding up to the building.
 Use **hurry** or **rush** when someone walks quickly:
 She hurried down the road to the shop.
 Use **wander**, **stroll**, **amble**, or **saunter** if someone walks slowly:
 Matt slowly wandered over to the door.

 Use **stomp** or **clump** if someone walks noisily:
 Tara stomped angrily out of the room.
 Use **creep**, **sneak**, or **tiptoe** if someone walks very quietly:
 I crept quietly downstairs, trying not to wake anyone.
 Use **limp**, **hobble**, **shuffle**, **stagger**, or **stumble** if someone can't walk very well:
 The old man hobbled along the street.
 Use **trudge** or **plod** if someone walks in a tired way:
 Wearily, we trudged home.
 Use **strut** or **swagger** if someone walks in a very proud way:
 I couldn't bear seeing him strutting about on the stage, so proud of himself!
 Use **hike** or **trek** if someone walks a long way over rough ground:
 We spent two weeks hiking in the mountains.

wander verb

We wandered around town all afternoon.
- **to roam**
- **to rove**
- **to drift**

want verb

1 *Do you want an ice cream?*
- **to fancy**
- **to feel like**
- **to need**
- **to desire** (formal)
- **to be dying for**
- **to be desperate for**
- **to wish for**
- **to long for**
- **to yearn for** →

a b c d e f g h i j k l m n o p q r s t u v **w** x y z

213

a
b
c
d
e
f
g
h
i
j
k
l
m
n
o
p
q
r
s
t
u
v
w
x
y
z

*Use **be dying for** or **be desperate
for** if you want something very
badly:*
*It's so hot! I'm **desperate** for a drink!*
*Use **wish for**, **long for**, or **yearn for**
if you want something badly but do
not think you will be able to have it:*
*She had always **longed for** a pony of
her own.*

2 *I **want** to be a professional footballer.*
* **to dream of** *I dream of being a
professional footballer.*
* **to set your heart on** *I have set my
heart on being a professional footballer.*

war noun
*For three years, there was **war** between
the two countries.*
* **fighting**
* **conflict**

warm adjective
1 *The water was **warm**.*
* **lukewarm**
* **tepid**
2 *It was a lovely **warm** day.*
* **hot**
* **mild**
* **sunny**
* **boiling hot**
3 *I was lovely and **warm** in my thick coat.*
* **hot**
* **cosy**
* **snug**
4 *We sat down in front of the **warm** fire.*
* **hot**
* **blazing**
* **roaring**
OPPOSITE cold

warn verb
1 *He **warned** us to stay away from the
old quarry.*
* **to advise**

* **to remind**
* **to tell**
2 *Someone had **warned** the police about
the robbery.*
* **to alert**
* **to tip someone off** (*informal*)
3 *This time I will just **warn** you. If you do
it again, you will be in big trouble.*
* **to caution**
* **to give someone a warning** *This
time I will just give you a warning.*

wash verb
1 *Go and **wash** your hands.*
* **to clean**
* **to rinse**
2 *You should **wash** more often.*
* **to have a bath**
* **to bath**
* **to have a shower**
* **to shower**
3 *I **washed** my hair.*
* **to shampoo**
4 *I'm going to **wash** the floor.*
* **to clean**
* **to mop**
* **to scrub**
* **to wipe**

waste noun
*Put the **waste** in the bin.*
* **rubbish**
* **litter**
* **junk**
* **refuse**
* **trash** (*American*)

watch verb
1 *I could feel that someone was
watching me.*
* **to look at**
* **to observe**
* **to stare at**
* **to gaze at**

Use **stare at** if you watch someone for a long time:
Ali was **staring at** the ship, trying to see who was on board.
Use **gaze at** if you are watching something beautiful or interesting:
We **gazed at** the dancers, amazed by their leaps and jumps.

2 Will you **watch** my things while I go for a swim?
  - **to keep an eye on** (informal)
  - **to look after**
  - **to guard**
  - **to mind**

water noun

1 Would you like a glass of **water**?
  - **mineral water**
  - **spring water**
  - **tap water**
2 We sat by the side of the **water**.
  - **a lake**
  - **a pond**
  - **a reservoir**
  - **a river**
  - **a stream**
  - **the sea**
  - **the ocean**
  - **a brook**

WRITING TIPS

Here are some useful words for writing about water.
- The water in the river **flowed** along smoothly.
- Water was **pouring** into the boat.
- Cold water **gushed** and **splashed** over the rocks.
- The water **trickled** and **gurgled** over the pebbles.
- A few drops of water were still **dripping** from the tap.
- The water of the lake **lapped** against the shore.

---

wave verb

1 She **waved** to me from the other side of the field.
  - **to signal**
  - **to gesture**
2 The flags were **waving** in the wind.
  - **to stir**
  - **to sway**
  - **to flap**
  - **to shake**
  - **to flutter**
3 He **waved** the stick over his head.
  - **to swing**
  - **to brandish**

wave noun

We played in the **waves**.
  - **a breaker**
  - **the surf**
    A **breaker** is a very big wave:
    Huge **breakers** crashed onto the shore.

way noun

1 Is this the **way** to London?
  - **a road**
  - **a route**
  - **a direction**
2 This is the best **way** to build a den.
  - **a method**   This is the best method of building a den.
  - **a technique**   This is the best technique for building a den.
3 He spoke in a very angry **way**.
  - **a manner**
  - **a fashion**
4 She ties her hair up in a very pretty **way**.
  - **a style**

weak adjective

1 She still feels quite **weak** after her illness.
  - **ill**
  - **poorly** →

a
b
c
d
e
f
g
h
i
j
k
l
m
n
o
p
q
r
s
t
u
v
w
x
y
z

a
b
c
d
e
f
g
h
i
j
k
l
m
n
o
p
q
r
s
t
u
v
w
x
y
z

- **feeble**
- **frail**
- **shaky**
- **delicate**

2 *You're too **weak** to fight against me!*
- **weedy**
- **puny**

3 *I think these wooden posts are too **weak**.*
- **thin**
- **flimsy**
- **fragile**
- **rickety**

4 *This orange squash is too **weak**.*
- **watery**
- **tasteless**
- **diluted**

OPPOSITE strong

wealthy adjective
*Her parents are **wealthy**.*
- **rich**
- **well-off**
- **prosperous**

OPPOSITE poor

weapon noun

WORD WEB
some types of weapon
- a bomb
- a bow and arrow
- a cannon
- a catapult
- a cutlass
- a dagger
- a gun
- a knife
- a pistol
- a revolver
- a rifle
- a sabre
- a spear
- a sword

---

wear verb
1 *He was **wearing** a smart blue jacket.*

- **to have on**
- **to be dressed in**
- **to be sporting**

2 *What shall I **wear** today?*
- **to put on**
- **to dress in**

weather noun
*What is the **weather** like in India?*
- **the climate**

weird adjective
*She wears some **weird** clothes!*
- **strange**
- **funny**
- **peculiar**
- **odd**

OPPOSITE ordinary

welcome verb
*We **welcomed** the guests at the door.*
- **to greet**
- **to receive**

well adjective
*I hope you are **well**.*
- **fit**
- **healthy**

OPPOSITE ill

well adverb
1 *You have done this work very **well**.*
- **carefully**
- **competently**
- **properly**
- **successfully**
- **thoroughly**
- **brilliantly**
- **excellently**
- **cleverly**
- **skilfully**

Use **brilliantly** or **excellently** if you do something very well:
Everyone in our team played **brilliantly**!
Use **cleverly** or **skilfully** if you do something in a clever way:
He painted each model **skilfully**.
OPPOSITE badly
2 They don't treat their pets very **well**.
• kindly
• lovingly
• caringly
OPPOSITE badly

well-known adjective
He's a very **well-known** pop star.
• famous
• celebrated
OPPOSITE unknown

wet adjective
1 My shoes are **wet**.
• damp
• soaked
• soaking wet
• dripping wet
• drenched
Use **damp** if something is slightly wet:
I wiped the table with a **damp** cloth.
Use **soaked**, **soaking wet**, **dripping wet**, or **drenched** if something is very wet:
My clothes were all **dripping wet** after I fell into the swimming pool!
2 The field is too **wet** to play on.
• muddy
• soggy
• waterlogged
3 It was a **wet** day.
• rainy
• drizzly
• showery
• damp
OPPOSITE dry

whisper verb
'Which way shall we go?' he **whispered**.
• to murmur
• to mutter
• to mumble
• to hiss
Use **murmur** if you speak very gently:
'I must be dreaming,' she **murmured** sleepily.
Use **mutter** or **mumble** if you speak quietly and not clearly:
The witch was **muttering** a strange spell to herself.
Use **hiss** if you speak in a loud or angry whisper:
'Get out of here!' he **hissed**.

white adjective
She was wearing a **white** dress.
• cream
• ivory
• snow-white

whole adjective
We ate the **whole** cake.
• complete
• entire

wicked adjective
1 The land was ruled by a **wicked** king.
• bad
• evil
2 That was a **wicked** thing to do.
• wrong
• bad
• immoral
• sinful
OPPOSITE good

wide adjective
We had to cross a **wide** river.
• broad →

a
b
c
d
e
f
g
h
i
j
k
l
m
n
o
p
q
r
s
t
u
v
w
x
y
z

217

- **big**
- **large**

OPPOSITE narrow

wild adjective

1 *They are **wild** animals and can be dangerous.*
- **untamed**
- **ferocious**

OPPOSITE tame

2 *Their behaviour can be a bit **wild** sometimes.*
- **noisy**
- **rough**
- **boisterous**
- **unruly**
- **rowdy**

OPPOSITE calm

will verb

1 *I **will** tell my teacher tomorrow.*
- **to intend to** *I intend to tell my teacher tomorrow.*

2 *I **will** help you.*
- **to be willing to** *I am willing to help you.*
- **to be happy to** *I am happy to help you.*

willing adjective

*Are you **willing** to help us?*
- **happy**
- **ready**
- **prepared**
- **eager**

OPPOSITE unwilling

win verb

1 *I was delighted when my team **won**.*
- **to be victorious**
- **to triumph**
- **to succeed**
- **to come first**

OPPOSITE lose

2 *She **won** a medal in the cross-country race.*
- **to get**
- **to earn**
- **to receive**

wind (*rhymes with* tinned) noun

*Outside, the **wind** was blowing.*
- **a breeze**
- **a gale**
- **a hurricane**

*A **breeze** is a gentle wind:*
*It was a hot day, but there was a lovely cool **breeze**.*
*A **gale** is a strong wind:*
*We couldn't play football because there was a **gale** blowing.*
*A **hurricane** is a very strong wind:*
*A lot of houses were damaged by the **hurricane**.*

WRITING TIPS

Here are some useful words for writing about wind.
- A **gentle** wind was **blowing** across the field.
- The **strong** wind **howled** and **roared** and **whistled** through the trees.
- The terrible wind **buffeted** the small boats on the lake.

---

wind (*rhymes with* find) verb

*She **wound** her scarf round her neck.*
- **to wrap**
- **to loop**
- **to coil**
- **to twist**

windy adjective

*It was a cold, **windy** night.*
- **breezy**
- **blustery**
- **stormy**

OPPOSITE calm

winner noun
> James is the **winner**!
> - **the champion**
> - **the victor**
> OPPOSITE loser

wipe verb
> 1 I'll **wipe** the table before we eat.
> - **to clean**
> 2 She used a duster to **wipe** the furniture.
> - **to dust**
> - **to polish**
> 3 Please could you **wipe** the mud off your shoes?
> - **to rub**
> - **to scrape**

wire noun
> There were electrical **wires** all over the floor.
> - **a cable**
> - **a lead**
> - **a flex**

wise adjective
> 1 My grandfather is a very **wise** man.
> - **clever**
> - **intelligent**
> - **sensible**
> 2 You have made a **wise** decision.
> - **good**
> - **sensible**
> OPPOSITE foolish

wish for verb
> I had always **wished for** a puppy.
> - **to want**
> - **to long for**
> - **to yearn for**

witch noun
> - **a sorceress**
> - **an enchantress**

wither verb
> The plants **withered** because I forgot to water them.
> - **to dry up**
> - **to shrivel**
> - **to wilt**
> - **to droop**

wizard noun
> - **a sorcerer**
> - **an enchanter**
> - **a magician**

wobble verb
> 1 The ladder **wobbled** as I climbed up it.
> - **to shake**
> - **to sway**
> - **to be unsteady**
> 2 The jelly **wobbles** when you move the plate.
> - **to shake**
> - **to quiver**

woman noun
> What was the **woman's** name?
> - **a lady**
> - **a girl**
> - **a mother** (a woman who has children)
> - **a widow** (a woman whose husband has died)

wonder noun
> We stared at the lights in **wonder**.
> - **amazement**
> - **admiration**
> - **awe**

wonder verb
> I was **wondering** what to do next.
> - **to think about**
> - **to consider**

a
b
c
d
e
f
g
h
i
j
k
l
m
n
o
p
q
r
s
t
u
v
w
x
y
z

wonderful adjective
> We had a **wonderful** time.
> • **great**
> • **amazing**
> • **brilliant**
> • **fantastic**
> • **marvellous**
> OPPOSITE terrible

wood noun
> 1 Our garden shed is made of **wood**.
> • **timber**
> • **planks**
> 2 We need more **wood** for the fire.
> • **logs**
> 3 We walked through the **wood**.
> • **woods**
> • **woodland**
> • **a forest**
> • **a copse**
> A **forest** is a large wood:
> They were scared to go into the huge, dark **forest**.
> A **copse** is a very small wood:
> We found a picnic spot near a little **copse**.

word noun
> I can't think of the right **word**.
> • **a term**
> • **a phrase**
> • **an expression**

work noun
> 1 Just sit quietly and get on with your **work**.
> • **a job**
> • **schoolwork**
> • **homework**
> • **a task**
> 2 What **work** do you want to do when you grow up?
> • **a job**
> • **an occupation**
> • **a profession**
> • **a career**
> 3 The **work** can be back-breaking.
> • **labour**
> • **toil**

work verb
> 1 We **worked** hard all morning.
> • **to be busy** We were busy all morning.
> • **to toil**
> • **to labour**
> 2 When I grow up I want to **work** in a bank.
> • **to be employed**
> • **to have a job**
> 3 The lift isn't **working**.
> • **to go** The lift doesn't go.
> • **to function** The lift isn't functioning.
> 4 I don't think your plan will **work**.
> • **to succeed**
> • **to be successful**

worried adjective
> 1 I was **worried** because they were so late home.
> • **anxious**
> • **concerned**
> 2 Are you **worried** about moving to a new school?
> • **nervous**
> • **apprehensive**
> OPPOSITE relaxed

worry verb
> Don't **worry**, everything will be all right.
> • **to fret**
> • **to be anxious**
> • **to be concerned**

a b c d e f g h i j k l m n o p q r s t u v **w** x y z

worry noun

I seem to have so many **worries** at the moment.
- **a concern**
- **a fear**

wound noun

He had a nasty **wound** on his arm.
- **an injury**
- **a cut**
- **a gash**

wound verb

The explosion **wounded** a lot of people.
- **to injure**
- **to hurt**

wrap verb

1 I **wrapped** the parcel in paper.
- **to cover**
- **to pack**
2 I **wrapped** my scarf round my neck.
- **to wind**
- **to loop**

wreck verb

1 The explosion **wrecked** several buildings.
- **to destroy**
- **to demolish**
- **to smash up**
2 He drove into a lamppost and **wrecked** his car.
- **to smash up**
3 You've **wrecked** my CD player!
- **to break**
- **to ruin**
- **to smash**

write verb

1 He **wrote** the word 'birthday' at the top of the page.
- **to print**
- **to jot down**
- **to scribble**
- **to scrawl**

Use **print** when you write something without the letters joined up:
He **printed** each word carefully in capital letters.
Use **jot down** when you write something quickly:
I quickly **jotted down** her phone number.
Use **scribble** or **scrawl** when you write something messily:
I **scribbled** a quick message to the others.
2 Please **write** your name here.
- **to sign**
3 I **wrote** a list of all the things we would need.
- **to compile**
- **to make**
4 Sometimes we **write** stories at school.
- **to make up**
5 We're going to **write** a piece of music.
- **to compose**
- **to create**

writer noun

I want to be a **writer** when I grow up.
- **an author**

🕸 **WORD WEB**

some types of writer
- a journalist (someone who writes for a newspaper)
- a novelist
- a playwright (someone who writes plays)
- a poet
- a scriptwriter (someone who writes scripts for films or television)

a b c d e f g h i j k l m n o p q r s t u v **w** x y z

wrong adjective

1 *The information that he gave us was wrong.*
- **false**
- **inaccurate**
- **untrue**
- **incorrect**

2 *I thought she lived here, but I was wrong.*
- **mistaken**

3 *It is wrong to steal.*
- **dishonest**
- **immoral**
- **bad**
- **wicked**

OPPOSITE right

a
b
c
d
e
f
g
h
i
j
k
l
m
n
o
p
q
r
s
t
u
v
w
x
y
z

Yy

yell verb

The man **yelled** at us to go away.
- to shout
- to scream
- to shriek
- to bawl
- to bellow

yellow adjective

The bridesmaids wore **yellow** dresses.
- lemon
- gold
- primrose

young adjective

1 I was too **young** to understand what was happening.
- little
- small
- immature
- childish

Use **immature** or **childish** when someone behaves in a way that seems too young: Stop being so **childish**!
OPPOSITE old

2 My dad is forty, but he still looks quite **young**.
- youthful
OPPOSITE old

a
b
c
d
e
f
g
h
i
j
k
l
m
n
o
p
q
r
s
t
u
v
w
x
y
z

a
b
c
d
e
f
g
h
i
j
k
l
m
n
o
p
q
r
s
t
u
v
w
x
y
z

Zz

zap verb
*You have to **zap** aliens in this game.*
• **to kill**
• **to shoot**
• **to destroy**
• **to blast**
• **to hit**

zero noun
1 *The temperature went down to **zero**.*
• **nought**
• **nothing**
2 *The other team won by three goals to **zero**.*
• **nil**

zoom verb
*The car **zoomed** along the motorway.*
• **to speed**
• **to race**
• **to tear**
• **to hurtle**

Word Explorer contents

Become a Word Explorer!

You don't need a map and a compass to be an explorer.
You can explore the world of words using your thesaurus.
For example, you can

* explore *new and interesting* words to use

* explore ways of making your *writing more interesting*

* explore ways of *building new words*

Have fun being a Word Explorer!

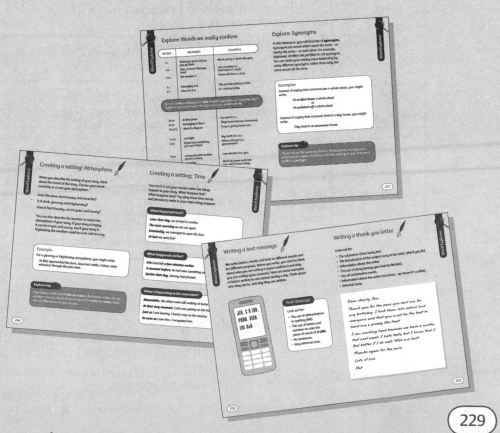

Explore: Building words and sentences

Punctuation

Use this guide to check your punctuation:

punctuation mark		when it's used	example
full stop	.	at the end of a statement	It's raining today.
question mark	?	at the end of a question	What's your favourite colour?
exclamation mark	!	at the end of an exclamation	I don't believe it!
comma	,	to separate items in a list or events in a sentence	Yesterday, when I went shopping, I bought flour, eggs, butter, and sugar.
apostrophe	'	to show that some letters are missing	I can't. He won't. She couldn't . They'll be here. It's time.
		to show ownership of something	John's coat. Anya's watch. The boys' books. The girls' pens.
speech marks	'' or " "	to show the words someone says	'I wonder what time it is,' said Raj. Tara replied, 'It's almost time to go home.' "Thank you for inviting me today," said Raj. Tara replied, "You are welcome."

Its or *it's*?

It's is short for *it is*. **Its** means 'belonging to it'.

To decide which you need, think about the question: can I turn it into *it is*? If you can, you need to write **it's**. If you can't, you should write **its**.

For example: It's (it is) raining today. The cat was eating **its** food.

Word classes

All the words in a sentence tell you different information.
The kinds of words are grouped together into word classes.

Common words classes are:

word class	what the word does in a sentence	example
noun	names things	The cat sat on the mat.
verb	tells you what is happening. Verbs tell you about *doing, being,* and *having.*	The cat sat on the mat and licked its face.
adjective	gives you more information about the noun which is often descriptive	The fluffy, grey cat sat on the ragged, dirty mat and licked its furry paws.
adverb	gives you more information about the verb. It tells you *how, when,* and *where* events are happening.	Meanwhile, the fluffy grey cat sat quietly on the ragged dirty mat and solemnly licked its furry paws.
preposition	tells you where things are	Meanwhile, the fluffy grey cat sat quietly on the ragged dirty mat and solemnly licked its furry paws with its pink tongue.

Explore: Prefixes

Word Explorer

PREFIX	MEANING	EXAMPLE
anti-	against or opposite	anticlockwise, antibiotic (a medicine that works against an infection in your body)
co-	together with someone else	co-pilot, co-author
de-	to take something away	debug, de-ice, defrost
dis-	opposite	dislike, disagree, disobey
ex-	in the past, but not now	ex-policeman, ex-wife
in- (also im-)	opposite	incorrect, insane, impossible, impolite
micro-	very small	microchip, microcomputer
mid-	in the middle	midday, midnight, midsummer
mini-	very small	minibus, miniskirt
mis-	badly or wrongly	misbehave, misspell
non-	opposite	non-fiction, non-smoker, non-stop
over-	too much	oversleep, overweight

PREFIX	MEANING	EXAMPLE
pre-	before	prehistoric (before the beginning of history), pre-school (before a child is old enough to go to school)
re-	again, for a second time	rebuild, reheat, re-open
semi-	half	semicircle, emi-final, semi-detached
sub-	under	submarine (a ship that goes under the sea), subway (a path that goes under a road)
super-	more than or bigger than	superhero, superhuman, superstar
un-	opposite, or not	unable, uncomfortable, undress, unknown, undo
under-	not enough	underfed, underweight, underdone

Explore: Suffixes

for making nouns

-hood	child childhood	father fatherhood	
-ity	stupid stupidity	able ability	pure purity
-ness	happy happiness	kind kindness	lazy laziness,
-ment	enjoy enjoyment	move movement	replace replacement
-ship	friend friendship	champion championship	partner partnership
-sion	divide division	persuade persuasion	
-tion	subtract subtraction	react reaction	

for making nouns that mean a person who does something

-er, -or	paint painter	write writer	act actor
-ist	science scientist	art artist	violin violinist

for making feminine nouns

-ess	actor actress	lion lioness

for making adjectives

-able	enjoy enjoyable	break breakable	forgive forgivable
-ful	hope hopeful	colour colourful	care careful
	pain painful		
-ible	eat edible	reverse reversible	
-ic	science scientific	photograph photographic	allergy allergic
-ish	child childish		

for making adjectives

-ive	attract attractive	compete competitive	explode explosive
-less	care careless	fear fearless	hope hopeless
-like	child childlike	life lifelike	
-y	hunger hungry	thirst thirsty	anger angry
	hair hairy		

for making adverbs

-ly	quick quickly	slow slowly	careful carefully
	normal normally		

for making verbs

-ate	active activate	pollen pollinate	
-en	damp dampen	short shorten	length lengthen
-ify	solid solidify	pure purify	
-ize, -ise	apology apologize	fossil fossilize	

Explore: Words we easily confuse

WORD	MEANING	EXAMPLE
to	when you go to a place, you go there	We're going to Spain this year.
too	also, or more than you need	He is coming too. Don't eat too much.
two	the number 2	There will be two of us.
its	belonging to it	The cat was eating its food.
it's	short for it is	It's raining today.

Hint: To decide which you need, think about the question: can I turn 'it' into 'it is'? If you can, you need to write 'it's', if you can't, you should write 'its'.

there	in that place	Go over there.
their	belonging to them	They have lost their homework.
they're	short for *they are*	They're going home now.
loose	not tight	My tooth is loose.
lose	If you lose something, you can't find it.	Where did you lose your jumper?
than	compared with another person or thing	I am shorter than you.
then	after that	We'll do some work and then we'll have a story.
whose	belonging to which person	Whose jumper is this?
who's	short for *who is*	Who's reading next?
your	belonging to you	Have you got your coat?
you're	short for *you are*	You're looking well today.

Explore: Synonyms

In this thesaurus, you will find lots of **synonyms**.
Synonyms are words which mean the same – or
nearly the same – as each other. For example,
frightened, *terrified* and *petrified* are all synonyms.
You can make your writing more interesting by
using different synonyms, rather than using the
same words all the time.

Examples

Instead of saying that someone **ate** a whole pizza, you might
write:

> *He wolfed down a whole pizza!*
> or
> *He polished off a whole pizza!*

Instead of saying that someone lived in a **big** house, you might
write:

> *They lived in an enormous house.*

Explorer tip

Try not to use the same word twice. When you've already used a
word once in a piece of writing, look that word up in your thesaurus
to find a synonym.

237

Explore: Related words

Some words are not synonyms, but are related to each other because they have similar meanings. For example, **flower** is a general word, which can mean any type of flower. The words **rose**, **daffodil**, and **tulip** are related words which have more specific meanings because they describe one specific type of flower.

It can help your reader to 'see' what you are writing about if you use more specific words rather than general words.

Examples

Instead of saying that a garden is full of **flowers**, you might write:

The garden was full of brightly-coloured lilies and sweet-smelling roses.

Instead of saying that someone was sitting on a **chair** reading a **book**, you might write:

He was sitting in a large armchair, reading a novel.

Explorer tip

Use your thesaurus to look up general words such as **chair**, **house**, or **flower** and see if you can choose a more specific and interesting word. These words are often in **Word Web** panels.

Explore: Words we use too much

When you read your writing, look out for words that you use over and over again. For example, read this postcard.

> Dear Ali,
> We're having a nice time here in Devon. The weather's good, so we've been to the beach a lot. Our caravan is nice, and there are good facilities on the campsite. The other people on the campsite are very nice, too, so I've made lots of friends.
> See you soon!

The words *nice* and *good* are **overused words**, because they are used over and over again. We can make the postcard more interesting if we use a different adjective each time.

> Dear Ali,
> We're having a **fantastic** time here in Devon. The weather's **warm and sunny**, so we've been to the beach a lot. Our caravan is very **cosy**, and there are **excellent** facilities on the campsite. The other people on the campsite are very **friendly**, too, so I've made lots of friends.
> See you soon!

Explorer tip

You can easily find **overused words** in this thesaurus. They are in special panels and have this symbol next to them.

There is a list of **overused words** at the front of the thesaurus.

Explore: Word building

Have you ever thought about making up a word?
If there isn't an exact word to describe something,
you could try creating your own by thinking what
it looks, smells, or tastes like and then adding one
of these endings.

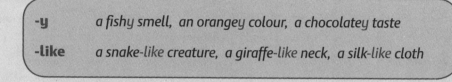

| **-y** | *a fishy smell, an orangey colour, a chocolatey taste* |
| **-like** | *a snake-like creature, a giraffe-like neck, a silk-like cloth* |

You can also make new words to describe what something looks,
smells, or tastes like using these endings:

-looking	*a strange-looking man, a fierce-looking dog*
-smelling	*sweet-smelling perfume, disgusting-smelling socks*
-tasting	*delicious-tasting soup, foul-tasting medicine*

Example

If you are describing an ogre, you could write:

He had thick leathery skin and huge shark-like teeth.
His eyes were small and evil-looking, and from his mouth
came foul-smelling breath.

Explore: Collective nouns

Collective nouns are words that are used to talk about a large group of things, usually animals. There is often more than one way to refer to the groups, but some common examples include:

- an army of . . .   caterpillars, frogs
- a band of . . .   gorillas
- a brood of . . .   chickens
- a colony of . . .   rabbits, ants, beavers
- a flock of . . .   sheep, birds
- a gaggle of . . .   geese
- a herd of . . .   horses, cows, goats, yaks, llamas, hippopotamuses
- a litter of . . .   pigs, kittens, puppies, cubs
- a murder of . . .   crows
- a nest of . . .   snakes
- a pack of . . .   wolves, polar bears
- a pod of . . .   walruses, seals, dolphins, whales
- a pride of . . .   lions
- a school of . . .   sharks, salmon, whales
- a shoal of . . .   fish
- a troop of . . .   monkeys, kangaroos
- a swarm of . . .   insects, bees
- an unkindness of . . . ravens

Explore: Place and position

in	out
high	low
on	off
in front	behind
far	near
above	below
between	through
under	on top off
left	right
inside	outside

Explore: Opposites

top	bottom
long	short
heavy	light
come	go
full	empty
loud	quiet
clean	dirty
fast	slow
most	fewest
high	low
light	dark
dry	wet
hot	cold
big	small
fat	thin
pretty	ugly
happy	sad
smooth	rough
hard	soft
wide	narrow
bad	good
easy	hard
new	old
up	down
open	closed

Explore: Writing stories

Top 10 tips

Before you write:

1 Plan your story carefully. Something must *happen* in a story.

2 Tell your story to a friend before you write. Would you want to read this story? Would your friend? Change your plan if necessary.

While you are writing:

3 Keep to your new plan when you write. Now is *not* a good time to change your mind.

4 Write in sentences and think about punctuation.

5 Don't forget paragraphs. If you need to begin a sentence with an adverbial clause of time (e.g. *Later that day . . . When it was all over . . .*) or place (e.g. Outside . . . In the woods) you probably need to start a new paragraph.

After you have written the first draft:

6 Use a dictionary to check your spelling.

7 Use a thesaurus to make sure you have chosen the best words.

8 Look at the overused words list. Try to use other words.

9 Can you add in some details about your characters to make your reader interested and want to know more about the characters?

10 Can you add more information about your setting to help your reader to 'see' it in their minds?

Creating a setting: Place

The first thing you must decide is *where* your story takes place.

Is it in a **forest** or on a **beach**?

Is it in a **castle** or a **house**?

Is it at **sea** or on an **island**?

Once you have chosen your setting, try to picture it in your mind and then describe all the details to your reader.

For example, are there **mountains** or **trees**?

Are there **people** or **animals**?

Every time you add a detail, try to use an adjective to describe it.

Example

If you are describing a forest, you could write:

All around us there were massive, ancient oak trees, with thick trunks and dense, dark-green leaves.

Explorer tip

Don't worry if you can't think of a good adjective straight away. Look up a common adjective such as **big**, **small**, **old**, or **new** and then choose a more unusual and interesting synonym.

Creating a setting: Atmosphere

When you describe the setting of your story, think about the mood of the story. Choose your words carefully to create your atmosphere.

Does the place seem **happy** and **cheerful**?

Is it **dark**, **gloomy** and **frightening**?

Does it feel **friendly**, or is it **quiet** and **lonely**?

You can also describe the weather to match the atmosphere of your story. If your story is happy, it can be **bright** and **sunny**, but if your story is frightening the weather could be **dark** and **stormy**.

Example

For a gloomy or frightening atmosphere, you might write:

As Max approached the dark, deserted castle, a bitter wind whistled through the pine trees.

Explorer tip

Try looking up the words **hot** and **cold** to find words to describe the weather. You can also look up words such as **rain** and **wind** to find lots of different words you can use.

Creating a setting: Time

You need to tell your readers *when* the things happen in your story. What happens first? What happens next? Try using these time words and phrases to make it clear when things happen:

What happened next?

Later that day, we arrived in London.

The next morning we set out again.

Eventually, we managed to open the door.

At last we were free!

What happened earlier?

Mika had left a few minutes earlier.

A moment before, he had seen something moving in the bushes.

Earlier that day, Sammy had phoned.

What's happening at the same time?

Meanwhile, the others were still waiting at home.

At that very moment, Carla was getting on the train.

Just as I was leaving, I heard a tap on the window.

As soon as I saw him, I recognized him.

Creating a character

To write good stories you must create interesting characters. First, think about your character's appearance.

Is your character **tall** or **short**?

Are they **fat** or **thin**?

Is their hair **long and straight** or **short and curly**?

Then, think about their personality.

Are they **kind** and **good-natured**?

Or are they **bad-tempered** and **mean**?

Think of three or four interesting adjectives to create a lively picture of your character.

Example

If you are describing a kind old man, you might write:

*Old Mr Brown was **short** and rather **plump**. He always seemed to be **cheerful** and **good-humoured**, and **beamed** at everyone when he spoke.*

Explorer tip

Try looking up common adjectives such as **fat**, **thin**, **happy**, and **grumpy** to find some interesting words for describing characters.

Describing action

When you are describing what happens in your story, try to use words which describe exactly how someone does something.

For example, does someone **march into the room**, **creep downstairs**, **stroll along the beach**, or **trudge home**?

Example

If you are writing about a person **running**, you might write:

> Tom *raced* home as fast as he could, and *dashed* upstairs to his room.

If you are writing about an animal, you might write:

> Little birds were *twittering* in the trees above me, then one *fluttered* down and landed by my foot.

Explorer tip

Look at the panels for **go**, **run**, and **walk** to find lots of different ways of saying how someone moves.

Look up the panels at words such as **car**, **boat**, **dog**, **cat**, and **bird** for specific action words to describe these things.

Writing dialogue

The words that your characters say in your story are the *dialogue*. When you are writing dialogue, remember to use speech marks correctly, and try to use different words for reporting what your characters say. Think about what your character is saying. Are they asking a question, giving an answer, or making a suggestion? Think about how they speak. Do they speak in a loud, angry voice or a quiet voice?

Examples

If someone is asking a question, you might write:

'Do you live near here?' she **enquired**.
or
'How old are you?' he **asked**.

If someone speaks in a loud, angry voice, you might write:

'You fool!' **yelled** Matt.
or
'Go away!' she **snapped**.

Explorer tip

Look up the word panel at **say** to find lots of interesting words you can use.

You can also look at the examples there to check how to use speech marks correctly.

Writing non-fiction

When you are writing non-fiction, it is important to think about **who** you are writing it for and **why** you are writing it. Is it a newspaper report to describe something that happened, or is it an advertisement to persuade people to buy something? If you are writing a newspaper report, choose words to make it interesting and accurate. If you are writing an advertisement, choose words to persuade people that something is good.

Examples

In a newspaper report of a robbery, you might write:

> *The thief assaulted Mrs Edwards in the street and tried to snatch her bag. He has now been captured by the police.*

In an advertisement, you might write:

> *This brand-new, cut-price phone has loads of fantastic features. Buy one today!*

Explorer tip

Write a draft of your text first, then go through it and underline the common adjectives and verbs that you have used. Look these up in the thesaurus to see if you can find some more interesting, accurate, or persuasive ones.

Writing a text message

We write letters, emails and texts to different people and for different purposes. Before you write, you need to think about who you are writing to (your audience) and why you are writing (your purpose). Here are some examples of letters written to one person during a day. Think about who they are to, and why they are written.

JEN, C U L8R.
PARK. 8ISH.
LOL XxX

Text message

Look out for:

- The use of abbreviations in spelling (*lol*).
- The use of letters and numbers to take the place of words (*C U L8R*).
- No sentences.
- Very informal tone.

Writing a thankyou letter

Look out for:

- The salutation (*Dear Aunty Jen*).
- The introduction of the subject early in the letter (*thank you for*).
- Information about the writer.
- The use of slang (*pressy; you must be the best*).
- Use of exclamation marks.
- Information about the writer (at school – we know it's a child).
- Informal tone.

Dear Aunty Jen,

Thank you for the pens you sent me for my birthday. I took them into school and everyone said that you must be the best to send me a pressy like that!

I am working hard because we have a maths test next week. I hate tests, but I know that I feel better if I do well. Wish me luck!

Thanks again for the pens.

Lots of love

Pat

Writing a formal invitation

Look out for:

- The salutation (*Mrs J. Davis*).
- The early introduction about the purpose of the letter.
- The information needed for the invitation to be successful.
- Tell the events as they will happen.
- RSVP (*Respondez s'il vous plait* is a formal French way of asking someone to reply).
- Very formal tone.

Mrs J. Davis,

Mr and Mrs E. Jones invite you to attend

the wedding of their daughter

Elizabeth

To

Jay Singh

The wedding will take place

At: The Palace Hotel, Northington

On: 23rd February at 3.30pm

RSVP

Writing a letter of complaint

Look out for:

- The salutation (*Dear Mrs Davis*).
- The introduction of the subject early in the letter.
- Information about the complaint.
- The expectation that the complaint will be sorted out.
- Signing off with *'Yours sincerely'*.
- Formal tone.

Dear Mrs Davis,

I understand that you are responsible for cooking the fudge in Ye Olde Fudge Shoppe. On the afternoon of 23rd November, I was passing the shop and I was attracted to the smell of your cooking. I came into the shop and, unfortunately, bought a bag of the fudge. I ate the entire contents of the bag within ten minutes. That evening, I found that I had put on a whole kilo in weight when I am on a diet and trying to LOSE weight. I hold you entirely responsible for my weight gain. It is thoughtless of you to leave the shop door open while you are cooking fudge since the smell is inevitably going to tempt passers by into your shop. I assume that you will now take steps to make sure that it doesn't happen again.

Yours sincerely,

Mrs Ethel Smith

Oxford Children's Dictionaries

Think Dictionaries. Think Oxford. www.oup.com